On Being a Christian and a Lawyer

On Being a
Christian
and a
Lawyer
Law for the Innocent

Brigham Young University Press

Thomas L. Shaffer

Publication of this volume has been made possible in part by a generous contribution from Brigham Young University Press employees through the University Together-for-Greatness Fund.

Library of Congress Cataloging in Publication Data

Shaffer, Thomas L   1934–
  On being a Christian and a lawyer.

  Bibliography: p. 251
  Includes index.
  1. Lawyers–United States.   2. Practice of law–United States.   3. Christianity and law.   I. Title.
KF298.S5   340'.023'73   80-25215
ISBN 0-8425-1833-9

Library of Congress Catalog Card Number: 80-25215
International Standard Book Number: 0-8425-1833-9
Brigham Young University Press, Provo, Utah 84601
© 1981 by Brigham Young University Press. All rights reserved
Printed in the United States of America
3/81 47337

For Cecil and Margaret Shaffer, who have shown me that there is joy in the first commandment with a promise attached.

The wisdom from above is in the first place innocent; and then peace-loving, considerate, and open to reason; it is straightforward and sincere, rich in mercy and in the kindly deeds that are its fruit. True justice is the harvest reaped by peacemakers from seed sown in a spirit of peace.
                                             James 3:17–18

Contents

Part One: Clients   1

1. The Ethics of Role   3
2. The Ethics of Isolation   13
3. The Ethics of Care   21
4. A Theology of the Client   35
5. The Problem of Revulsion   45
6. The Problem of Representing the Guilty   57
7. The Problem of Ministry to the Guilty   71
8. The Problem of Collaboration   81
9. An Example on the Problem of Collaboration   93

Part Two: Advocacy   105

10. The Practice of Reconciliation   111
11. Advocacy of the Person   121
12. Moral Discourse and the Community   127
13. The Administration of Justice   135
14. On Being Effective   143

Part Three: Lawyer Culture   153

15. A Theology of Lawyer Culture   155
16. Moral Moments in Law School   165
17. Law Faculties and the World   177

Part Four: Institutions   185

18. Thomas More's Skill   189
19. Thomas More's Hope   199
20. Franz Jaggerstatter's Hope   207
21. Tragic Communities   217

Afterword	227
Acknowledgments	229
Chapter Notes	231
Bibliography	251
Index of Names	263

PART ONE
Clients

But now, quite independently of law, God's justice has been brought to light. The law and the prophets bear witness to it: it is God's way of righting wrong.

Romans 3:21–22

CHAPTER ONE
The Ethics of Role

My marketability in law teaching is the law of the dead—wills, trusts, and death taxation. Part of the law of the dead is an old but still developing body of rules on the disinheritance of a spouse. I have for years posed an issue on disinheritance for my students with this example:

> A middle-aged, wealthy woman says to you, "I want to give all that I have to the Christian Anti-Communist Crusade, and nothing to my husband or children."

This is a useful example for teaching about the American legal rules which force inheritance within the family. In the nineteenth-century system, the only inhibition on disinheriting spouses was the law of dower and curtesy. It applied only to real estate; if our client's wealth were in stocks and bonds and if dower and curtesy were the applicable law, no legal rule would prevent her from doing what she proposes.

Modern American law on the subject is different. Most American states now have forced-share statutes which preserve an interest for a surviving spouse, regardless of the will of the dead spouse, and regardless of whether the property involved is real estate. But the forced-share statutes operate only on testamentary transfers—that is, on wills. If our client were willing to make her transfer in some other form—in a gift made now, for example, or in a trust which would be set up now—she could do what she wants without interference from the law.

There are, though, movements of reform. Transfers during life can now be reached by disappointed spouses in a few states. It does not matter, in these states, what the form of wealth is, and it does not matter whether the gift is made at death, in a will, or in a trust, or by outright transfer during life. But these rules of reform do not completely frustrate our client, because there are some forms of transfer they do not reach. Life insurance is an example. She could, if she wanted, convert her wealth into cash, use the cash to pay life-insurance

3

premiums, and make the Christian Anti-Communist Crusade her life-insurance beneficiary. This would probably frustrate any of the American legal rules which protect husbands from disinheritance. Since there is no American law protecting adult children, she could probably disinherit them with what in the trade is called a simple will.

This exercise leaves law students feeling capable and clever, which is not a bad result in the law-school classroom, Professor Kingsfield to the contrary notwithstanding. But I usually reserve ten minutes or so, toward the end of the class, to ask one further question:

> Now that you know you *could* do this for this client, I wonder whether you *would* do it.

Students who answer that question fall into two categories, leaving aside the few who are not listening closely enough to realize that their teacher has begun to talk about morals. The first group of students—usually the larger—says, "Yes, we would do it. We may disagree with what this woman is doing—meaning either that we wouldn't do it to our spouses or that we think it is immoral for her to do it to hers—but one of a lawyer's functions in society is the preparation of wills, whether he agrees with them or not."

The second group—usually the smaller—says, "No, we would not do it. We feel as we do because we think what she is doing is unwise or immoral or both; we would advise her that she should not or cannot do what she proposes."

Both sets of students (and their professional elders) answer the moral question by answering another, implicit question: "What does a lawyer do?" Two answers to that question are, "A lawyer does what his client wants," or "A lawyer tells his client what to do." In this context, one lawyer says, "Whatever you want," and drafts the will; another says, "No, that's not what you want," and then tells the client what the client, or her family, or her society, really wants. This latter operation is often more sophisticated than I make it sound. Lawyers of the second persuasion may advise this client that wills such as she proposes are vulnerable to will contest as "unnatural," and that, whatever the legal rules provide, a jury may decide that she lacked testamentary capacity when she made the will or was under the "undue influence" of her co-religionists or was defrauded. Transfers during life are subject to somewhat the same sort of lawsuits. Even life insurance is. Some few of these lawyers may even say that the law will not allow such a will (which is a bit of a lie) and hope the client will let it go at that. When such tactics are challenged, these lawyers will say that their highest duty is to give clients what they need and that this woman and her family certainly do not need a lawsuit. In this way, it may become necessary for the lawyer who believes he should dissuade his client from such a will to act with moral justification. The justifications I have heard are all more or less paternalistic; in one way of saying it, the lawyer here "protects the client from herself." In another, he justifies interference with her freedom of action for reasons which refer to her welfare, good, happiness, needs, interests, or values. The American Bar Association's *Code of Professional Responsibility* uses the word "benefit."

The first and larger group of lawyers—those who give clients what they want—also have moral arguments. (Few lawyers say that they do what they do without regard to morals; the question—the *ethical* question—is whether their moral reasons make sense.) The first group might say that lawyers are, like hardware-store clerks or plumbers, providers of services. They need not worry about the rightness of what the clients want, because interests are balanced against one another in the adversary system. That is, the lawyer gives his client what the client wants, and the government sees to it that the client gets what the client should have or what is for the good of society or what serves the interests of justice. People who understand this argument see it as similar to a physician's treating a patient regardless of what the patient's character is or what the patient, when well, may do with his health. Laymen (and lawyers) who do not understand this argument say that it is a principle of suspended conscience applicable only to lawyers: Only lawyers, in the adversary system, need not account morally for what they do. The client is seen as asserting what he wants and the professional lawyer as providing services in reference to what the client wants. The only limit on the lawyer is that he must act within the bounds of the law, because lawyers should not offend the system they serve.

The choice to serve what the client says he wants appears to be a choice against paternalism. When this choice takes on a moral justification it is in defense of competitive politics, or free enterprise, or the adversary system. This justification does not remove paternalism; it moves the role of pater from the professional to the government or "the system." A particularly appealing justification of this type appeared in early literature growing out of the War on Poverty in the United States. In one example, a young poverty lawyer named Steven Wexler looked at his welfare clients in terms suggesting a choice about needs and wants. He rejected being paternal toward these clients and then decided that they should be taken at their word: "The lawyer must remember that he is where he is in order to help poor people do their thing.... The way in which decisions are made about what the lawyer does must reflect a full understanding that the lawyer is there to do what poor people want.... A lawyer must help them do *their* thing, or get out." I discover a similar reaction among most law students when I ask them about the will benefiting the Christian Anti-Communist Crusade.

The psychological difference between serving what the client wants and serving what the client should want is the imposition on the client of what the professional wants—the professional's political views as well as more selfish interests. The conversation in which the client states what he wants avoids the imposition, but it is like a conversation in a catalogue store; the professional is the person who takes notes. The conversation in which the client is told what he wants is like a conversation in the nursery, a conversation in which Pater says, "No, that's not what you need. Let me tell you what you really need."

Either choice here is, I think, a matter of asking and answering the ethical question, "What does a lawyer do now?" rather than asking and answering the question, "What do I do now?" In terms which are common in the literature of legal counseling and legal ethics, either choice involves a role-determined answer to a moral issue. The lawyer facing a client sees himself; he sees his client; he sees his client looking at him; and he sees himself looking at his client and at himself the lawyer. He has expectations of himself. He knows that the client has expectations of him. In trying to discover and cope with those two sets of expectations he asks himself, "What does a lawyer do now?" That is a role question. American legal education is filled with role questions and role answers.

(I kept score, once, in a class discussion of what should be done when the client presented a moral question. My notes indicated that my students saw lawyers as people who are honest and thoughtful, know the law, yell at people on the telephone, tell people what to do, control the time and place in which they deal with clients, are all business, take over, make decisions, sit behind the desk, pay attention, are interested in facts, are very careful, do battle for clients, avoid moral questions, and resolve moral questions. The students thought that clients want lawyers to give them a sense of security, to tell them the answers, to lay everything out, to take care of their troubles, and to make clients feel trusting and dependent.)

So dominant is this role-associated approach to morals in law practice that moral debates within the profession usually assume that the moral issue is as my wills students understand it to be—that is, the choice is between doing what the client wants and telling the client what the client wants. Those who argue for doing what the client wants invoke adversary ethics.

The American school of adversary ethics grew up after the Civil War. If you look into professional opinion at the time of the first American attempt to codify moral rules for lawyers—David Hoffman's Baltimore "Resolutions" of 1836—you will find a vehement denial of the idea that a lawyer may suspend his conscience. "My client's conscience and my own are distinct entities," Hoffman said. "I shall ever claim the privilege of solely judging to what extent to go." Four decades later, in the lectures which are said to form the historical basis for the American Bar Association's *Code,* Judge George Sharswood of Pennsylvania said, "It is not every case in which a man has a *legal* that he has a *moral* right to claim the benefit of . . . laws." There are cases, Judge Sharswood said, which "counsel ought to hold up in their proper light to those whom they advise, and wash their hands of the responsibility of them." It was part of the office of lawyers, he thought, to urge clients toward "the spirit of high and pure morality which breathes through the sermon on the mount."

But even the leaders of the bar now argue for the principle of suspended conscience. John P. Frank, Arizona lawyer and articulate commentator, writing about Mr. Justice Brandeis, says "the lawyer's personal attitude toward his client's cause is immaterial." Former Justice Abe Fortas, writing about his law partner, Thurman Arnold, says, "Lawyers are agents, not principals; and they should neither criticize nor tolerate criticism based upon the character of the client whom they represent.... They cannot and should not accept responsibility for the client's practices. Rapists, murderers, child-abusers, General Motors, Dow Chemical—and even cigarette manufacturers and stream-polluters—are entitled to a lawyer; and any lawyer who undertakes their representation must be immune from criticism for doing so." There is no significant difference in this regard between the codified rules which govern law-office practice and those which govern work in the courts. An attempt was made to codify such a distinction in the 1969 *Code,* but the attempt failed.

One reaction to the dominant adversary ethics, from within the profession, comes from modern "public interest" lawyers. A public-interest lawyer is committed to realizing certain substantive interests. He claims the right to decide whether a client's purposes are worthy or unworthy, moral or immoral. These lawyers have decided that some social objectives are sound and some not. They devote their professional energies to the realization of the social goals they agree with. They are to be distinguished from poverty lawyers, of whom Mr. Wexler is an example, or civil-liberties lawyers of the old school, who seek to provide representation where it would otherwise not be provided and then adopt the adversary ethic in representing their clients. Hoffman and Sharswood would understand these modern "public-interest" lawyers, or at least Hoffman and Sharswood, if they disagreed with them, would disagree on moral grounds which refer to the goals public-interest lawyers have. They would argue, that is, for moral positions and would agree that the public-interest lawyers are right to assist causes they agree with and to refuse causes they do not agree with. Hoffman, Sharswood, and the public-interest lawyers would probably tell our wills client she should not give her property to the Christian Anti-Communist Crusade. Their reasons would differ, but each would approve of the other's making his own decision in the matter.

There are two ethical points to notice about the comparison of needs and wants as professional ethical positions: (1) In either case, the process of decision turns on an untruthful idea of what lawyers do, that is, on a delusion about professional role; and (2) either resolution of the tension serves what Paul called "government and authority ... power and dominion" (Ephesians 1:21).

Delusions about role. The argument justifying either approach is an argument which says, "A lawyer is a person who (does what his client wants) (tells his client what to do)." If the statement is made in the first form (wants), it is justified by (Social) Darwinian or *laissez faire* or adversary-ethic arguments which say that the clash of wants between citizen and citizen will be resolved by nature or by the government, and there resolved for the best. If the statement is made in the second form (needs), it is justified, as Toqueville justified the legal profession in the United States, by saying that an aristocracy is in order to impose moral, or at least orderly, behavior on ordinary people. In one case (wants) the delusion is that the lawyer has no conscience. In the other (needs) the delusion is that the client has no conscience (or, to be fair, perhaps as if the client's conscience does not matter). Both positions are delusions because they pretend that conscience has little to do with the case.

Serving power. In either situation, the lawyer is seen as a person who serves the system. Mr. Wexler's case for welfare mothers, and arguments in defense of the adversary system, comfort the guilty consciences of lawyers by saying that lawyers are entitled to suspend judgment, in serving what their clients want, because the adversary system (i.e., the government) requires naked assertions of purpose in order to locate truth and justice and thereby to rule. Lawyers serve the government by taking on the duties of adversaries in this system.

Arguments from the public-interest bar, that lawyers should restrain their business clients out of respect for economic or political ideas about fair distribution of wealth, or the preservation of community interests, are arguments that lawyers should serve in the same way elected representatives or public officials are expected to serve. The argument sometimes relates public service to the interests of clients by implying that what clients need is better society and that lawyers in seeking a better society serve their clients. The public-interest argument, like the poverty-law argument—one an argument from needs and the other an argument from wants—seems to me to depend on the assumption that lawyers' fealty is to power. The lawyer who serves needs is ostensibly more a servant of the system than the lawyer who serves wants, but both are servants of the system. The moral justification for serving the system is that the system is a source of goodness. Generalized, principled fealty to the system is fealty to power, which assumes that power is a relatively dependable way to goodness. The assumption that power is the way to goodness is not truthful; it depends on a delusion about people—clients and lawyers—and a delusion as well about society and its history, about government, and about the nature of worldly kingdoms. Such delusions are the occupational hazards of professionalism. Professionalism as an ethical orientation is unable to cope with the truth about power or to suggest adequate ways for lawyers and clients to talk to one another about the moral limits of power. Professionalism makes assumptions about power which are based not on right and wrong but on force and fear. These assumptions are not a sound way for deciding what the conversation between lawyer and client should be like. They do not even involve a significant moral conversation.

I don't argue that power is evil but only that power is not dependably good. There are various ways for a Christian to explain this wariness of government. One can be historical and describe evident excesses and sins of worldly power—the Holocaust, Hiroshima, Dresden, or Vietnam. One can draw on Anabaptist traditions, and the sometimes impressive biblical exegesis which supports them (John Howard Yoder's *Politics of Jesus,* for example), and see the Christian life as one which stands apart from "government and authority ... power and dominion." And one can say, with Karl Barth, that government is no more evil than any other institution, but that no institution merits a Christian's trust. "We are engaged," Barth said, "in life's revolt against the powers of death that enclose it. We cannot longer allow ourselves to be *wholly* deceived by the theories with which those powers have surrounded themselves and by the facts which seem to point to their authority. There is something fundamental in us that denies those powers." Barth is able, then, to meditate on Genesis 1:31 (God "saw everything that he had made, and behold it was good") and Colossians 1:16 ("by him were all things created ... thrones ... principalities ... powers: all things were created by him, and for him") and to conclude with a claim of freedom—"a humble but purposeful and really happy freedom of movement"—and a respect for government as creature. "Destroy it not, for a blessing is in it."

I can see a modern American lawyer asserting a moral position of freedom from government (as Barth defines it), with arguments from our own traditions (common law, Puritan, and frontier) of suspicion of power; from empirical conclusions from such things as "the lesson of Watergate"; and from a Jewish and Christian theology which says that the God of Abraham, Isaac, Jacob, and Jesus is both the source of all power and the only source of power that can be trusted. None of these reasons leads necessarily to a witness against power, but each of them argues against the idea that service to worldly power is a dependable way to goodness, and against the idea that fealty to worldly power—as adversary or in the public interest—is an adequate justification for professional behavior. A more positive way to put this, and a way I will explore in the next two chapters, is that this freedom from government is also freedom for a professional life of ministry to clients.

* * *

A footnote to this first chapter is necessary on the assumption which I am making about what lawyer-client conversations are. My argument here assumes that law-office conversations are almost always moral conversations. This is so because they involve law; law is a claim which people make on one another—that is, a claim resting on obligation, a moral claim—and for which they may seek the sanction and coercion of the state. (My jurisprudence on this point is one I borrow from my colleague and teacher, Robert E. Rodes, Jr.) In this derivative sense, a conversation about rights and duties is by definition moral.

In an empirical and psychic sense, also, the law-office conversation usually involves issues of what to do about rights and duties, and of consequences to third persons. Often the moral content is implicit—whether to file a claim for damages for physical injury, whether to probate one's father's will—but moral content is always present. The claim for damages or the distribution of a dead person's property rests on an *ought* as well as on a rule. And when one takes advantage of the rule he has decided that he ought to take advantage of it. He might have decided that he ought not. Law-office choices and decisions often involve consideration of the social effect of what clients do and of the effect on the character of a particular institution, such as a family or a business or the civil community. If it is possible for a serious conversation, between a lawyer and a client, in a law office, to be without moral content, I cannot think of an example.

I am interested here in personal relationships between lawyers and clients. I exclude the case in which the lawyer does not see his work as representing a person. Abe Fortas said, as reported by Anthony Lewis in *Gideon's Trumpet,* that he did not meet his client, Clarence Earl Gideon. Fortas seemed not to want to meet Gideon. Law-reform and civil-liberties litigation, taken as lawyers often describe it, involves the representation of political positions to which clients are incidental. Such litigation is best treated in discussions of the abstract political discourse characteristic of the constitutional system in the United States, which takes place in courts. Its claim to be representative of particular persons is a formal claim only; it is representation only because access to the courts requires a formally interpersonal dispute.

The Ethics of Role

Professional representation by a lawyer commonly involves a personal, narrow focus on some aspect of the client. The *Code* expresses this narrow focus as "the benefit of his client ... free of compromising influences and loyalties." This means at least that lawyers see their clients; that they see them one at a time, in a relatively intimate environment; and that lawyer and client work together periodically and interpersonally, since the benefit to be discovered is that of a person, not a thing. The focus on benefit implies that neither lawyer nor client sees the other as merely a member of a group and that the lawyer does not see the client merely as a means to an end. When the *Code* goes beyond benefit, to aspire to law-office decisions which are "morally just as well as legally permissible," it seems to aspire to a deeper level of interpersonal conversation.

If I exclude from consideration the interpersonal and political "representation" in which lawyers sometimes engage, and if I notice that lawyers aspire to a personal association deep enough to make both moral admonition and free choice possible, I must also notice that any professional association is, by definition, limited. It may be helpful to say that lawyers are, or should be, concerned about the "whole persons" of their clients, but it is not helpful to say that a lawyer *represents** the whole person of his client. There should be something personal about a lawyer's representation, but:

1. A lawyer does not, in court or negotiation, say: "I represent Harrison Tweedy, a 50-year-old white, male Episcopalian with wife, children, and membership in the country club. I have here personal descriptions of him from his parents and his rector, and I offer all of this because my client is a person and a unique and valuable individual." The lawyer talks, instead, depending on the case, about Mr. Tweedy's property, or business, or injured body.
2. A profession, by definition, does not serve *all* of a person. A professional is set apart from other people by his claim to serve limited aspects of people—their property, their injured bodies, their business health, their learning. Professionalism assumes a caring community in which each of a person's needs is met somewhere and in which the community itself sees to it that each of its members' needs is attended to. Therefore, an aspiration to be a professional and to serve *all* of a person's needs is futile.

The claim to serve the client as a person means that the lawyer aspires to serve some limited aspect of his client, but to do that in a way which represents the client as unique—as a person, or, as a Jew or a

---

*"Represent" is used here, and generally in the legal profession, to include both advocacy and service to clients which does not involve advocacy.

Christian might add, as a child of God. The law office conversation is personal but limited. Its moral dimensions have always to be defined or negotiated.

CHAPTER TWO
The Ethics of Isolation

A colleague of mine was the only customer in a neighborhood drugstore one evening when a shabby, hirsute young man came to the pharmacist and said, "My wife is a diabetic. We are out of needles for her insulin injections. I would like to buy a package of needles." The pharmacist located a package on the shelf, handed it to the young man, and collected the price of the needles. When my colleague and the pharmacist were alone, the pharmacist said, "You know, I didn't believe him. He is going to use those needles to shoot heroin." He shrugged. "But what can you do?"

I asked a second pharmacist if this situation arises frequently in the drugstore business, and he said that it does. But, the second pharmacist said, he does not handle the situation as the first pharmacist did. He does not sell needles to such customers. I asked how he distinguishes an eligible customer from an ineligible customer, and he said he asks questions about diabetes and the medication which is administered through needles. The answers to these questions tell him if the diabetes is genuine. If the diabetes is not genuine, this second pharmacist will not sell the needles. I asked him what he says when he refuses to sell the needles, and he said he believes in being honest; he says to the customer, "I will not sell you the needles, because I think you are going to use them to shoot heroin."

The moral quality of the refusing pharmacist's answer to the hirsute young man seems to me different from the moral quality of the answers of the two groups of students who responded to my questions about the woman who wanted to give everything to the Christian Anti-Communist Crusade. The first pharmacist, in giving the young man the needles, justified his conduct by saying in effect that pharmacists are in business to give customers what they say they want. The dynamics of toxicology will do for his customers what the adversary system does for the clients of lawyers. The answer of the first pharmacist appears to have been a role-determined answer of the "whatever you want" sort. A role-determined answer of the "let me tell you what you want" sort is possible here, too. But I don't think that is the sort of answer this refusing pharmacist gave. When he says, "I am not going to sell you the needles because I think you are going to use them to shoot heroin," he is saying "I am not going to do that for you *because I think what you propose to do is wrong.*" The refusing pharmacist is asserting that conscience is relevant to his professional activity.

One way this refusal is different is that it is honest. The pharmacist, having concluded that the young man wanted the needles for heroin, might have said that the drugstore was out of the kind of needles the customer wanted. He might have proposed to sell a kind of needles that will not work for heroin, or he might have said that he required a physician's prescription for the needles, even though the law did not require a prescription. In the same way, the wills lawyer might say that the client's proposal is not allowed under the law of elective spouses' rights or is unwise because of the law of undue influence. These are paternal answers (as well as dishonest answers); all are defended, if at all, in terms of the client's need. I would put them in the second category discussed in Chapter 1.

Another way the refusing pharmacist was different is that he asserts conscience openly. The wills lawyer might have said "I will not draft a will which disinherits your husband and children." Neither of these would be paternal answers; they are what the late Dr. Eric Berne would have called adult-to-adult answers. They can be defended in terms of client need, but there is a moral quality about them which is different from the avuncular judgment that what the client needs is not what the client is asking for. This moral quality is the assertion of the conscience of the professional. Candid refusers make a claim of conscientious objection. Each of their answers is an announcement of what the professional's conscience will not allow him to do. The pharmacist will not be implicated in the use of heroin. The wills lawyer will not be a party to such a drastic disinheritance. These claims are personal to the professional. They are not statements about the client at all.

The opposites of these answers would not be "whatever you want" answers. They would be "if you think it's right" answers. In the ethics which seems to be invoked by the refusing pharmacist, the opposite of asserting conscience against the client's purpose would be accepting the client's conscientious defense of his purpose. The pharmacist-customer dialogue might be:

P: I think you're going to use the needles for heroin.
C: Well, yes, I am. But, you see, I have to have heroin; I will die without it. The reasons I need new needles are that my old needles are dull and damage my skin more than is necessary, and they are dirty and may give me hepatitis.

P: All right. It's up to you.

The wills lawyer might say, "Have you thought about your family?" The wills client might answer in terms of devotion to the work of Christian anti-communism. In this case, too, the answer might then be, "It's up to you." These answers are not the same as saying, "Whatever you want." The difference lies in the fact that the professional raised a moral issue, in terms of his own conscience, and raised it candidly. This issue provoked a (more or less candid) reply from the client, in terms of the client's conscience. The lawyer listened to the reply and decided whether the client's explanation made the claim of conscientious objection unnecessary.

If the professional had persisted in expressing misgivings, even after hearing about the state of the client's conscience, there would have been in each case a further issue about the conscience of the professional. The difference between the two sets of answers ("It's up to you" and "I won't do it") would then be that one turns on the conscience of the client while the other turns on the conscience of the lawyer. They differ from role-determined answers because conscience has been placed in issue. Conscience is being asserted. The characteristics of these answers are (1) they make conscience relevant, (2) they are not reasoned and may be opaque, (3) they assume moral insularity, and (4) they do not involve risk.

Conscience. The client's conscience comes into the case either because the client volunteers it or the lawyer asks about it. In law-office cases such as the one I have put, my observation is that the client usually volunteers an explanation, such as her devotion to the Christian Anti-Communist Crusade. These answers are almost always serious and interesting and are often persuasive. When you think about it, there is much to be said by and for a person who proposes to give her wealth to religious charity. In social terms, this is one of the oldest issues in the law of wills and trusts. We tend to talk about it in class under the heading of "mortmain" laws; it is the issue which gave to our subject trite phrases about control by "the dead hand." In personal terms it involves deep attachments, intimations of eternity and of the will of God, and, more negatively, resentments toward family members who have neglected the client and affection for co-religionists who have not. My choosing Reverend Hargis and his radio evangelism in this example is, in other words, not caustic; when we reach the point at which conscience becomes relevant—when we are past the typical lawyer-client dialogue, which doesn't consider conscience—it becomes important to think a bit about our client's deeper feelings and about the lawyer's feelings toward enterprises such as Christian anti-communism.

At this point serious conversation, even negotiation, might begin but, in the ethics of isolation, does not. As soon as the assertion of conscience is clear it is non-negotiable; one side or the other accepts it (gives up, if you like). My principal recent experience of exchanges of this morally insular sort has been in observing ethics discussions in law school, where the teacher says, "What would you do in this situation?" and the student answers, "I would do this, and I would do it because of the way I was brought up."

Not reasoned and may be opaque. Conscience is asserted here, rather than offered. Conscience is a way of saying, "This is the way I feel; I cannot do anything about it." In the sense in which I prefer to use the words, the conversation is moral but not ethical. It deals with right and wrong, but it does not deal with dealing with right and wrong; it is not a conversation about right and wrong but is only an assertion about right and wrong. If the client does not like the lawyer's assertion, he can either get another lawyer or change his mind about what he wants. If the lawyer elicits the client's moral assertion and then decides he will not cooperate with it, he moves the assertion from the client's moral isolation to the lawyer's moral isolation; he says, "It's up to me," instead of, "It's up to you." The client does not come to understand the lawyer's moral assertion and is therefore not persuaded by it. He is not convinced; he is only overruled.

Professional discussion, when it invokes the possibility that conscience might be relevant in a law office, tends to assume that moral problems are for lawyers only. (Geoffrey Hazard's insightful recent book *Ethics in the Practice of Law* is an example.) Discussion is then limited to gathering the information which the lawyer must have if he is to resolve his conscience, either toward doing for the client what the client wants or should have done *for* him (a role-determined answer) or toward refusing to act for the client at all. The ABA *Code* says, "The professional judgment of a lawyer should be exercised ... solely for the benefit of his client." This sounds like the *Code* expects the lawyer to be the moral decision maker, and even if the *Code* is open to a different reading, lawyers often behave as if the *Code* read that way. The *Code* enjoins lawyers to advise (meaning, at least, inquire) on "the practical effect" of client decisions. Lawyers have to decide for themselves what is "within the bounds of the law" and what is not; certain decisions in litigation are reserved for lawyers, as certain decisions in surgery are reserved for physicians. Lawyers are to see to it that clients consider their decisions soberly. Lawyers are to inquire whether clients' decisions are "morally just as well as legally permissible."

Therefore, it is frequently the case that moral dilemmas are seen more as problems for the lawyer than as subjects for moral discourse with the client—more as the end of lawyer-client discussion than as a beginning for it. A lawyer then has one of two choices, depending on whether his ethics are role determined. He can decide between dominating the client or being dominated by him (the ethics of role), or he can decide whether to exercise a right of conscientious objection and refuse to work with the client at all. From the client's point of view this is an adversary system in which he is not allowed to be an adversary. His position is defined by his lawyer and accepted or rejected by his lawyer. Conscience is involved, but not the conscience of the client.

This is probably another instance of lawyers behaving as they learned to behave in law school. Student answers in law-school moral conversation tend to be of the form, "I would/would not do that." Those of my students who are in the second and smaller group in the Christian Anti-Communist case are an example. Sometimes answers are of the form, "I *just* would/would not do that. I'm sorry about it, but it's the way I am, and I am the way I am because I was raised (in the South) (in parochial schools) (by a good Baptist mother)." The dialogue has valuable potential in its acceptance of student feelings, but its ethical content, beyond an implied principle of civility, is flimsy at best and fatalistic at worst. From an intellectual point of view, the professor is a classroom scorekeeper.

Discourse of the "I would/would not do it" sort, in law school, has value, if only because it establishes that there must be moral reflection in a profession. It at least establishes that the moral feelings of students are relevant; so often moral argument in law classes is turned aside with a Kingsfield-like disdain for "fuzzy thinking." But the habit of asserting and accepting moral positions in this bald and unreasoned way implies to students that there is no discipline in moral discourse, that one cannot engage in it with the same hope that he engages in discourse about the arcane rules of property law. One cannot hope to come out with understanding. He cannot hope to be able to say of a moral position, "That is a good position," as he can of a rule of property law. He cannot hope to develop skill for conducting moral discourse with clients.

There is a story about a reception at which the late theologian Reinhold Niebuhr met the late Justice Felix Frankfurter. The judge introduced himself as a reverent agnostic; the theologian introduced himself as an irreverent believer. Reverent agnosticism is the issue in bald assertions of moral position—in law school, in law office, or anywhere else. Reverent agnosticism seems to me to be useless in office or university (whatever value or propriety it has in court). Irreverent belief is more appropriate.

Assumption of moral insularity. The *Code,* after defining in several ways the obligation a lawyer has to inquire into the conscience of his client, emphasizes that ultimate moral decisions are for the client, not the lawyer. However, in both Canada and the United States, professional ethics affirm that no lawyer need participate in a case offensive to his conscience. In practice, therefore, the *Code* doesn't mean what it says. Regardless of who makes the prevailing moral judgment, when client self-determination and lawyer conscientious objection come together they imply that the client and the lawyer, while they may talk to one another, are not likely to influence one another. When the conversation is resolved by the moral assertion of the client, the profession is likely to talk about the lawyer as representing the interests of his client and to defend itself by references to the adversary system. When the conversation is resolved by the moral assertion of the lawyer, the profession is likely to talk about the lawyer as representing the interests of society and to defend itself by talking about the social responsibility of lawyers. The assumption in either case is that the lawyer and client both operate in moral worlds but that their worlds are isolated from one another.

This moral isolation is, to some extent, the delusion of our culture. Modern North Americans come out of a frontier tradition which exalts the rugged individual, values a diversity of cults, and celebrates the economic myth that each person is a unit of production and consumption. We are supported in these assumptions by affluence and help-those-who-help-themselves notions of social welfare. We tend to act as though each of us was an island.

But isolation in America is not a fact and never has been a fact. The spiritual history of the United States is the history of pilgrims yearning to be a people, of a religious pluralism which has always sought to deny itself. The story of any lawyer's life is a story of moral influence on clients—sometimes paternal, sometimes what I am here calling conscientious objection, sometimes a deeper influence which depends on conversation. To suppose that clients are morally isolated, and that lawyers are incapable of changing the consciences of clients, is not truthful. Isolation as a moral idea is therefore inadequate. Nor are lawyers morally isolated. Lawyers tend to take on the values of their most important clients—and this not as the result of conversation with them but of assumptions about their client's purposes. Mr. Wexler's comments about poverty law are an example at one end of the American class structure. The lawyer fiction of Louis Auchincloss is an example from the other end. Lawyers are not the moral agents they and the professional rules about lawyers suppose them to be. Even when seen as public moral leaders, lawyers are not isolated.

Donald Shriver, who is a theologian, pastor, and president of Union Theological Seminary, and Carl Ostrom, a pastor and psychologist, collaborated in a recent and good little book called *Is There Hope for the City?* They sought to discover correlation between religious faith and public concern. They found that people who maintain a strong, interpersonal religious life and are active in social concerns are more happy and more effective (in their faith *and* in their efforts toward reform) than people who maintain one without the other. They claim that rugged individualism in America is a product both of affluence and strong social support—that is, that moral autonomy is an illusion and that moral independence is not possible without economic and social interdependence. This is to say, I think, that moral independence is not possible at all: "The righteous cannot live by faith alone, if by faith we mean a steadily held, strong-minded, interior spiritual tilt. Such individuals, our data overwhelmingly indicate, are likely candidates for lives of quiet desperation. Without the links of friendship, worshiping community, a community for political discourse, and associates for their public action, the faithful are also the frustrated." Donne was right; no man is an island.

Moral isolation does not involve risk. Moral isolation is an arrogant idea as well as an untruthful idea. There are two reasons for this. First, choices based on the delusion of moral isolation are often made carelessly. The moral judgment which the refusing pharmacist makes about the hirsute young man reasons recklessly from appearances and then comes to a conclusion based on stereotypes about heroin users. The moral judgment of the wills lawyer (if he refuses to draft the will) draws similar conclusions based on a stereotype (a vindictive or deceived old woman) that might fall before insight into the complex and frustrating lives which the client and the rest of us lead. Second, the moral judgments are typically made without a hint of doubt about the principles or the experience on which they rest. Another example from the lore of testamentary counseling illustrates how the dialogue in the wills case might proceed:

"A lawyer told me about an elderly widow who had one living child and two grandchildren, and who told the lawyer that she wanted her estate divided into three parts and to give one part to each descendant. He said he told her she shouldn't do that. What she should do, he said, was give half to the child and one-fourth each to the grandchildren. That, he said, was the proper way.

"I told the lawyer that I was appalled at the way he imposed his idea of propriety (and at its source, which is apparently the seventeenth-century English Statute of Distributions). I asked him if he always did things like that, and he said that he did—always." This is the ethics of isolation. In their untruthfulness and in their arrogance, they deserve the misgivings of Karl Barth: "He who takes the risk of counseling must be prepared to be counseled in turn by his brother if there is need of it. Such mutual counseling in a concrete situation is an event. It is a part of the ethos which is realized ethics. The ethos ... implies that he refrain from attempting too much and becoming thereby a lawgiver."

Similar objections can be made about assuming moral isolation in clients. What seems to follow the "It's up to you" professional reply is a series of rationalizations: there is no real evidence that heroin is that harmful; there is nothing I can do about it anyway; it really is important to avoid hepatitis; she will only go to some other lawyer and get her will. Because of this tendency to rationalization, it is important to realize the inadequacy of the idea of moral isolation, and to distinguish it from the ethics of interpersonal care (which I discuss in the next chapter). Moral isolation is such an appealing delusion. It is such a tempter from responsibility. When moral insularity is assumed in the client, a lawyer is tempted to the comfort of irresponsibility. When moral insularity is assumed by a lawyer, the lawyer is tempted to a paternalism which diminishes the moral growth of clients and erodes the possibility of humility and openness in the lawyer. The delusion of isolation is appealing because it tolerates moral propositions and the appearance of moral concern. It seems so much nobler than the morality of role. Isolation is, though, a moral life without risk, since in it the lawyer's views are not made vulnerable. ("He who takes the risk of counseling must be prepared to be counseled in turn.") Isolation is, finally, a grim and joyless way to live. Geoffrey Hazard sketched a picture of the morally isolated lawyer in a 1975 essay on professional ethics. "The picture of the lawyer," he said, "is that of a lone practitioner who must judge for himself what is right while engaged in intense competition with his fellow professionals and with outsiders who want to intrude on his professional domain. The controls on his conduct, in the contemplation of the rules of professional conduct, are almost entirely those of self-governance under the guidance of rules and the strictures of conscience." My view is that Hazard's picture is a false picture as a matter of fact and an inadequate one as a matter of ethics.

Isolation implies that morals are a private affair; they are asserted, not talked about, which is to suppose that morals are not important, literally not *worth* talking about. When morals become unimportant, power fills the vacuum; might becomes right; and one's law office is conducted in result if not in concept—but very likely in both result and in concept—on the ethics of fear.

CHAPTER THREE
The Ethics of Care

We must learn again to speak to each other with authority and not as the scribes. For the present we are all much too clever and unchildlike to be of real mutual help.

Karl Barth

The beginning and end of a lawyer's professional life is talking with a client about what is to be done. My claim is that this is a moral conversation. I am suggesting three ethical orientations which seem to govern the conversation, and then trying to weigh the adequacy of each of the three orientations.

The first orientation is one governed by *role,* that is, by an idea about the function in society of the legal profession, and the function of a lawyer in the profession. Most discussions of legal ethics in the profession, and most notably the debate between public-interest lawyers and adversary-ethic lawyers, is carried on within this first ethical orientation. I claim that the role orientation pretends that the law-office conversation is not a moral conversation. Because the conversation is moral, whether or not lawyer and client see it as moral, the role orientation is not truthful.

The second orientation is one governed by *moral isolation,* that is, by the idea that the law-office conversation is one in which moral positions are asserted and either accepted or rejected. The profession respects this orientation and has officially provided for it in rules which urge lawyers to seek and to honor the moral decisions of their clients, and announce for lawyers a right to refuse or withdraw from employment when client decisions offend the consciences of lawyers. This second ethical orientation respects the moral quality of what lawyers and clients say to one another and is therefore more nearly truthful than role orientation. Moral isolation is inadequate, though, because it does not admit two facts—that lawyer and client influence one another, and that moral life is a life of openness and risk. The problem with the ethics of moral isolation is partly that they are not truthful and partly that they are too safe.

The third orientation is one governed by an aspiration to *care* for the client and to be cared for by him. It admits that the law-office conversation is moral and that those who speak to one another in law offices are interdependent and at risk. It aspires to moral discourse as an exercise of love—that is, of what Aquinas called fraternal correction, what Barth called conditional advice, what Martin Buber saw as the soul of relationships.

The ethics of care, like the ethics of isolation, allow for a moral conversation; they make conscience relevant. But care goes beneath and beyond the ethics of isolation; it denies that lawyer and client are moral islands. Lawyer and client depend on one another and influence one another. I assert that as a fact, as well as a norm; the ethics of care is a procedure in which the fact of moral interdependence is the basis of conversation.

Stories offer the most distilled examples of moral conversation, especially stories about strong people making up or changing their minds. The "realist" novels of Trollope and Snow are my favorites. In *The Duke's Children,* Plantagenet, who is Trollope's study of the gentleman in England, comes to agree to his daughter's marriage, after initial, strong opposition; in *The Warden,* Septimus Harding decides to surrender economic security for himself and his daughter because he understands the justice of arguments made by his enemies. In Snow's *The Affair,* a group of English academics decide to support the cause of a colleague who challenges their deepest values and is personally repugnant besides. The process these novelists describe is inevitably moral, inevitably interpersonal, inexhaustibly fascinating. But even a first-year law student, who probably could not describe the process, can, as he pretends to be an office lawyer, illustrate how it works:

L: Have you had any dealings with this broker?
C: No, only in the purchase of this property.
L: And you had no written agreement with him concerning this deal (acquiring a tenant), only his request to you for this money, after the fact.
C: Yes. That's right. He didn't say anything about getting a sixpercent commission till after the tenant was in. As far as I was concerned, I shouldn't have to pay him anything. I don't know if I really have to. However, I assume I do. I don't know.... Do I have an obligation to pay?
L: Under our law ... any arrangement or agreement which is made between you and a broker which is not written down is not enforceable....

C: And I could have told him good-bye and leave me alone.
L: There was nothing he could do about it.... I think also you have some extralegal considerations that you shouldn't lose sight of ... in terms of your business reputation, in terms of if you are ever going to have dealings with other brokers....
C: What are you telling me then? That I should pay him or that I shouldn't?
L: Well, I'm not telling you that you should pay him or not pay him, but I think ... in making your decision you have to consider not just your legal obligations but also other considerations which are up to you, to decide how significant they are to you. You see, the point is that we don't know how difficult it would have been for you to get somebody to become a tenant in that building, and, after all, he did go out of his way to get somebody in that building, and that person is now paying you for leasing. So you're getting a benefit conferred on you right now. Now, it's true that you may not technically be liable to him, and we're not saying that that shouldn't be an important consideration to you, obviously.
C: Well, all right. I said before I suppose I have to pay him.

A novelist would want to find out more about the lawyer, and more about the client, and especially more about their sudden relationship. But even a first-year law student, uncoached and extemporaneous, demonstrated here how a moral conversation in a law office proceeds. It is not a contrivance; it happens every day and routinely. The art of moral conversation is more a matter of removing obstacles—of forgetting to speak like the scribes and of allowing oneself to be childlike—than it is a matter of sophistication.

The most celebrated of all legal-counseling cases is called "The Case of the Rabbi and the Horsewhip Lawyer." It involves a young wife and mother who has found her dutiful, dull husband less exciting than her passionate Italian lover and has come to a lawyer to get a divorce so that she can marry her lover, who, she says, is also getting a divorce.

"My reaction to all of the above was that Mrs. G was a silly, stupid person," the lawyer recalled. "[S]he could use an old fashioned horse whipping and I told her so frankly. I told her that she had sex confused with love. I told her that I did not think there was any future in the proposed divorce. I told her that I felt that if the third person was such an individual that he would abandon his own wife and two sons, I could not see any hope in the future of a home with him and her three children. In short, I attempted to dissuade her from the idea of divorce. However, she insisted that her happiness was with Mr. X and that she still wanted my services in trying to secure a divorce and custody of the children."

Negotiations then began between Mr. G's lawyer and the Horsewhip Lawyer. They resulted, at one point, in Mrs. G and her lover, Mr. X, agreeing to talk with Mrs. G's rabbi; the result of that conversation was an agreement—each would go his separate way and try to fill his legal and religious obligations without seeing each other for a year. However, after about two weeks of this, Mrs. G called the rabbi and told him that she would have to break her promise because her love for the third person was so great.

"I might say that I am a poor counselor in this sort of situation because I felt that Mrs. G was being used. I told Mrs. G that I felt that the lover never had an intention of marrying her, that he was putting a veneer on a sordid arrangement, that she was heading straight to destruction—even worse. I pointed out that marriage and life was not just sex, that marriage was economic, family, societal, etc., and not merely lovers coming together.... My reaction was one of such complete disgust that I had all I could do to keep from tossing Mrs. G out of my office on her ear.... If she was not agreeable to my counsel and advice, she might try another lawyer."

Mrs. G took only the last suggestion. She got another lawyer, and she got her divorce; her husband got custody of the children and was required to pay very little alimony; Mr. X, the lover, did not get a divorce. The Horsewhip Lawyer, who had spoken not with authority, but as the scribes, turned out to be right in his prediction of what would happen. Much of the criticism of the Horsewhip Lawyer turns on the assertion that he did not respect his client's freedom of choice; in the analysis I am suggesting, he operated during the first phase of the relationship from the ethics of role, subtopic "let me tell you what you want," and, in the second phase, from the ethics of isolation, subtopic "I won't do it." In suggesting a third ethic for such a case, I propose to talk first about the goal in the relationship and then about two kinds of moral risk in it—the risk of openness and the risk of mutuality.

Goal. Any human relationship has a tendency. It is going somewhere. To the extent that the parties are conscious of the tendency, the goal can be a matter of moral conversation. Mrs. G was not *seeking* an immoral goal; she said, no doubt, that she realized that what she was doing was against moral rules she believed in or respected, but she probably also said she could not help that, that love conquers all, and that she and Mr. X would try to work out the divorce with the least pain to its victims (two inoffensive spouses and five children). The Horsewhip Lawyer answered that she was kidding herself. The conversation, to this extent, was characterized by moral isolation—and that was where the relationship ended. In an ethics of care, the Horsewhip Lawyer might have thought more about what his goal for Mrs. G was and about whether there was any possibility of thinking about this goal honestly and broadly enough for there to be some possibility of negotiating a purpose for the lawyer-client relationship—not a purpose for her, or a purpose for him, but a purpose for *them*.

Much of modern philosophical ethics talks in terms of autonomy as being the moral destination we should respect and seek in one another. The substantive moral idea involved is freedom. Those who write on the subject do not talk about particular virtues; they talk instead about providing information, time for thoughtful choice, and institutional (and professional) procedures which forbid coercion. Autonomy is a different ethical concept; moral thinkers whom I respect say that it is impossible to seek autonomy and that, given all that bears on a person's moral life, autonomy is an impossible moral position. I believe it can be treated as a possible goal for a professional relationship, if it is defined carefully and if we are honest about the fact that our morality is more a matter of what we are than of what we choose.

At any rate, the goal of autonomy does not preclude deep moral conversation. That is to say that there is a difference between freedom and isolation. The aspiration to autonomy assumes moral conversation because it assumes that moral decisions are important and that none of us makes his moral decisions alone. Autonomy (etymologically rule-of-self) assumes a certain amount of independence, but it is not an ethics of isolation. As Gerald Dworkin puts it, autonomy is independence *plus* authenticity. "We need characterization," he says of the moral agent, "of what it is for a motivation to be *his,* and what it is for it to be *his own.* The first is what I . . . call authenticity; the second independence." There are times, he says, "when we really don't want to know. But we do resent being manipulated in our own interest." He could, I think, have been speaking for Mrs. G.

An ethics of isolation would say, "It is he who *decides.* It's up to him." An ethics of autonomy can say, "It is *he* who *decides.*" Autonomy focuses on the pronoun (the person) as well as on the verb (the action or, as we say in law school, "the problem"). The result of autonomous ethical reasoning can be thought of in terms of the deeper beliefs of the moral agent—so that the "landlord" from the contracts class thinks, finally, that paying for benefit conferred is more important to him than the protection of the law, or even so that Mrs. G decides that her family is more important to her than her lover.

Autonomy allows for, and may even require, Aquinas's "fraternal correction" or Barth's "conditional advice." Immanuel Kant, who is the source of the ethics of autonomy, emphasized that the autonomous moral agent exercises a "self control," which overcomes both an array "of outside forces" *and* "one's own phenomenal self . . . one's empirical inclinations." Autonomy is open to moral conversation in a deeper way than isolation is, because autonomy involves the self of the client as well as the client's dilemma. Dworkin prescribes a number of standards for the conduct of institutions in such a way as to show respect for autonomy. These can to some extent be applied as well to a professional's showing respect for and seeking moral conversation with his client. I notice three of Dworkin's guidelines which are of interest for the law office:

[1] Methods of influence [should be used] which are not destructive of the ability of individuals to reflect rationally on their own interests.
[2] Methods which rely essentially on deception, on keeping the [client] in ignorance of relevant facts, are to be avoided.
[3] [One should prefer] methods of influence which work through the cognitive and affective structure of the [client], which require the active participation of the [client] in producing the change, [over] those which short-circuit the desires and beliefs of the [client] and make him a passive recipient of the changes.

I think these could be stated positively as standards requiring (1) time, space, and environment for reflection, (2) full information, and (3) collaboration. Dworkin would probably emphasize legal-counseling tactics which seek out the authenticity of the client over tactics of influence; but he admits that his theory is basically a procedural one and is consistent with the moral agent's admitting to himself, and accepting, the moral influence of another person. At the very least, though, the moral conversation has to begin where the parties are, with the feelings they have, and with the pain they feel.

It is possible, in Dworkin's view, for a client to be influenced but nonetheless autonomous. Dworkin provides for that with his distinction between procedural and substantive independence. Either kind of independence becomes autonomy when coupled with the client's authenticity. I conclude from this that some influences violate freedom and some do not. Another way to say it would be that interpersonal influences are data for decision. "The compassionate or loyal or moral man [has authenticity but] is one whose actions are to some extent determined by the needs and predicaments of others," Dworkin says. "He is not independent or self-determining."

Autonomy can make room for moral influence, both indirectly, as the client considers others (the broker, the inoffensive husband), and directly, as the client opens himself to fraternal correction or conditional advice. The moment in which this openness occurs, Barth would say, is the moment in which law-office conversation becomes an adult, self-conscious, moral enterprise: "It is a part of the ethos which is realized ethics."

Still, it is possible to hope that my client will leave me with more moral gain than the ethics of autonomy seems to allow for. It is possible to seek a *conversion* of my client to a situation which is not only freedom but freedom *for*. If the object of law-office discourse, as moral discourse, is to serve the goodness of the client, then many of us feel that there is more to goodness than autonomy. Born-again Christian lawyers whom I know tell their clients about Jesus Christ as savior; some of them have told me that they ask clients to pray with them. The practice of turning to scripture for legal guidance is as old in the Jewish and Christian tradition as Moses himself. I, who am a Christian, would say that my hope for my client is that he respond to the redemption which God has accomplished for him. And if that is my hope, then it is my duty, no doubt, to say something about it. At least it is my duty to deal with my client as a child of God, and, when I speak to him, to speak to "the One in the other."

The point at which this aspiration to conversion and the aspiration to autonomy connect is the fact that conversion begins in the relationship, in the human connection, and proceeds in and through freedom. Conversion is not imposed or called down upon a weak, fumbling, hurting person. "Human freedom is not realized in the solitary detachment of an individual in isolation," Deitrich Bonhoeffer said. "Only in encounter and in communion may I receive the gift of freedom. God is *pro me* because He is *pro nobis*." And all of this is true along with the truth that "there is no 'being-free-from' without 'being-free-for.' There is no dominion without serving God. Without the one, man necessarily loses the other. Without God, without his brother, man loses the earth." If my goal for my client (and for myself and for our relationship) is conversion, then I must realize that conversion (which means growth) begins in freedom. I cannot ignore freedom, whether I call it autonomy or something else, and I cannot ignore the theology of the matter, which says that my client and I are converted to freedom together. "Only in encounter and in communion . . . may I receive the gift of freedom."

But even a minimal ethics of autonomy, without any idea about conversion, implies a goal, some tendency beyond freedom itself. I say this not so much to convince my lawyer-reader of what his professional goal should be as to suggest that he admit that there is a goal in the law office—that he has a goal in his law office and that goal is not merely freedom. The goal of autonomy is, if honestly considered, more than autonomy. The goal of conversion, if honestly considered, is more than autonomy, but it is never less.

For example, a useful ministry to Mrs. G would accord her more compassion than the Horsewhip Lawyer accorded her.* "Compassion"

---

*"Ministry" is used here as a way to describe an ideal of interpersonal service and not in its clerical sense.

is a common word and also (therefore) a theological word. It is close to the essence of Christian morals because it is close to the essence of the Incarnation and to the Jewish ethical tradition in which Jesus stood. It is a matter both of God-with-us and of loving one's neighbor as oneself. Compassion includes the realization—at least that, at least this intellectual idea—that it is hard to be good. "When I want to do the right, only the wrong is within my reach. In my inmost self I delight in the law of God, but I perceive in my bodily members a different law, fighting against the law that my reason approves and making me a prisoner under the law that is in my members" (Romans 7:21-22).

"By the law, through which I know God, I am enabled *to will to do good*," Barth commented, on this text. "By the same law, through which I am known by God, my success in *doing evil* is exposed. Thus my noblest capacity becomes my deepest perplexity; my noblest opportunity my uttermost distress; my noblest gift, my darkest menace." Christian faith, in Barth's view, includes accepting what God has done about this dilemma. Ministry recognizes the dilemma, in the minister and in his client. Dworkin puts the cases of the smoker who wants to stop smoking and the drug addict who does not want to stop taking drugs. The smoker is authentically a nonsmoker; the addict is authentically an addict. This is not a theoretical schizophrenia, nor is it a Manichean notion. Christian theologians are at some pains to avoid that impression: "It is one man that wills and does not perform; one man that does not will, and yet performs; within the four walls of the house of sin dwells but one man," Barth says. He makes this one, integrated person an object of discourse—of professional service and of self awareness—when he talks about addressing "the One in the other."

The risk of openness. Moral discourse in professional relationships does not require that either party consciously change; it is possible for two people to discuss an issue of conscience, and to discuss it deeply, even though neither of them comes to change his mind. One who meets the other in a deep way, who meets the One in the other, is changed by such a meeting, but this change need not include a conscious change of mind. However, the assumption of moral discourse is that each of the discoursers is *open* to change. Martin Buber said of the I-You* relationship that the tendency of the relationship was "as far as possible to change something in the other, but also to let *me* be changed by him." Change is the model in moral discourse, and the poetic paradigm as well, but it is openness to change—vulnerability, risk—which is the essence of moral discourse. Buber said that this openness was in essence a

---

*This is commonly referred to as the "I-Thou" relationship, but the modern English translation (Kaufmann's) uses the modern English second-person pronoun, which grates for a while but makes sense. We no longer say, "I love thee."

belief that there is something in the other (e.g., client) that one can come to trust: "The worst in him and the best in him are dependent on one another ... what we may call the good, is always only a direction. Not a substance."

This means, of course, that even in an I-You relation, even after all of the skills that Dworkin's guidelines imply, the lawyer may have to retain his conscientious objection. He may have to refuse to go further with the client. This is not, though, a retreat to the ethics of isolation—for two reasons: First, the dialogue has taken place, and that means that the lawyer has left his island and asked the client to leave his island. As a matter of behavior, isolation has been left behind. Second, the actors have influenced one another; the matter may be in the hands of God, but it is there in a way it would not be if either lawyer or client had retained his isolation. It makes a difference that the lawyer has spoken: "Only by declaring the truth openly do we recommend ourselves, and then it is to the common conscience of our fellow men and in the sight of God" (2 Corinthians 4:2). The point Barth makes when talking about "realized ethics," and the point Buber makes in his ontology of relation, is that the act of witness is a fact, a phenomenon. Something has happened, whether we know it or not, and a believer must, I think, say that his act in this respect is never futile even though it may not appear to be effective.

The risk of openness is a risk involving the person of the client, and acceptance of the principle (and of the fact) that even in "representation" it is not only an argument or interest being asserted, but a person and a relationship being not asserted, but lived. Another way of saying this is to say that the professional relation should be, at least to the lawyer, an end in itself and not merely a means to an end.

The result of making the person central is that the professional relation is tentative. "Every I-You relationship is a situation defined by the attempt of one partner to act on the other so as to accomplish some goal that is condemned never to be complete." It is risky, too; attitudes defined by professionalism (that is, by role) are less changeable, clearer, and more secure. Moral isolation makes one less vulnerable. What compels an ethic of care, in the face of clarity and relative security elsewhere, is an interest in living professional life in a truthful way. The risk in trying to live truthfully is not the loss of self but the loss of security. The price of openness is "not the I but that false drive for self-affirmation which impels man to flee from the unreliable, unsolid, unlasting, unpredictable, dangerous world of relation into the having of things." What is possible, given the maintenance of moral discourse, is the discovery of truth, and that requires an openness to the other which is almost like passivity. It is a sense of being more than a sense of doing.

Buber is occasionally mystical in describing the I-You relationship as a way to truth. More than mystical, his view of relationship is ontological; it is only in relationship that a person comes to be at all. There are less mystical illustrations of the idea, the most common of which, in the law, is probably the Socratic dialogue. The "Socratic method" in modern legal education has come to mean a manipulative device in which the student (client) comes to discover what the master (lawyer) knew all along. But to Socrates the method was a conversation in which people discover one another, and each discovers himself, and each seeks the true and the good. "We shall unite the officer of judge and advocate in our own persons," he said. In other words, discourse was, to Socrates, not a method so much as a relation.

The professional consequences of this view of moral discourse are in part a need for skills—counseling techniques if you like—for being open and honest. A lawyer who wants moral discourse in his office will attend primarily to what in fact worries the client, rather than to what should worry the client—to hepatitis in the case of the needles, evangelical zeal or family resentment in the will case, romance in the Horsewhip Lawyer case. He will learn to listen to what his client says, attend to what his client feels, find out about the client's values (his authenticity, to use Dworkin's term).

The broader professional consequences could be revolutionary: Lawyers would have to become morally attentive, attending, that is, to the persons of their clients as much as to the problems clients bring to them. Law students would come to insist on education which trains them in the skills of sincerity, congruence, and acceptance. Every level of the legal enterprise would come again to think of moral development as part of its task, all toward a professional ethic of receiving as well as giving—of unfolding, rather than imposing, to use Buber's phrase. Parents give; children receive; adults give *and* receive.

The risk of unrealized mutuality. The ethics of care is distinctive in its mutuality and interdependence. "Humanity is attained by self-determination and other-determination in mutual dependence," Paul Tillich said. "Man strives for his own humanity and tries to help others reach humanity, an attempt which expresses his own humanity." But this mutuality is rarely realized in professional relationships; it may not even be possible to realize it. Buber, pressed in his old age to give vocational application to his great insights on human relationship, tended to salvage what he could for professionals, but finally, I think, saw the professional relationship as a poor model for "I and You." "He [the client] is foundering around, he comes to you ... but he is not interested in you as you. It cannot be.... I see you *mean* being on the same plane, but you cannot.... There is ... a certain situation ... which may sometimes be tragic, even more terrible than what we call tragic.

You *cannot* change this." If a lawyer seeks the relationship with his client that calls him and his client into being, and seeks being only there, he will probably finish in frustration. But, in my view, if he seeks anything less he will not do as much as he can to nourish moral discourse in his practice of law. Even in law offices the moment of surprise is possible.

This anticlimactic concern with mutuality is, here, as Barth said his theology was, "the description of an embarrassment." Barth asked whether a person could be a preacher—"not How *does* one do it? but How *can* one do it?" The answer, out of his Calvinist tradition, was a sense of being under judgment: "If God has chosen us—miracles being *possible* with *him*—and if he will justify us *as* ministers even *in* the church situation [as lawyers even *in* the system of power we inevitably serve], we may be certain that he will do so only *when* we come under *judgment,* when the church [system] comes under judgment, and when our ministry comes under judgment." Barth's image is the high priest in Leviticus, offering the bullock for himself and for his house before he offers the goat in atonement for the sins of the people. The image is important to an understanding of his concept of conditional advice.

Barth's view, gloomy as it may sometimes be, seems to me more productive than a postulate which requires lawyers, as William May reads it, to "reach for that justice and fairness of which the law itself is but an approximation," *unless,* as May also suggests, the reaching is out of the relation—a reaching which sees the goodness of the client as more significant than good decisions made or imposed by the lawyer. At least it is possible to regard one's client as being an end, not merely a means, and to regard him as having infinite value. He is unmediated; he is beyond all categories and concepts; he is uncaused; "I become aware of him, aware that he is different from myself, in the definite, unique way which is peculiar to him, and I accept whom I thus see," Buber said. This attitude may finally be a matter of faith; Buber saw it as a way to fathom the silence of God. "I can recognize in him, know in him, more or less, the person he has been (I can say it only in this word) created to become."

And it is possible, given a mutual commitment to be honest (what I call above the risk of openness), to seek my client's growth, and to seek my growth as well as I deal with my client. Buber was so sure of this possibility that he saw relationship as the one thing in creation which was not subject to entropy.* He speaks of me and of my client—he

---

*This emphasis on the human person implies the wariness toward government which I suggested in Chapter 1, and the wariness toward professional groups which I will suggest in Part Two. "The more unrelated individuals are," Buber said, "the more consolidated the State becomes, and vice versa.... The collective aims at holding in

speaks for each of us, even in a law office—when he says: "Surrounded by the air of a chaos which came into being with him, secretly and bashfully he watches for a Yes which allows him to be and which can come to him only from one human person to another. It is from one man to another that the heavenly bread of self-being is passed."

My concern in these first three chapters has been to ask, "Is it possible to be a Christian and a lawyer?" My answer is that it is possible to be a Christian and a lawyer only if the question remains unsettled—so that the tentative nature of the answer is an admonition to attempt in the practice of law more than the practice itself, the conventional professionalism of it, can bear. To the extent that one determines to conduct his practice as moral conversation, his advocacy as moral discourse, his lawyer skill as the virtue of hope, his life as an affirmation that justice is a gift and not a commodity one has from the government, I think it is possible to be a Christian and a lawyer. Seen that way, the law is a calling in which "we are saying something that we do not know, that *is* true only when it *comes* true" (Buber). As Saint Paul put it:

> I pray that your inward eyes may be illumined, so that you may know what is the hope to which he calls you, what the wealth and glory of the share he offers you among his people in their heritage, and how vast the resources of his power open to us who trust in him. They are measured by his strength and the might which he exerted in Christ when he raised him from the dead. *Ephesians 1:18-20*

Among other things, Paul's is a calling to moral discourse with clients, a calling which impeaches the self-deceptions that allow lawyers to suppose that either the ethics of role or the ethics of isolation are adequate. It calls us to a conversation in which we speak to one another with authority but not as the scribes. If role and insularity, being clever and unchildlike, are adequate, it is not possible to be a Christian and a lawyer. It is not possible for a Christian:

1. To serve an adversary system on the assumption that the government can provide justice.
2. To serve the conventions of civil society, or the demand for social justice, on the assumption that clients must be duped or coerced into good behavior, that an investment in the goodness of clients is not appropriate to the practice of law.
3. To determine one's moral answers outside the human relation which provokes moral questions, on the assumption that moral questions are not worth talking about in a law office.

---

check the inclination to personal life. It is as though those who are bound together in groups should in the main be concerned with the group and should turn to the personal partners, who are tolerated by the group, only in secondary meetings."

My claim is that the ethics of care, which are the ethics of Jews and Christians, have relevance in law offices, and that the ethics of care are not served by either deference or paternalism.

CHAPTER FOUR
A Theology of the Client

The view of the lawyer's calling as ministry distinguishes the ethics of care (Chapter 3) from the ethics of role (Chapter 1) and the ethics of isolation (Chapter 2). This view is a *theology,* in two respects: It provides a theory of purpose for the professional relationship (autonomy or conversion or something in between), and it provides a theory about who the client is.

It is possible to come with the tools of secular ethics to much of what Martin Buber (and Aquinas and Barth) taught and implied about the purpose of a professional relationship. It is possible to do that without theology. Secular scholars of Martin Buber have come of late to call him an anthropologist—not a theologian at all, but a student of mankind. Buber himself, as I have tried to show, and regardless of what he called himself, came to his view of the relationship between two people with and out of faith. "I can say it no other way." The approach of some Buber scholars suggests that they view his theology as an eccentricity; in their view, acceptance of his theology is not necessary to acceptance of his ideas about the I-You relationship.

It seems to me that the Buber scholars are, in this respect, wrong. It is not possible for Buber, or for any of us, to explain insight and at the same time to set aside the richness of a thinker's life and spirit. In Buber's case richness and spirit included his Judaism. But, just possibly, the general question can be left open. Perhaps, at least, one can describe a view of lawyer-client relationship and prescribe for the lawyer a morality of care, without saying much about each lawyer's purpose in entering upon a life of ministry in the law. Perhaps, for example, it is possible to pursue this calling with the object of helping one's client to moral autonomy, to a freedom *from,* without interfering concern for a spiritual destiny which is more than autonomy, which is freedom *for.* *Perhaps.* It is a point on which I cannot be helpful, because I am not a nonbeliever.

A second point of difficulty on the issue of whether the practice of law as a ministry is possible without a theology to teach and nurture it is one's theory of the client. It is a question about who this other person, this You (Thou) is. My theological proposal is that this You is a letter of recommendation from God. I propose to develop the point with an excursion into Paul's endless difficulties with the Christians in Corinth, and then to ask whether theology makes any difference on the issue of who the client is.

Paul went to Corinth for the first time on his second missionary journey (about A.D. 50). Corinth was a teeming, turbulent port city fifty miles from Athens. Paul had been to Athens and had failed in his evangelism there. His clever attempt to convert the intellectual Greeks there, by comparing the risen Christ with their Unknown God, had not worked. He was alone, and weary, and maybe even unwell, when he came to the synagogue in Corinth and began, as was his more usual custom, to attempt to attract Jews to the Christian faith.

Those who attended the synagogue were a fractious lot, compounded of the orthodox, refugees from Claudius's expulsion of the Jews from Rome, many members of the lower classes, and, probably, some Gentiles who were attracted to Judaism but had not been circumcised. "My brothers," Paul later said to these people, "think what sort of people you are, whom God has called. Few of you are men of wisdom, by any human standard; few are powerful or highly born" (1 Corinthians 1:26). "Make no mistake: no fornicator or idolater, none who are guilty either of adultery or of homosexual perversion, no thieves or grabbers or drunkards or slanderers or swindlers, will possess the kingdom of God. Such were some of you" (1 Corinthians 6:9–11). The Bible scholar William Neil says Corinth was "the cesspool of Greece.... It is difficult to know, as we read this letter and its sequel, whether to be more astounded at the dauntless faith and magnificent courage of the apostle, who might have given up in despair, or whether to be more heartened that it was upon such unpromising foundations that God built a world church."

Paul was with these people about two years. His approach through the synagogue was not successful. The leaders of the synagogue brought a Roman prosecution against him. He prevailed in court and then shook the dust of the synagogue from his feet by taking up residence in a Gentile household. His approach to the Gentiles was more successful and, when he left Corinth to return to Antioch, a Corinthian church had been established. But the church was promptly embroiled in bickering and schism; it split itself into at least four parties. During Paul's subsequent year in Antioch, and then during his two years in Ephesus, he heard repeatedly of the sad condition of the followers of Christ in Corinth. He wrote to them four times and made one quick visit there, all in attempts to heal their divisions in an approach which, Neil says, "mingles irony with reproach, tenderness with severity, and pride with humility."

Second Corinthians is the fourth letter he wrote to Corinth and is apparently the last. It was written after he had heard enough to give him some cautious optimism about the future of the Corinthian community. In it he addresses the question I am interested in, the question of who these people are.

"Do we, like some people, need letters of introduction to you, or from you? No, you are all the letter we need, a letter written on our heart; any man can see it for what it is and read it for himself. And as for you, it is plain that you are a letter that has come from Christ, given to us to deliver: a letter written not with ink but with the Spirit of the living God, written not on stone tablets but on the pages of the human heart" (2 Corinthians 3:1-3). "Not the man who recommends himself, but the man whom the Lord recommends—he and he alone is to be accepted" (2 Corinthians 10:18).

The theology of the matter, if we can apply such thoughts to the array of relatively respectable people with whom lawyers deal, is that my client was sent to me by God; God proposes to deal with me through my client. We are told that we have to deliver one another. James Burtchaell may exaggerate this theology a little, but he makes the point boldly when he says, "The only place one can find the Father is in one's brother, and in the transactions of goods and services which will help that brother to become nourished and to grow."

Consider, for example, the duty a lawyer has to respect the confidences and secrets of his client. Geoffrey Hazard, in a recent essay on the origins of the attorney-client privilege, sees this professional rule as "the pivotal element of the modern American lawyer's professional functions," on the two theories that a lawyer cannot act in litigation unless "the client is free to disclose everything, bad as well as good," and that the lawyer's function as a counselor requires that the client be free to make full disclosures to him. The *Code* justifies Canon 4 ("A lawyer should preserve the confidences and secrets of a client") somewhat more broadly, referring to "the fiduciary relationship existing between lawyer and client" and to "the proper functioning of the legal system."

The *Code* extends the requirement of confidentiality to all knowledge which comes to a lawyer "acquired during the course of the representation"; to information learned from third persons; and to information learned before and after the lawyer's employment.

ABA opinions under the 1908 *Canons,* predecessors to the 1969 *Code,* referring seminally to the client's "freedom from fear" with regard to what his lawyer will tell others, extended the requirement of confidentiality to the client's hideout when the client was a fugitive; to informing physicians and hospitals to whom the client owed money that the client had received money in payment of a judgment; to concealing from the court fatal defects in the client's case; even to situations where, when the evidentiary privilege is narrower than the ethical rule of confidentiality, the lawyer will have to go to jail unless he testifies against his client. "It is not justifiable under any circumstances for a lawyer to double-cross a client who employs him," one of the unpublished opinions said. On the other hand, and in some ways more indicatively, the rule did not prohibit disclosure of what the lawyer needed to say in order to collect his fee, or to information the lawyer had in some capacity other than his capacity as lawyer, or to protecting himself from the client's attack on him for professional dishonor or incompetence. The rule as it is at present worded does not extend to the client's stated intention to commit a crime, but it does not require that lawyers report their clients who intend to commit crimes; it merely permits lawyers to do so.

There is a valuable professional tradition at work here, and a psychologically sophisticated social value. There is a strong secular ethic—patent humanism—in the idea that the lawyer must be his client's loyal confidant, even where the price of preserving the value is the frustration of the judicial process, injustice to third persons, and punishment of the lawyer who does his duty. Hazard reflects what is probably a prevailing opinion among modern lawyers, that confidentiality goes to the heart of the professional relationship and to the soul of the professional function. The state has acted, in developing the evidentiary privilege and in ordering a rule of confidentiality for lawyers, in such a way as to say that confidential legal counsel is more valuable *to it* than the discovery of truth is. A lawyer can be disciplined—by the state—if he tells his client's secrets, and his client can demand the lawyer's silence about them, even in court. The evidentiary privilege is the broadest of all evidentiary privileges (broader, for example, than the physician-patient or priest-penitent privileges and more general than the psychologist-client privilege) and, Canon 4 says, the lawyer's duty to respect confidences is broader than the privilege maintained in the law of evidence.

The reason for confidentiality as a professional rule for lawyers is nonetheless narrowly professional. It is for lawyers. It exists so that lawyers can carry out their professional function, and it disappears if confidentiality is interfering with the professional function (as, for example, if the client attacks the lawyer or won't pay his fee or announces that he is setting out on a criminal enterprise). The ABA *Code* pegs the rule, in part, to "the fiduciary relationship existing between lawyer and client," but it limits the fiduciary relationship to professional ends—broadly defined ends, but professional ends all the same.

Hazard has demonstrated that the evidentiary rule has only recently come to serve professional ends. Its history is a history of service to governmental ends. Its origin traces to the fact that a trial lawyer in England is "not merely an 'officer' of the court but a member of it." He cannot testify as to what his client told him, in the case he is pleading, because that will interfere with his carrying out the duties the court designated him to carry out. As late as 1743, in a case in which the client wanted his lawyer to prosecute the client's relative for murder in order to prevent the relative from inheriting ahead of the client, the English court refused to allow the privilege to cover anything except facts relevant to a case the lawyer was employed to plead (and the lawyer there did not plead the trumped-up murder case). The justification of the privilege, at about the time of the American Revolution, was this: "[I]n court the client could not speak for himself and therefore had to inform someone to speak for him." It was equally limited in early nineteenth-century American cases; David Hoffman's Baltimore "Resolutions" of 1836 do not mention confidentiality as a moral duty, although Hoffman devotes a long footnote to the law of lawyer-client privilege.

The rules were invented for governmental reasons and survive for both governmental and professional reasons. (There is some empirical evidence that the rules are not necessary for adequate representation and advice, that clients will disclose what is necessary to the lawyer's professional function whether what they say is held confidential or not.) The risks exist, that is, for the convenience of lawyers and because the state finds it more functional to have such things as evidentiary privileges than not to have them; protecting confidences does more good than hiding the truth does harm.

If, tomorrow, the state decided—as it might, for its own good reason—that evidentiary privilege is not more important than forcing facts from lawyers, the privilege would disappear. (It may be important to notice that privilege has had a much more tenuous history, and has been stated with more exceptions, where the professional has been a clergyman or physician or psychologist.) If, tomorrow, the legal profession decided that the rule of Canon 4 should be abolished (perhaps because of empirical evidence that it does not bring about more disclosures from clients to lawyers), the professional justification would disappear.

Of course there are secular moral arguments to be made to the state and to the profession on why the privilege and Canon 4 should be retained. One secular moral argument is that the state should recognize the interdependence of people. There is something about human beings, in their emotional need for one another, that the state cannot duplicate or find a substitute for. The best thing for the state to do is respect that need and respect what people do in response to it. It is best because people whose need for people is met are better citizens than people who are lonely. People need lawyers to stand between them and the power of the state; they need lawyers to help them through stressful interpersonal combat; they need lawyers to help them face the realities of death and taxes. Even secular morality—even the state—can perceive that the relationship between two people is a valuable and fragile thing which is, for the most part, beyond the power of government and immune from the blunt instruments of law. On sound political principles, the state should leave such relationships alone and should seek to protect them from outside intrusion, especially from intrusion by the state itself. The current debate over whether lawyers should disclose to government untrue statements from their business clients in securities registration is a debate which invokes this argument; the argument against disclosure is not that business people should be able to lie with impunity, but that lawyers functioning within the business relationship can do more for sound morals than government can. (I take up this subject again in Chapters 8 and 9.)

Another secular moral argument is that the state receives useful service from professional relationships. Lawyers encourage obedience to the law; the clergy encourage good moral behavior; physicians encourage good health. These valuable results occur as a result of professional relationships, which relationships depend to some extent on interpersonal intimacy. There is something useful in the relationship between a person who is hurting and a person who proposes to be helpful in bearing the hurt; there is a social utility in "helping person" relationships. These relationships are entitled to respect and protection from government for the same reasons government allows, protects, and even subsidizes secular functions in church-related schools. These services contribute to the common (secular) good; if the schools did not do them, the state would have to do them.

A third secular moral argument is that it is a good thing for human difficulties to be resolved in the arena which involves the fewest people and the least social machinery. The quiet resolution of disputes saves public energy and public money. Even casting aside such aspirations from political philosophy as the principle of subsidiarity, this is a matter of economy. A Christian who specially adheres to Paul's injunctions against repairing to the secular courts saves the state time and money, as does a Jew who takes his family dispute or his dispute with his neighbor to a rabbinical court rather than to the civil courts. Common-law courts, and even administrative agencies, respect the dispute-settlement apparatus within a family or company or school.

Government gives grants to social experiments which create neighborhood mediation services. There is a social value in the engines of reconciliation men and women invent; the professional relationship between the lawyer and client is one of these and is important to the success of some of the others.

These arguments for social good justify both the traditional lawyer-client evidentiary privilege, which was narrow, and the modern rules on confidentiality, which are remarkably broad. We lawyers have a duty, a duty generally respected even in the law of evidence, not to speak of what our clients tell us. This duty is as broad as the need which brings people to us.* It is a duty with social value; our function as professionals depends on it, because our function as professionals requires that we learn the truth as often as we can. Because our function is valuable, the means we must have to perform it well are also valuable.

These are political arguments; none of them would stand up as a sound moral reason for confidentiality, although there may be moral reasons behind them. The reason they are not sound moral reasons is that they depend on the proposition that the state and the organized legal profession are dependable sources of goodness. None of these reasons contains or refers to the ways in which a moral actor can judge whether the profession or the state are right in preferring confidentiality over truth in particular cases. They are, like the adversary ethic and the argument for public-interest lawyers, arguments for a social role which do not contain the means for deciding if a person's acting in that social role is a good thing to do.

The 1743 English case suggests an example for analysis: Henry comes to me and asks me to bring suit against his neighbor Sam for violation of Henry's property boundaries. I establish that there is some ground for such a suit—some slight encroachment by Sam on Henry's property—but then I say, "Now, Henry, I do not think that is the real reason you want me to sue Sam. Tell me the real reason." The profession argues that I need to know the answer to that question so that I can do my duty (which duty includes discouraging senseless litigation and not allowing the courts to be used for ignoble purposes). The state says that I may receive Henry's answer in confidence (without fear of having later to testify about it) because "the proper functioning of the legal system" requires that I have it. Both the profession and the state, or apologists for them, might add one or more of the three secular

---

*I reflect, for example, on cases in which I have represented indigent criminal defendants and prisoners in the Indiana State Prison, people who are usually by definition guilty. My recurrent problem has been to convince the client in that situation that I am on his side. He sees me as part of the machinery which put him behind the bars and wants him to stay there. He tells me what he thinks the judge wants to hear.

arguments I have suggested above. I, therefore, am relatively free to say to Henry: "Don't worry about my telling any of this; I am required to keep your statements confidential."

With or without this assurance, Henry tells me that the real reason he wants to sue Sam is that Sam is of the wrong race and Henry wants Sam to sell out and move away. I balk; Henry goes to another lawyer, who files the suit; Sam counterclaims against Henry, seeking damages for abuse of process, and calls me as a witness. The truth is that Henry used property law for an illegal purpose, and my testimony is necessary to prove that truth.

The evidentiary privilege may keep me from testifying. The traditional privilege would not; the lawyer in the 1743 case was required to testify. The modern American common-law rule would probably keep me from testifying, but the codified (reformed) rule of evidence makes an exception where the client proposes to commit a tort (which is what Henry did; the tort is abuse of process), and out of all of this comes the result that the state, after wavering for centuries, may well require that I testify. I can refuse to do so only on pain of contempt of court.

But the professional rule to which I adhere as a lawyer is broader than the evidentiary privilege. I consider whether I am required by a professional rule to risk jail by refusing to testify. The existing rule (Canon 4) makes an exception for client statements of intention to commit crimes, but not, as the reformed evidentiary rule does, for statements of intention to commit torts.* As matters stand, my profession might require me to go to jail; I could be disciplined by my profession if I did not. The *Code* might call me to a position of moral risk.

But not for long. The committee of the ABA charged with drafting the new *Rules of Professional Conduct* proposes to eliminate the differences between the duty of confidentiality and the evidentiary privilege. The chance that I will have to go to jail for following my *professional* duty stands to be eliminated. If it is eliminated, and if the evidentiary rule which is applicable is the modern one, I will be required to testify, and I will be told by my profession that testifying is the moral thing to do, even though, twenty years ago, both the rules of evidence and professional consensus would have told me not to testify. So much for reliance on the powers of this world, and so much, too, for moral arguments that depend on the goodness of the state and the legal profession.

---

*The *Code* also makes an exception for disclosures "required by law or court order." It is not clear to me whether a trial judge's interpretation of the common-law privilege would be a "court order" within the meaning of this exception. My example assumes it would not.

If I decide, despite the new rules, that I will not testify, and if I want to justify my decision, I will have to argue from moral rules which run deeper and run with more consistency than those provided by the state, the profession, or the secular morality which is used to justify official rules on confidentiality.

This is not yet a point at which a theology of the client is unavoidably necessary. Secular morality could lead me to say that there is more to the human personality of my client, Henry, than the state and the profession is prepared to honor with respect for secrecy. Another human person is an unfathomable mystery; he is indivisible and infinitely valuable. My entry into the life of that other person is sacred (somehow). It is possible to think all of this without also thinking of Henry as a child of God and a letter of recommendation from Christ; it is possible to think all of this without also thinking that God comes to me in people like Henry (or–a more frightening thought–that God comes to Henry in people like me).

Secular morality may explain *that* I should take this risk for Henry, but it does not tell me *why* I should. The risk in refusing to testify does not turn on my view of human personality; it turns on the possibility that Henry can grow. If he cannot grow, why would I risk going to jail in order to protect his nasty little secret? Is it possible, even, and even without a theology of the client, to be optimistic about Henry's abandoning his racism and amounting to something? A moral justification of confidentiality here goes back to Henry's coming to me in the first place and to the possibility of Henry's beginning, right there in my office, to do something better than to bring a racist lawsuit to get rid of his neighbor. If there is not that possibility and that justified risk, my morality of human dignity is something that does not matter. If the possibilities in Henry's life do not include that turn to the light, my theories about his human dignity are held against the evidence.

They are held against the evidence unless, of course, I have the kind of hope which allowed the solitary tent-maker and street preacher from Antioch to suppose that the low-lifes of Corinth would ever amount to anything. It is at the point where growth is the issue–a point beyond social justification and beyond theories of human dignity–that it becomes necessary to have a theology of the client. It may require a theology to be able to look at someone who is so evidently despicable as Henry is, and as the children of God in Corinth were, and be able to say of him: You are my letter of recommendation from Christ, a letter written not with ink, but with the spirit of the living God. To anticipate an idea I will attempt to develop more fully later (Chapter 18 and 19), optimism in the face of Henry's lawsuit is not enough; truth is needed, a truth which can admit Henry's evil design and still think that he might amount to something, or, even if he does not, that he is worth my time and effort because God has redeemed him. Optimism without truth is despair, as much as truth without optimism is. Optimism with truth is what Jews and Christians call hope.

I am willing to say to all of my professional colleagues that reliance on a theory of confidentiality depending upon what the legislature or the American Bar Association has done does not evidence sound morals. Such reliance may be logical; it may accord with sound social policy, for the moment; but it is not sound morals. I am willing to say to those of my professional colleagues who hold humanistic theories of human dignity, which would permit them to refuse, even against the rules, to betray a client's trust, that I admire their theories. But I would have to add that, as a matter of moral reasoning, I cannot understand how those theories could lead to risk and sacrifice for a character like Henry. When it comes to characters like Henry, some of us feel the need for theology.

* * *

There are, of course, obstacles to being able to work with Henry. Reason will not overcome them, but reason might be able to indicate what they are like and why trying to overcome them is worth the effort. One obstacle is that Henry is repulsive, one is that he is guilty, and one is that he proposes to do evil. The following five chapters will consider these obstacles.

CHAPTER FIVE
The Problem of Revulsion

Serving the guilty is probably the oldest and most persistent of moral questions for lawyers. Its age and persistence are evidenced by the vehemence with which nonlawyers condemn us for serving the guilty and by the energy and sophistry we use in defending ourselves. I pose the question first in terms of the fact that guilty people are repulsive, and I do that by reference to a quaint but thorough treatment of it in the character of Thomas Furnival, barrister and member of Parliament in Anthony Trollope's novel *Orley Farm*. Trollope's reaction to Furnival is in many ways the reaction new law students have to us lawyers when they first come to law school and ask us whether it is possible to represent guilty clients. Furnival's reaction to himself is like the reaction law professors have to that question.

Orley Farm is the story of a guilty woman, Lady Mary Mason, who has forged what appears to be a codicil to the will of her dying husband, Sir Joseph Mason. She has done this twenty years before the novel begins. The codicil has been proved, in litigation, through Lady Mason's testimony. As a result, her son Lucius is in possession of the devise at issue, Orley Farm. Sir Joseph's eldest son, Joseph Mason, has been cheated out of the farm. He is a child of Sir Joseph by a former marriage; Lucius is Lady Mason's only child. Her forgery is like the misdeed of the biblical Rebecca; she has acted dishonestly to benefit her child.

A scheming and vengeful solicitor named Dockwrath has, as he believes, been mistreated by Lucius. Dockwrath sets out to prove the forgery from old documents which will show how Lady Mason got through the will contest. What she did was this: On the day the codicil was supposedly executed the witnesses to it signed another document for Sir Joseph–a partnership deed. Lady Mason gave the codicil that same date; the witnesses to the deed thought (and testified) that what they signed was the codicil. Dockwrath produces the partnership deed and the aging witnesses, and the witnesses are prepared to say that they signed only one paper. Dockwrath succeeds in getting Joseph Mason and his respectable London lawyers to agree to prosecute Lady Mason for perjury, based on her testimony in the will contest. That is the suspense in the story. Trollope thought it was his best plot in forty-seven novels.

Lady Mason returns to the barrister who represented her in the will contest—Thomas Furnival. Furnival represents and befriends her even though he comes quickly to see what happened and to believe that his client is guilty of forgery and perjury. He serves the guilty with misgiving and professional bluster, as we justify to our students the fact that we and our colleagues serve the guilty. I pause, now, for a while, over these loyalties and emotions of Thomas Furnival.

Lady Mason is an attractive client—pretty, upright, dependent, pathetic but appealing in her pathos. This elemental human attraction is part of the reason Furnival serves her. Another part is that Furnival has been through this issue once before and then managed to suppress his doubts about her and get her a verdict, a result which convinces Furnival that he was right to suppress his doubts then and would be right to suppress them again:

> Twenty years ago, at the time of the trial, he had at one time thought,—it hardly matters to tell what, but those thoughts had not been favorable to her cause. Then his mind had altered, but he had learned,—as lawyers do learn—to believe in his own case. And when the day of triumph had come, he had triumphed loudly, commiserating his dear friend for the unjust suffering to which she had been subjected.

But the first stages of dealing with Lady Mason on the second occasion raise the old doubts—and, because Furnival is sharp, he can see what happened. Nonetheless:

> Mr. Furnival did think that he might induce a jury to acquit her; but he terribly feared that he might not be able to induce the world to acquit her also. As he thought of all the case, he seemed to put himself apart from the world at large. He did not question himself as to his own belief, but seemed to feel that it would suffice for him if he could so bring it about that her other friends should think her innocent. It would by no means suffice for him to secure for her son the property, and for her a simple acquittal. It was not that he dreaded the idea of thinking her guilty himself; perhaps he did think her so now—he half thought her so, at any rate; but he greatly dreaded the idea of others thinking her so.

So there were three things working on Mr. Furnival—personal attraction, what he thought of as loyalty to Lady Mason's broader interests, and a zeal born of professionalism. In all of these ways and in each of them a lawyer comes to believe in his own case. Trollope makes an interesting distinction. Furnival is attracted to Lady Mason; he feels a loyalty to her which is more than professional loyalty. He wants to save her from the world's disapproval—which means that Furnival knows that the world cannot forgive her as he does. "He wished he could know whether or no she were innocent, without knowing whether or no she were guilty."

> He said to himself that he could forgive the fault. That it had been repented ere this he did not doubt, and it would be sweet to say to her that it was very grievous, but that yet it might be forgiven. It would be sweet to feel that she was in his hands, and that he would treat her with mercy and kindness. But then a hundred other thoughts forbade him to think more of this. If she had been guilty—if she declared her guilt to him—would not restitution be necessary? In that case her son must know it, and all the world must know it. Such a confession would be incompatible with that innocence before the world which it was necessary that she should maintain. Moreover, he must be able to proclaim aloud his belief in her innocence; and how could he do that, knowing her to be guilty—knowing that she also knew that he had such knowledge? It was impossible that he should ask any such question, or admit of any such confidence.

Mr. Furnival cannot face up to the consequences of Lady Mason's guilt—neither the consequences to her nor the consequences to himself. If she is guilty, and if he remains by her side, then he is guilty too. It is necessary *to his function* that she remain, as we lawyers say, *not guilty*. She need not be innocent, but she must be not guilty.

The importance of Lady Mason's being not guilty becomes more prominent as the trial approaches. Mr. Furnival's ardor cools. It bothers him that the nature of the case requires him to engage two criminal trial lawyers whom he secretly regards as not honorable. At the trial, it is neither ardor nor his client's respectability which pulls him through, but professionalism. In other words, it is not her being innocent which pulls him through; it is her being not guilty:

> [O]n these three days—seeing that he had not shaken the matter off, he rose to his work as though he still loved her, as though all his mind was still intent on preserving that ill-gotten inheritance for her son. It may almost be doubted whether at moments during these three days he did not again persuade himself that she was an injured woman. [But:] [A]s he sat down he knew that she had been guilty! To his ear her guilt had never been confessed; but yet he knew that it was so, and, knowing that, he had been able to speak as though her innocence were a thing of course. That those witnesses had spoken truth he also knew, and yet he

had been able to hold them up to the execration of all around them as though they had committed the worst of crimes from the foulest of motives. And more than this, stranger than this, worse than this,—when the legal world knew—as the legal world soon did know—that all this had been so, the legal world found no fault with Mr. Furnival, conceiving that he had done his duty by his client in a manner becoming an English barrister and an English gentleman.

That is all possible, we lawyers say, because Lady Mason, although not innocent, was entitled to a lawyer who would treat her as not guilty.

Trollope editorializes in that fashion, but, great novelist that he is, he makes his point better by comparing Furnival with other lawyers in the story—particularly with his junior colleague Felix Graham and with Mr. Chaffanbrass, a wily criminal defense lawyer, brought down from the Old Bailey, whom Trollope regards as typical. Graham is unable to be in the case, he says, unless he believes Lady Mason to be innocent. He disapproves of the way English lawyers face questions of guilt and innocence. He believes that a trial lawyer should seek to find and demonstrate truth, and not seek to serve guilty clients. Furnival has to pretend to Graham that he, Furnival, believes in Lady Mason's innocence. Chaffanbrass has contempt for Graham. Trollope uses Graham and Chaffanbrass to frame Furnival's moral problem. When Furnival first suggests to Chaffanbrass that they retain Graham as their junior helper:

> "Felix Graham is very much interested in the case," said Mr. Furnival, "and is as firmly convinced of her innocence as—as I am." And he managed to look his ally in the face and to keep his countenance firmly.
> "Ah," said Mr. Chaffanbrass. "But what if he should happen to change his opinion about his own client?"
> "We could prevent that, I think."
> "I'm not so sure. And then he'd throw her over as sure as your name's Furnival."
> "I hardly think he'd do that."
> "I believe he'd do anything." And Mr. Chaffanbrass was quite moved to enthusiasm. "I've heard that man talk more nonsense about the profession in one hour, than I ever heard before since I first put a cotton gown on my back. He does not understand the nature of the duty which a professional man owes to his client."

Graham is diffident in the trial, of course; Chaffanbrass growls at him, and Trollope says that he can understand why Chaffanbrass would feel as he does. "Considering the lights with which he has been lightened, there was a species of honesty about Mr. Chaffanbrass which certainly deserved praise. He was always true to the man whose money he had taken, and gave to his customer, with all the power at his command, that assistance which he had professed to sell. But we may give the same praise to the hired bravo who goes through with truth and courage the task which he has undertaken. I knew an assassin in Ireland who professed that during twelve years of practice in Tipperary he had never failed when he had once engaged himself. For truth and honesty to their customers—which are great virtues—I would bracket that man and Mr. Chaffanbrass together."

Neither Chaffanbrass nor Graham struggles with the moral problem. Graham, like some of our youngest students, would establish a system in which accused people have no defense if lawyers think them guilty—a system in which lawyers, not juries and judges, decide questions of guilt. Graham would deprive us of our right to regard our clients as not guilty. Because Graham is self-righteous in his adherence to the purity of this principle, he has to be duped by his colleagues and he has to avoid personal contact with his client. The world has to hide itself and to pretend, for his benefit.

Mr. Chaffanbrass does not believe that guilt has anything to do with the case. He supposes his clients to be guilty even when they are innocent (as in his defense of Phineas Finn, in another Trollope novel, *Phineas Redux*). He is the sort of lawyer our youngest students disapprove of; he seems to have no morals. He acts as if lawyers have a license to ignore both the truth and the consequences of what they do.

Mr. Furnival is neither a hired bravo nor a Pharisee. He gets no comfort from sitting in judgment and none from refusing to sit in judgment. Furnival struggles. In the end he resolves his struggle through self-delusion. When erotic attraction has cooled, and when there is no joy left in loyalty to his client, he comes to believe in his case because he sees advocacy as a job. It is service which saves Mr. Furnival, but not service to his client. He is saved by service to the government.

There are three moral questions here: One is that Lady Mason has cheated her stepson. One is that she continues to do so. And one has to do with a social fact: The guilty are repulsive. Lady Mason, as pretty and respectable as she is, comes to be repulsive to everyone in the story, even to herself. Her neighbor and friend, Sir Peregrine Orme, loves her and is at one point engaged to marry her, but he gives her up when he learns of her guilt; he withdraws his household from her and becomes a dying recluse because the tragedy of her guilt is his tragedy, too—a tragedy he believes he cannot share with her but must bear alone. Lady Mason's closest friend, Sir Peregrine's daughter-in-law, Mrs. Orme, still comforts Lady Mason, but Mrs. Orme also urges her to confess her guilt and make restitution. Lucius, Lady Mason's son and the beneficiary of her treachery, says at the end, "She can never be my mother again." And Lady Mason herself, although she is acquitted, admits her guilt, restores the farm to Joseph, and banishes herself to Germany.

"She bowed her head and kissed the rod, she prayed that her release might come to her soon."

Revulsion and the New Testament. The social and personal reality I am concerned about in this chapter is revulsion. The New Testament is filled with repulsive people; one of the most prominent things the New Testament does is provide an answer to the issue of revulsion. But the New Testament answer is a difficult answer. The problem of whether to serve the guilty is answered with stories of Jesus having lunch with tax collectors and choosing his friends from among prostitutes, thieves, violent revolutionaries, and Samaritans—"many bad characters," Matthew says (9:10). Evidence that the New Testament answer is difficult is available in the fact that few Christians follow Jesus' example in this respect, and almost as few can understand it. It may be that the processes by which the world condemns people are important and useful processes. It may be, as is often the case with New Testament answers, that Jesus' solution is painful.

Emile Durkheim noticed, nearly a hundred years ago, that crime is "an integral part of all healthy societies." It is, he said, "a movement of the public temper" more than it is an assault on the community. It is a process for clarifying values more than it is a challenge to values. It is both the stimulus and the product of a society's need to stand for something. If we didn't have criminals we would have to invent them; without criminals we would have no public morals. Seen in this sociological perspective, Lady Mason, in her crime, contributed to the maintenance of the private-property economy of Victorian England and to the tradition which provided for the families of dead men by having their property devolve on their eldest sons. She gave her society an opportunity to reaffirm these values.

Kai Erikson compared Durkheim's theory of deviance with the criminal-court records of the Massachusetts Bay Colony. He discovered that that earliest definitional American society defended and defined itself through three "crime waves," each of which occurred when it had a need to draw itself together, and each of which served to locate and underline important social values. The first of these crime waves was the antinomian controversy of the 1650s, the second was the immigration of the Quakers about five years later, and the third was the witch trials at the end of the seventeenth century. Erikson noticed several things about these processes of definition which are important in understanding why it is that New Testament stories on serving the guilty provide a painful answer to the problem of revulsion.

Criminality is conferred. It is not accurate to define crime as you would define a disease—as if society were a body and misconduct were pathological. Ann Hutchinson and others who were identified as criminal in the antinomian crisis were not markedly unusual in their behavior, but their behavior came at a time when it was important to support the authority of the leaders of the colony. The Quakers were, in their theology and their political objectives, similar to the Puritans, but they came to the colony at a time when its theocratic principles were at risk. In each case, and in the case of the witches, who arose when expansion of the colony was threatening its political integrity, criminals gave the colony a needed opportunity to reinforce values which were central to its survival.

Crime is not a game, as some deviance processes are. We have ways of establishing good manners and civility without condemning people, but the criminal law is not one of them. Criminal law is played out on the borders of the community; it is a confrontation between those who are at the limits and those "whose special business it is to guard the cultural integrity of the community." The utility provided by criminal law was, given the importance of real property and of inheritance in the island economy of England in 1860, equally true of Lady Mason and of what she was accused of doing. She forged the will, and then lied about it, because she thought it was wrong of her husband to give nothing to her child. She knew, too, that she had confronted one wrong by committing another.

The criminal and those who seek to punish her are cooperators. The criminal cooperates in the process by condemning herself; each side nourishes the other. There is something to be said for Felix Graham's concern for honesty and decency in his society. And there is something to be said for Lady Mason's role in helping Felix get his values straight. The deviant "is not a bit of debris spun out by faulty social machinery, but a relevant figure in the community's overall division of labor."

Criminals are sometimes evil and sometimes not. The powers of the world condemn the deviant out of the world's needs, so that, during the fervor of war, the conscientious objector is as much an outcast as the thief. And if, occasionally, the outcast becomes a successful revolutionary or reformer, the prosecutors of yesterday become the outcasts of today. The important point about the sociological analysis is that *power, serving as always to perpetuate itself by processes of fear, causes the criminal to become repulsive.*

The community, which always has and always needs processes of condemnation, *seems to lack processes of reconciliation.* It always manages to throw people out—it always *has* to do that—but it lacks ways to get them back in again. Mrs. Orme, who was Lady Mason's comforter, knew that; that is why she is a model of virtue in her care for Lady Mason. But she is also the person who insists on repentance, and the person who knows that, repentant or not, Lady Mason cannot get back in. Mr. Furnival sees that fact, too, and determines to save Lady Mason from public suspicion of guilt. Sir Peregrine, who loves Lady Mason, sees the same fact and his knowledge throws him into despair. The price of being a criminal, of cooperating in the society's important task of defining itself, is a tragic price; the stories of Jesus, while they may say something to those of us who propose to serve the repulsive, do not make them any less repulsive. Sometimes there is nothing for God to forgive (Ann Hutchinson, or the biblical leper), and sometimes the criminal has done something sinful (Lady Mason, the good thief), but even if God forgives them, or doesn't need to, and we are supposed to forgive them, or don't need to, the world is not likely to forgive them. *Repentance is not a way back in; repentance is tragic.*

The point of Mr. Furnival's concern to vindicate Lady Mason publicly, as well as judicially, is just this point. If she is found out, her respectability is finished. When Mrs. Orme insists that Lady Mason must admit her guilt, Mrs. Orme knows, and Lady Mason knows, that the results of repentance will be tragic. Lady Mason will lose her respectability, once and for all, and Lucius will lose both his respectability and Orley Farm. Repentance is not a way back into the community. Mrs. Orme practices what Aquinas called "fraternal correction"—the virtue of charity. She is a good friend, in all senses of the word; she is unconditionally caring. But she does not hide the truth, not from herself and not from Lady Mason. "Love does not keep a record of wrongs; love is not happy with evil, but is happy with truth" (1 Cor. 13:6). Mrs. Orme knows and says that Lady Mason cannot get back in.

Jesus forgave the woman taken in adultery and saved her from capital punishment. He sent her away shriven and redeemed, but she was no less an adulteress (John 8:1-11). The *social* effects of repentance, in other words, are not redemptive; God's kingdom is not of this world. This is the contrast between two orders. The powers of this world turn criminals out—communities turn people out—they do it inevitably. They do it in the process of defining and defending themselves; turning people out is implicit in the definition of a community which is formed by the powers of this world. Jesus' answer to that fact is to say that his kingdom is not part of the community formed by the powers of this world; the world of power through fear is not part of his kingdom. His alternative is stark and tragic: He gathers his followers around him, but he does the gathering on Calvary. His kingdom, as John Howard Yoder puts it, *is* the Cross.

Jesus does not re-socialize social outcasts. He does not offer this service to the community. Mrs. Orme knew that, and Lady Mason knew that. He redeems outcasts. The tax gatherer who became Matthew was not turned into a respectable Jewish citizen; neither was Cornelius, the Roman officer to whom the Lord sent Peter (Acts 10); nor was the woman who had been taken in adultery. When Jesus touched the leper, Jesus became a leper. Jesus was then forbidden to enter the city openly.

He was required, like the leper, to live outside, and to call out "unclean, unclean" (Leviticus 13:45; Mark 1:42-45).

The stories of Jesus and the guilty people of his day offer an answer to the question of how a lawyer is to serve the guilty, but it is a hard, hard answer. Jesus offers comfort, but his is the comfort of one who is, as Karl Barth put it, wholly other. It is the comfort of a kingdom which is wholly other. The comfort is the comfort of Cross and Resurrection. It involves, for a Christian lawyer, the agony of living, working and wielding power in the worldly kingdom and seeking at the same time to stand with the outcasts under the Cross.

Lawyers' answers. All of Trollope's three lawyers were Christians but not one meets the problem of serving the guilty with a New Testament answer. Mr. Chaffanbrass claims for himself the benefits of the adversary ethic. He takes advantage of a license, which no other citizen enjoys, to overlook the consequences of what he does. Those who argue for such a license claim that it is essential to the purposes of the government that lawyers be given this special license: The government will do justice only if every person called to book before the government has an advocate. Mr. Chaffanbrass would say that Lady Mason must have her case argued fully, so that judge and jury can do justice, and that it is the mission of other lawyers to argue the case for the prosecution. Neither set of lawyers need worry about the outcome; that is the government's worry. Mr. Chaffanbrass's moral claim is the one Trollope, who was a man of the world and the son of a trial lawyer, could not understand; but it is the dominant principle in our *Code,* and, for the most part, the answer we law professors give to our youngest students when they wonder how lawyers can serve the guilty.

Felix Graham does not stand on Calvary either. He argues, as modern "public-interest" lawyers often argue, that lawyers should see to the benefit of the community. It is more important, in Felix's view, for Lady Mason's lawyer to get at and proclaim the truth than it is for him to argue for Lady Mason's acquittal. The reason it is more important to find and proclaim the truth is that a lawyer is a public servant. "It all resolves itself into this," Felix says. "Let every lawyer go into court with a mind resolved to make conspicuous to the light of day that which seems to him to be the truth. A lawyer who does not do that—who does the reverse of that, has in my mind undertaken work which is unfit for a gentleman and impossible for an honest man." But, Trollope says, "No living orator would convince a grocer that coffee should be sold without chicory; and no amount of eloquence will make an English lawyer think that loyalty to truth should come before loyalty to his client." And, therefore, Felix is not professionally successful. Mr. Chaffanbrass, who is successful, condemns Felix as unprofessional.

Furnival, who is both respectable and successful, does not trust Felix. He has to lie to Felix and protect him from the lies of others.

Thomas Furnival feels a little of the agony of trying to serve the kingdom of the world and also stand on Calvary, or at least he feels agony which is like that agony. He resolves his agony illegitimately, though—at first through the memory of a past triumph and an erotic attraction to his client, and then through the familiar juices of competition. Furnival, finally, longed to beat Joseph Mason a second time, and he did; the excitement of the courtroom carried him through. His client was an incidental professional necessity. He resolved the agony as lawyers, I think, often do—through the emotional dynamics of a demanding, intricate game—a game which, I will say for myself, I find more engrossing than any other game I have ever played.

None of these lawyers has an answer which will stand up to moral analysis. Mr. Chaffanbrass takes advantage of a license to be immoral. He doesn't bother to argue why he should have such a license; those who do argue say that the professional privilege is necessary in order for a lawyer to serve the state. A modern American lawyer might even say that he does not serve the guilty at all; he serves the Constitution. The problem with that as a moral position is that it provides no way to decide if the system is worth serving. Service merely to power can end one up in Buchenwald—not as a victim but as an executioner.

Felix Graham claims a dispensation from Mr. Chaffanbrass's loyalty to Lady Mason, but his claim is essentially the same claim Mr. Chaffanbrass makes. Felix also rests his morality on duty to the state. He seeks to serve the public interest in much the same way an elected official or a civil servant seeks to serve the public interest. His system does not offer, any more than that of Mr. Chaffanbrass, a way to evaluate what the state is up to.

And Furnival—poor Thomas Furnival—suffers from his passions. (That is how one refers, in the Thomistic tradition, to being subject to lust, jealousy, anger, and pride; it is suffering from one's passions.) He makes no clear moral claim at all, and, because he does not, all of his decisions are made for him. He stands firmly in midair. Many lawyers work out the problem of serving the guilty in this way. The ambivalence of it is expressed in our official rules on serving the guilty. ("Ambivalence" is a word derived from chemistry and means being pulled simultaneously in two directions.) On the one hand, "It is ethical for a member of the bar to represent the accused even if he knows the latter to be guilty. In fact, it may be on occasion an ethical duty to do so." But, on the other hand, "There are certain inherent limitations.... There must be no relationship between them except purely that of attorney and client; counsel must retain control of the presentation of the case, and neither the client nor any outside person may dictate to him how to conduct the case.... Counsel is not expected to stultify himself in an attempt to advance his client's interest. The attorney is justified in withdrawing, where, during the progress of the litigation, the client engages in conduct that tends to degrade or humiliate the attorney."* This is what you sound like when you rationalize your service in the courts of the world. In the courts of the world, respectability—honor, if you like—is of first importance. It is difficult to serve there and at the same time to stand on Calvary. On Calvary, we are in the service of adulteresses, lepers, prostitutes, thieves, Samaritans, tax gatherers, publicans, and heathens—and we are so much in their service that we risk being regarded by the world as they are regarded. That is the Christian life, and there may be no honor in it.

Two tentative thoughts on a theology of serving the guilty. An adequate moral answer to the problem of serving the guilty would, I think, involve first a turning *toward* the guilty. It would involve a more generous response than our official rules allow for; it would involve even a loving relationship, an I-Thou relationship, as Martin Buber put it. The gospel seems to say that we *have* to do that; we are commanded to do it. The Christian system for approaching outcasts is manifestly a system for, above all, *being with* them.

A second tentative thought is that we should be honest about looking for the fact or force which makes it hard for us to serve the guilty. The criminal law is, at least in large part, a system for adding coercion to an agreed-upon set of social rules. It is in some ways a system of sin but it is not a system of redemption, because, as Kai Erikson demonstrates, it offers no way back in. It is, in that sense, not a moral system so much as it is a system for protecting power. Erikson's most remarkable finding in the criminal-court records in colonial Massachusetts was that crime rates were stable. When the fever broke out and people were prosecuted for disobedience, or for Quaker theology, or for black magic, the incidence of other crimes declined. The amount of social energy given to prosecution remained stable. There seemed to be fewer thieves, more witches, fewer murderers, more Quakers. One offense became less important as another became more important. The amount of energy the world devoted to its system of right and wrong was constant. That energy was always directed to the offense which most threatened the maintenance of power. The method and the product of that social system was fear. You were supposed to become as afraid of disobedience as you would be of theft.

Another way to put it is that the kinds of crime which showed up in the records were related to the things which power feared most— disobedience as the colony began to become diverse; unacceptable

---
*These quotations are from a recent annotation in the *American Law Reports.*

liberalism in belief as liberalism began to gain ground in Mother England; alliances with the devil as the theocratic regime began to crumble. Evil appeared as the elders lost authority, and as the elders lost authority evil appeared. "Men who fear witches," Erikson says, "soon find themselves surrounded by witches." In Lady Mason's case: "Men who become jealous of private property soon encounter eager thieves."

The first problem for us Christian lawyers is not: How *can* we serve the guilty? It is: Why *don't* we serve the guilty? Why do we need excuses such as the Constitution or the *Code* or the integrity of the legal profession when we have the story of Jesus? I think we fail to serve the guilty because we are afraid. Whether the criminal law is a system of morals or not, it is a system of fear and power. First and always it is a system which defends itself through fear. Stanley Hauerwas, in his *Theology Today* essay, expressed what I mean here: "[B]y learning to be forgiving we are enabled to view other lives not as threats but as gifts. Thus in contrast to all societies built on shared resentments and fears, Christian community is formed by a story that enables [Christians] to trust the otherness of the other as the very sign of the forgiving character of God's kingdom." It is not guilt which keeps us from serving the guilty. It is fear.

CHAPTER SIX
The Problem of Representing the Guilty

Is there a difference between the guilty who are really guilty and the guilty who are victims of the pretensions and delusions of power and fear? Ann Hutchinson did only what appears, to modern eyes and ears, to be the use of her considerable intelligence on matters of faith and morals. A conscientious objector to war or some other governmental adventure–Thomas More, for example (Chapters 18 and 19), or Franz Jagerstatter (Chapter 20)–were yesterday's criminals but are heroes today. The seventeenth-century Quaker in Massachusetts was purer than his Puritan persecutors and the witches who were killed in Salem were at worst what we would today call mentally ill. These people were not guilty, not really guilty; they were victims of the social needs of their own generations. They were not the same, morally, as a Mafia don or Lady Mason, both of whom are really guilty.

This comparison underlines the point that a theology of serving the guilty can only go so far with the deviance theories of Durkheim and Kai Erikson. Sociologists describe a system in which the victims of fear and the really guilty are treated alike; all are cast out, none gets back in. Jewish and Christian theology distinguishes between those who are victims and those who are really guilty; there is such a thing, in theology, as guilt. "Do not suppose that I have come to abolish the law," Jesus said. "I did not come to abolish, but to complete" (Matthew 5:17). He served both the leper and the adulteress, but to the adulteress, and not to the leper, he said, "Go and do not sin again" (Mark 1:40-45; John 8:11). The difference I notice here is the difference between the leper and the adulteress.

The tension Trollope describes in Thomas Furnival, and then frames in comparing the torn conscience of Felix Graham with the hardened conscience of Mr. Chaffanbrass, is a real tension. Our arguments to law students, that our services are needed to protect the innocent and those who are the victims of tyranny and fear, leave law students wondering about professional services–including Furnival's argument for acquittal and his sarcastic cross examination of honest witnesses—for people such as Lady Mason, people who are really guilty. I attempt a description of this tension in terms of the situation of American lawyers, in this chapter, and look at it as a theological tension in the next chapter.

Geoffrey Hazard points out that the elementary idea of professional service in the law is a scandal to lay people—the idea that the professional, claiming to serve the community and the government, can prefer one person over another. In America all persons are equal; that is a principle of moral behavior, as well as a political principle, and one who announces special preference for one person over others is suspect, particularly if he proposes to exercise that preference in return for money. That, I think, is the basic moral tension lying behind the problem of representing the really guilty; it is aggravated by the two facts that the really guilty seem not to deserve representation (the issue I discussed in Chapter 5) and that the really guilty deserve condemnation.

This tension runs through the history of the profession in America. England had worked out a way of solving it, by treating trial lawyers, those who plead for the guilty, as officials in the governmental agency charged with clearing the jails; in Hazard's phrase, an English barrister is not so much an officer of the court as a member of it. The English barrister travels with the judge. He first meets his client in court. He is isolated from his client by another professional (the solicitor), whose function it is to interview the client and other witnesses, explicate a legal theory of the case, and see to the barrister's fee. There are many reasons why this system has endured in England and many reasons why it did not survive in this country—but this official function in the barrister, and the distance between him and his client, help to explain it. In America the lawyer was a general practitioner. He met his client in jail. Judges here were many and of varying qualifications. (In England judges were, and are, few and of high qualifications). As the nineteenth century wore on, American judges were even subject to popular election and to all of the egalitarian and anti-intellectual forces of Jacksonian democracy, one of which forces was government by contention.

The earliest tension (dating this bit of history from the American Revolution), as I see it, was the tension between the English ideal of the trial lawyer and America's attempt to build or discover a national community, built on a constitutional system fashioned by lawyers—on law and not on men—to fulfill the promise implicit in the ringing Jeffersonian prose of our Declaration of Independence. On the one hand, such specifically professional ideals as American lawyers could find to announce were English. Professional admonitions of the period 1817-54 are filled with references to lawyer heroes in England; the jurisprudence was Blackstonian; the precedents were English common law. On the other hand, Americans—lawyers in the midst of them, and perhaps most of all—were working on the national edifice Martin Marty calls a "Righteous Empire."

The English-barrister ideal exalted the narrowest sort of loyalty to the client, but only in the narrowest lawyer-client context. Lord Brougham's speech to the House of Lords in the Queen Caroline case is the famous (and probably most hyperbolic) example: "[A]n advocate, by the sacred duty which he owes his client, knows in the discharge of that office but one person in the world, that client and none other. To save that client by all expedient means, to protect that client at all hazards and costs, to all others, and among others to himself, is the highest and most unquestioned of his duties; and he must not regard the alarm, the suffering, the torment, the destruction which he may bring upon any other. Separating the duty of a patriot from that of an advocate, he must go on, reckless of consequences: though it should be his unhappy lot to involve his country in confusion."

The other force on American lawyers was the idea that America was God's new Israel; that the Millennium would begin on these shores; that God's design for the world was being worked out in a special way in this country. This idea of Righteous Empire was not the invention only of frontier evangelists; it was also a logical (and expressed) consequence of Jefferson's theory of moral improvement among people who had new opportunity for growth and property; the phrase "God's new Israel" was Jefferson's phrase. The Righteous Empire was compounded of enlightenment optimism and Christian millennial thinking—they happened, on that one point, to agree. The revival itself, from its earliest Methodist origins in the 1740s, was strongly ethical—always more ethical than theological—and, during the first half of the nineteenth century, was ethical in terms of social goals and social policy, including the law. David Hoffman, the first American lawyer to attempt a codification of legal ethics, was a formidable Bible scholar; George Sharswood, whose essay and lecture on legal ethics formed the basis of the ABA *Canons,* was a Presbyterian Sunday-school teacher all during the most turbulent and exciting years of the revival of 1840-57. And the revival was nowhere more turbulent than among Presbyterians. Perry Miller quotes Samuel Chapin saying (1829) that law is "not a combination simply for the protection of life and property; but it is an association for moral improvement." The religion of the revival was a social religion; it rested on a broad nondenominational consensus;* it beat back theological notions which were incompatible with

---

*The consensus was Protestant. One of the reasons jurisprudes of this era relied so much on "natural law," despite its associations with Roman Catholic theology, was that their natural law came from Blackstone, who was dependably Protestant. After large numbers of Roman Catholic immigrants began to arrive, in the 1850s, there was

democratic "free will" dogmas about salvation ("Old Light" Calvinism for example); and it did not shrink from bringing its vision of empire into government. European visitors said that American government and this American state religion were for all practical purposes inseparable.

In terms of religious ethos, "the question before each community was whether it was acting as a community" (Marty). The tension for American lawyers was between the narrow idea of client loyalty which came to them from the largely alien professional culture of London and the idea that the American community was a Righteous Empire—the kingdom come or at least the kingdom coming. Anthony Trollope's mother, Frances, visited America during these years and complained of the stifling effect of this consensus. "Religious tyranny," she called it. The tension was resolved by framing the question in terms of the best interests of the community and in reference to generally held ideas about personal morality.

I would like to consider this resolution in reference to the theories of David Hoffman and George Sharswood. Hoffman (1774–1854) practiced law in Baltimore until middle age; he was prosperous and successful when, at the age of 40, he reduced his practice to become a law teacher in the newly founded University of Maryland. In preparation for his new career he prepared an outline of law study for those who proposed to become lawyers, one section of which was devoted to telling students how they should behave as lawyers. This was the first essay on legal ethics published in America. (It was first published in 1817, then expanded and published for both law students and lawyers in 1836; I am using the 1836 version, which has apparently not been reprinted since 1953.) The problem of representing the really guilty was a prominent one for him, and he answered it as one who saw the problem in terms of community interest. Here are Resolutions 10, 15, and 33, from his 50 "Resolutions in Regard to Professional Deportment."

> Should my client be disposed to insist on captious requisitions, or frivolous and vexatious defences, they shall be neither enforced nor countenanced by me. And if still adhered to by him from a hope of pressing the other party into an unjust compromise, or with any other motive, he shall have the option to select other counsel.

* * *

> When employed to defend those charged with crimes of the deepest dye, and the evidence against them, whether legal, or moral, be such as

---

a Catholic revival which was similar in method and even in aspiration to the older American Protestant revival; an interesting piece of evidence is that one of the most florid Catholic revival preachers, Redemptorist Father Clarence Walworth, was converted at a Protestant revival meeting.

The Problem of Representing the Guilty

to leave no just doubt of their guilt, I shall not hold myself privileged, much less obliged, to use my endeavors to arrest, or to impede the course of justice, by special resorts to ingenuity–to the artifices of eloquence–to appeals to the morbid and fleeting sympathies of weak juries, or of temporizing courts–to my own personal weight of character–nor finally, to any of the overweening influences I may possess, from popular manners, eminent talents, exalted learning, etc. Persons of atrocious character, who have violated the laws of God and man, are entitled to no such special exertions from any member of our pure and honourable profession; and indeed, to no intervention beyond securing to them a fair and dispassionate investigation of the *facts* of their cause, and the due application of the law: all that goes beyond this, either in manner or substance, is unprofessional, and proceeds, either from a mistaken view of the relation of client and counsel, or from some unworthy and selfish motive, which sets a higher value on professional display and success, than on truth and justice, and the substantial interests of the community. Such an inordinate ambition, I shall ever regard as a most dangerous perversion of talents, and a shameful abuse of an exalted station. The parricide, the gratuitous murderer, or other perpetrator of like revolting crimes, has surely no such claim on the commanding talents of a profession, whose object and pride should be the suppression of all vice, by the vindication and enforcement of the laws. Those, therefore, who wrest their proud knowledge from its legitimate purposes, to pollute the streams of justice, and to screen such foul offenders from merited penalties, should be regarded by all, (and certainly shall be by me,) as ministers at a holy altar, full of high pretension, and apparent sanctity, but inwardly base, unworthy, and hypocritical–dangerous in the precise ratio of their commanding talents, and exalted learning.

* * *

What is wrong, is not the less so from being common. And though few *dare to be singular,* even in a right cause, I am resolved to make my own, and not the conscience of others, my sole guide. What is morally wrong, cannot be professionally right, however it may be sanctioned by time or custom. It is better to be right with a few, or even none, than wrong, though with a multitude. If, therefore, there be among my brethren, any traditional moral errors of practice, they shall be studiously avoided by me, though in so doing, I unhappily come in collision with what is (erroneously I think) too often denominated the policy of the profession. Such cases, fortunately, occur but seldom, but when they do, I shall trust to that moral firmness of purpose which shrinks from no consequences, and which can be intimidated by no authority however ancient or respectable.

Hoffman's is a principle of diminished representation–almost, by modern standards, no representation at all. Presumably he would, unlike Felix Graham, have consented to represent Lady Mason, but he would not, like Mr. Chaffanbrass, have done his best for her, nor, like Thomas Furnival, have argued her innocence or challenged the testimony of her accusers. He prefers to honor "the course of justice ... a fair and dispassionate investigation of the *facts* ... and due application of the law." It is important to remember, of Hoffman, what "the law" meant, and the Righteous Empire it served, and his view, within that empire, of his "pure and honourable profession."

Hoffman taught at Maryland until 1833, when he fell into a dispute with university authorities and went to Europe, although his resignation from the faculty there was not accepted until 1843. He spent much of the rest of his life in Europe and in a new law practice in Philadelphia; he was a prolific writer, especially on law and legal education, but also on such things as contemporary politics and a Christian history of the world. He died in New York, on the way back to Europe, in 1854.

The religious ethos brought by the revival continued after 1840 and enjoyed a monumental burst of energy about 1858, but the character of the revival, and of the ethos, changed. Timothy Smith has shown how the revival in this period laid the foundations for the twentieth-century social gospel, but in the period itself there was less identification of the kingdom of God with the American experiment. The Righteous Empire faded. There were many causes of this—the immigration of Roman Catholics and Jews, the transcendentalist and utopian movements, the moral agony over slavery, the tendency of settled local Christian congregations to serve local interests, the sharp trend toward industrialization and urban growth, and a cynicism growing out of the nation's most harrowing war. The result of all of these forces, in the legal profession, was the loss of a sense of the law as serving higher purposes. Early in the nineteenth-century revival it was a common sentiment that lawyers should "bring the spirit of Christianity into our courtrooms," that there could be a national religion without a state church; Hoffman's theory of diminished representation belongs, I believe, to that early sentiment.

By the time Judge George Sharswood gave his lectures on professional ethics in Philadelphia (1854) Righteous Empire was beginning to be replaced by what Perry Miller called "government by negotiation"—by the idea that law was a matter of depravities contending with one another and that the officers of the law were referees in the contention. The ethical tendency from that theory is, usually, to state operative principles as secondary principles—as rules of procedure—and to see the law as a way to find protection from human savagery. Given the steady identification of the leaders of the American bar with businessmen, that latter point came out meaning that the principal business of the law was to protect property; Sharswood spent most of the first half of his lectures on ethics explaining that the law was above all a protection against force and a bulwark of private property and that the best thing for the lawmaker to do—especially the legislator—was to limit himself to those offices.

George Sharswood (1819–1883), a lifelong Philadelphian, was a lawyer, legislator, trial-court judge, and justice (later chief justice) of the supreme court of Pennsylvania. He was the virtual founder of the University of Pennsylvania Law School, taught there for years, and was its dean for sixteen years. (He was dean when he gave the lectures on ethics.) His 1854 lectures on professional ethics went through five editions (the last published after his death) and formed the basis for the 1908 ABA *Canons*. The lectures were apparently last published by the ABA in 1907. On the question of representing the really guilty they evidence less faith in government; a clearer tolerance for the idea of loyalty to clients, even guilty ones; a substantial change in Hoffman's concept of diminished representation; and, perhaps, a bit of the perspective of the judge.

> That lawyers are as often the ministers of injustice as of justice, is the common accusation in the mouth of gainsayers against the profession. It is said there must be a right and a wrong side to every lawsuit. In the majority of cases it must be apparent to the advocate, on which side is the justice of the cause; yet he will maintain, and often with the appearance of warmth and earnestness, that side which he must know to be unjust, and the success of which will be a wrong to the opposite party. Is he not then a participator in the injustice?
>
> * * *
>
> Now the lawyer is not merely the agent of the party; he is an officer of the court. The party has a right to have his case decided upon the law and the evidence, and to have every view presented to the minds of the judges, which can legitimately bear upon the question. This is the office which the advocate performs. He is not morally responsible for the act of the party in maintaining an unjust cause, nor for the error of the court, if they fall into error, in deciding it in his favor. The court or judge ought certainly to hear and weigh both sides; and the office of the counsel is to assist them by doing that, which the client in person, from want of learning, experience, and address, is unable to do in a proper manner. The lawyer, who refuses his professional assistance because in his judgment the case is unjust and indefensible, usurps the functions of both judge and jury.
>
> As an answer to any sweeping objection made to the profession in general, the view thus presented may be quite satisfactory. It by no means follows, however, as a principle of private action for the advocate, that all causes are to be taken by him indiscriminately, and conducted with a view to one single end, *success*.

* * *

[E]very case must, to a great degree, depend upon its own circumstances, known, peradventure, to the counsel alone; and it will often be hazardous to condemn either client or counsel upon what appears only. A hard plea—a sharp point—may subserve what is at bottom an honest claim, or just defence; though the evidence may not be within the power of the parties, which would make it manifest.

* * *

There are a few propositions, however, which appear to me to be sound in themselves, and calculated to solve this problem practically in the majority of cases; at least to assist the mind in coming to a safe conclusion *in foro conscientiae,* in the discharge of professional duty.

There is a distinction to be made between the case of prosecution and defence for crimes; between appearing for a plaintiff in pursuit of an unjust claim, and for a defendant in resisting what appears to be a just one.

Every man, accused of an offence, has a constitutional right to a trial according to law; even if guilty, he ought not to be convicted and undergo punishment unless upon legal evidence; and with all the forms which have been devised for the security of life and liberty. These are the panoply of innocence, when unjustly arraigned; and guilt cannot be deprived of it, without removing it from innocence. He is entitled, therefore, to the benefit of counsel to conduct his defence, to cross-examine the witnesses for the State, to scan, with legal knowledge, the forms of the proceeding against him, to present his defence in an intelligible shape, to suggest all those reasonable doubts which may arise from the evidence as to his guilt, and to see that if he is convicted, it is according to law.

* * *

It is not to be termed screening the guilty from punishment, for the advocate to exert all his ability, learning, and ingenuity, in such a defence, even if he should be perfectly assured in his own mind of the actual guilt of the prisoner.

* * *

[I]t is one of the most striking advantages of having a learned profession, who engage as a business in representing parties in courts of justice, that men are thus brought nearer to a condition of equality, that causes are tried and decided upon their merits, and do not depend upon the personal characters and qualifications of the immediate parties. Thus, too, if a suit be instituted against a man to recover damages for a tort, the defendant has a right to all the ingenuity and eloquence he can command in his defence, that even if he has committed a wrong, the amount of the damages may not exceed what the plaintiff is justly entitled to recover. But the claim of a plaintiff stands upon a somewhat different footing. Counsel have an undoubted right, and are in duty bound, to refuse to be concerned for a plaintiff in the legal pursuit of a demand, which offends his sense of what is just and right. The courts are open to the party in person to prosecute his own claim, and plead his own cause; and although he ought to examine and be well satisfied before he refuses to a suitor the benefit of his professional skill and learning, yet it would be on his part an immoral act to afford that assistance, when his conscience told him that the client was aiming to perpetrate a wrong through the means of some advantage the law may have afforded him. "It is a popular but gross mistake," says the late Chief Justice Gibson, "to suppose that a lawyer owes no fidelity to any one except his client, and that the latter is the keeper of his professional conscience. He is expressly bound by his official oath to behave himself, in his office of attorney, with all fidelity to the court as well as the client; and he violates it when he consciously presses for an unjust judgment, much more so when he presses for the conviction of an innocent man.... The high and honorable office of a counsel would be degraded to that of a mercenary, were he compelled to do the biddings of his client against the dictates of his conscience."*

* * *

[T]here may and ought to be a difference made in the mode of conducting a defence against what is believed to be a righteous, and what is believed to be an unrighteous claim. A defence in the former case should be conducted upon the most liberal principles. When he is contending against the claim of one who is seeking, as he believes, through the forms of law, to do his client an injury, the advocate may justifiably avail himself of every honorable ground to defeat him. He may begin at once by declaring to his opponent or his professional adviser, that he holds him at arm's length, and he may keep him so during the whole contest. He may fall back upon the instructions of his client, and refuse to yield any legal vantage-ground, which may have been gained through the ignorance or inadvertance of his opponent. Counsel, however, may and even ought to refuse to act under instructions from a client to defeat what he believes to be an honest and just claim, by insisting upon the slips of the opposite party, by sharp practice, or special pleading—in short, by any other means than a fair trial on the merits in open court. There is no professional duty, no virtual engagement with the client, which compels an advocate to resort to such measures, to secure success in any cause, just or unjust; and when so instructed, if he believes it to be intended to gain an unrighteous object, he ought to throw up the cause, and retire from all connection with it, rather than thus be a participator in other men's sins.

Sharswood makes it fairly clear that a lawyer is free to refuse his services for reasons personal to himself. This was one of the clearest differences between American lawyers and English barristers. (Canadian lawyers have taken the American position on the question and have by and

---

*Rush v. Cavenaugh, 2 Barr 189.

large eliminated the distinction between barristers and solicitors.) It is a tradition of the English bar that a barrister should not refuse a case for any but administrative reasons, a tradition which emphasizes the principle that a lawyer is not morally accountable for what his client has done or for what, within the law, is done in his client's defense. That difference is an important one to notice at this point, since some modern scholars of legal ethics would accept the fullness of the English-barrister ideal and even go beyond it in resisting all moral accountability, provided that the lawyer feels free to decline to represent a client in the first place. The lawyer's right of conscientious objection, particularly at the point at which the lawyer-client "contract" is made, is clear and fundamental in American legal ethics.

Sharswood retains the concept of diminished representation, but not in criminal defense. It is possible for him, as it was for Hoffman, to defend the idea that a lawyer would appear in his client's cause but not do everything he could do for his client; the difference is that Sharswood would limit diminished representation to defense against civil claims which ought to be paid. Diminished representation is not a prominent idea in modern legal ethics, but there are a few vestiges—in, for example, the apparent consensus on how a court-appointed lawyer conducts a criminal appeal for a convicted indigent—and there is a continuing strong argument that office lawyers should exercise a greater moral witness against their clients' purposes than trial lawyers should. Generally, though, Judge Sharswood outlined the principles which continue to govern defense of the really guilty. Those principles would say that Felix Graham's conscience was too tender and Mr. Chaffanbrass was too cynical. Thomas Furnival need not have worried over what he did in court for Lady Mason; Anthony Trollope, for all his worldly wisdom, simply does not understand lawyers.* When America's preeminent modern scholar of legal ethics, Henry Drinker, talked about *Orley Farm* (in 1950, to the Grolier Club in New York City), he said, "Trollope still persists in his insistence that (lawyers') principal function consists in 'turning black into white.' This he does in his portrayal of the hero, Felix Graham ... and in his indignation against the

---

*The contrast may be suggested by Hoffman's and Sharswood's views of the morality of pleading the Statute of Limitations on a debt which the client owes. "[I]f my client is conscious he owes the debt," Hoffman said, "and has no other defence than the *legal bar,* he shall never make me a partner in his knavery." Sharswood, in the generation which had come to see the courts as places where depravity contends with depravity, argued at some length that lawyers have a duty to remind their clients of the moral course in such cases, in the hope that "the spirit of high and pure morality, which breathes through the Sermon on the Mount, prevailed more extensively," but he did not argue that a lawyer who used the limitations defense for his client was acting immorally.

conduct of Mr. Furnival in continuing to defend Lady Mason after he suspects that she is really guilty.... [W]hile no lawyer should knowingly promote an untruth, a lawyer who presumes to prejudge a case disregards the whole theory and basis of our legal system, which is to ascertain the truth by having able advocates present the two sides to an impartial judge and jury.... The Felix Grahams in actual life are usually found, on graduation, serving as Assistant Secretaries of Uplift Societies ... they never do much uplifting."

The 1908 ABA *Canons* deal with the defense of the really guilty in three places, and in all three reflect the influence of Judge Sharswood. In Canon 5, the principle permitting representation of those whom the lawyer believes to be guilty is defended, perhaps more broadly than Sharswood would have defended it but in reference to the ideas contained in his 1854 lecture: "It is the right of the lawyer to undertake the defense of a person accused of crime, regardless of his personal opinion as to the guilt of the accused; otherwise innocent persons, victims only of suspicious circumstances, might be denied proper defense. Having undertaken such defense, the lawyer is bound, by all fair and honorable means, to present every defense that the law of the land permits, to the end that no person may be deprived of life or liberty, but by due process of law."

Canon 15 set limits upon advocacy, denying that a lawyer may do "whatever may enable him to succeed in winning his client's cause," but affirming that a lawyer is required to be vigorous and thorough, "to the end that nothing be taken or be withheld from [the client], save by the rules of law, legally applied.... In the judicial forum the client is entitled to the benefit of any and every remedy and defense that is authorized by the law of the land, and he may expect his lawyer to assert every such remedy or defense." The limits on this conception of zeal were two: (a) Lawyers were forbidden to violate the law and were barred from "any manner of fraud or chicane," and (b) The lawyer "must obey his own conscience and not that of his client." The latter limit sounds broader than it is. Hoffman's idea of diminished advocacy for the guilty had disappeared. A lawyer was free to seek the acquittal of a guilty person, because the prosecutor could be wrong and because even the guilty are entitled to due process. The lawyer's conscience was appropriately exercised in choices of tactics, but not so as to deny the client the benefit of every legal device. If the lawyer felt that the client should not be defended at a level of intensity that ignored guilt, he was free to refuse the case.

These principles were applicable to civil cases as well as to criminal defense; in fact, the only reason to separate the two kinds of cases may have been to state that guilt was irrelevant to the morality of defense.

Canons 30 and 31 apply to all cases in affirming the lawyer's right of conscientious objection. Canon 30 sets mandatory standards of refusal that are prior to the exercise of this right, but Canon 31, which is like the last sentence of Canon 15 in this respect, gives a general dispensation from English-barrister ideas that a lawyer is to be available to anyone who wants him. "The lawyer must decline to conduct a civil cause or to make a defense when convinced that it is intended merely to harass or to injure the opposite party or to work oppression or wrong. But otherwise it is his right and, having accepted retainer, it becomes his duty," says Canon 30, "to insist upon the judgment of the Court as to the legal merits of his client's claim." Canon 31, a broad statement of the right of conscientious objection, says that "No lawyer is obliged to act either as adviser or advocate for every person who may wish to become his client. He has the right to decline employment. . . . The responsibility for advising as to questionable transactions, for bringing questionable suits, for urging questionable defenses, is the lawyer's responsibility. He cannot escape it by urging as an excuse that he is only following his client's instructions."

It is fair to say that modern standards would not admit of Sharswood's distinctions or Hoffman's reservations. Monroe Freedman has it right when he says that the point at which the profession still clearly allows a lawyer to consider the justice of his client's cause is the point of original employment. "[A] lawyer should . . . have the freedom to choose clients on any standard he or she deems appropriate. . . . [The choice] can properly be subjected to the moral scrutiny and criticism of others, particularly those who feel morally compelled to persuade the lawyer to use his or her professional training and skills in ways that the critics consider to be more consistent with personal, social, or professional ethics.

"[H]owever, once the lawyer has assumed responsibility to represent a client, the zealousness of that representation cannot be tempered by the lawyer's moral judgments of the client or of the client's cause." In their 1980 comments to the proposed new *Rules,* the ABA drafting committee quotes Broughman's hyperbolic statement of this ethical idea from early nineteenth-century England: "Responsibility to a client requires subordinating of the* other interests to vindicating the client's cause. In the classic statement of this loyalty, it was said: 'An advocate, in the discharge of his duty, knows but one person in all the world, and that person is his client . . . [etc.].' Properly understood, this statement means that a lawyer should permit no consideration of political interests or concern for the personal or financial interests of others to detract from duty to the client."

---

*I wonder whether the draft at some point said here *"all* other interests."

The ABA's criminal-justice standards say that "the basic duty the lawyer for the accused owes to the administration of justice is to serve as the accused's counselor and advocate with courage, devotion, and to the utmost of his or her learning and ability and according to law.... The duties of a lawyer to a client are to represent the client's legitimate interests, and considerations of personal and professional advantage should not influence the lawyer's advice or performance."

These statements are careful not to say, as Freedman does, that consideration of conscience cannot interfere with professional function, but Freedman's view is probably the prevailing one, even among those who drafted these statements. Most American lawyers would probably agree with the *American Law Reports* generalization that I quoted in Chapter 5: "It is ethical for a member of the bar to represent the accused even if he knows the latter to be guilty. In fact, it may be on occasion an ethical duty to do so."

CHAPTER SEVEN
The Problem of Ministry to the Guilty

> [T]he significant unit of thought and action in the realm of historical encounter is not a mind but a self.
>
> Reinhold Niebuhr

The development in American legal ethics of a theory for representing the guilty begins and ends in Lord Brougham's defensive mandate to loyalty—"to save that client by all expedient means, to protect that client at all hazards and costs." The profession is as uncomfortable with the answer now as it was at the beginning of the Republic—even less comfortable, perhaps, because we have lost our innocent trust in the government's ability to do justice with its adversary system. We have retained the English-barrister model, but we have lost the vision of Righteous Empire which, in nineteenth-century America, sustained for us a confidence in the goodness of government.

In any event, this license to *represent*—what Murray Schwartz calls the two principles of professionalism and nonaccountability—does not go to the sort of ministry which is envisioned by the ethics of care (Chapter 3). The modern American rule on representation is summarized in the annotation in *American Law Reports*: "It is ethical for a member of the bar to represent the accused even if he knows the latter to be guilty. In fact, it may be on occasion an ethical duty to do so. . . . This is necessarily true because every defendant in a criminal case is entitled to be represented by counsel, and the trial cannot proceed without counsel unless this privilege is affirmatively waived." Monroe Freedman puts it more grandly: "Before we will permit the state to deprive any person of life, liberty, or property, we require that certain processes be duly followed which ensure regard for the dignity of the individual, irrespective of the impact of those processes on the determination of truth." The emphasis is on the conduct of government. "[T]he trial cannot proceed" unless "certain processes be duly followed."

The profession struggled, in America, with the English-barrister model; we departed from it, briefly, in theories of diminished representation which were sustained not by fealty to power but by the innocent vision of America being "God's new Israel." We repented and came back to Lord Brougham, but not—not ever—in terms of *ministry* to the guilty; our ethic is stated only in terms of representation of the guilty before the powers of government and as part of the function of government. In this way the profession has been able to do what the government needs to have done but can still claim for itself the aura aristocracy requires. Hoffman said that "persons of atrocious character, who have violated the laws of God and man, are entitled to no ... special exertions from any member of our pure and honorable profession." Sharswood's disagreement was limited to the function the government required: "He has no alternative then, but to perform his duty. It is his duty ... as an advocate merely ... to use all fair arguments arising on the evidence. Beyond that, he is not bound to go in any case."

The *American Law Reports* annotation accepts only the least vestige of diminished representation by modern American lawyers: "There are certain inherent limitations ... on counsel who represents a defendant whom he knows to be guilty. *There must be no relationship between them* except purely that of attorney and client; counsel must retain control of the presentation of the case, and neither the client nor any outside person may dictate to him how to conduct the case in court.... Counsel is not expected to stultify himself in an attempt to advance his client's interest. The attorney is justified in withdrawing, where, during the progress of litigation, the client engages in conduct that tends to degrade or humiliate the attorney" (emphasis added). Or, as Freedman puts it, representation of the guilty is limited to "the needs ... imposed by the adversary system."

American legal ethics would, as Henry Drinker said it would, vindicate Thomas Furnival's uneasy but vigorous representation of Lady Mason. It would tolerate Mr. Chaffanbrass's moral philosophy of advocacy. It would disapprove only of Felix Graham, who, Drinker said, is not fit to be a lawyer but fit only to be employed by a moral uplift society. *It would ignore Lady Mason herself.* In the novel, she ends up acquitted—and therefore, by worldly lights, well served by her lawyers—but self-condemned, self-banished, and miserable. "I may, perhaps be thought to owe an apology to my readers in that I have asked their sympathy for a woman who had so sinned as to have placed her beyond the general sympathy of the world at large. If so, I tender my apology, and perhaps feel that I should confess a fault," says Trollope at the end of the novel. "But as I have told her story that sympathy has grown upon myself till I have learned to forgive her, and to feel that I too could have regarded her as a friend. Of her future I will not venture to say anything. But no lesson is truer than that which teaches us to believe that God does temper the wind to the shorn lamb." That tender message did not reach Lady Mason; no human being brought that comfort to her. If, as Trollope hoped, she was to find comfort in her future, it would be after she was finished with lawyers.

It seems that the issue of *representing* the guilty is not an awesome issue at all. It is a question of governmental administration, and government always manages to administer itself somehow. The issue of representing the guilty is one which engages law students, for a while, and it engages those who must rationalize the profession's behavior in codes of ethics written (as Hoffman's and Sharswood's were) for law students. Lawyers in practice resolve the issue with a psychology of partisanship, with the effects of competition and of fear; we almost always come to find the zeal required for advocacy, even for the guilty, if only because the stakes are high and there is another lawyer on the other side. It may be, as James Gustafson has observed, that in Europe practical ethics is worked out by thinkers and theologians, but in America the partnership has been between thinkers and actors; American ethics have a way of rationalizing what we do.

There is a degree of paradox in our official reverence for the English-barrister model. American lawyers have not had the sort of law practices English barristers have. American lawyers have in fact spent time with their clients and shared the agonies of their clients—even the guilty ones. There has been a ministry to the guilty, acted out in the lives of American lawyers, which the official rules on representation of the guilty do not seem to contemplate. Trollope's barristers in *Orley Farm* were of no use to their client; Trollope's other intensely legal novel, *Phineas Redux,* illustrates the same point and the same kind of lawyering. Phineas there faces the gallows and has no comfort from his lawyers and no growth at their hands. But novels about American lawyers are not like that. The trial lawyers of American fiction live and suffer through the pain of their clients, those who are guilty and those who are not.* William Faulkner's lawyer, Gavin Stevens, has his most extensive exposure as a trial lawyer in the *Intruder in the Dust,* a murder defense which is not about the administration of justice in Mississippi but is about the relationship between an establishment white lawyer

---

*This is true of *some* English lawyers, too, but not in court. Soames Forsyte's career, to the extent we see it, is a career built of service to his clients and to the members of his extensive family. C. P. Snow's Lewis Eliot is a lawyer who enters into the agonies of the people he serves, from George Passant in the first volume of *Strangers and Brothers* through the scruffy young communist at peril in *The Affair* to the repugnant terrorists in *The Sleep of Reason,* the ninth and next to last volume of the series— but when Eliot is seen in court (as in *The Conscience of the Rich*) it is not to good effect and in a scene in which the client is incidental.

and an unfortunate old black man. Faulkner's story is deeply about that society and about the fact that the black man is in a sense guilty and in a sense not, but it is about that society as it is affected by relationships. It is not about a mind; it is about a self. Harper Lee's Atticus Finch (in *To Kill a Mockingbird*) works in a similar society, in a similar case, with a similar client; the message—the sense of the story and the point it has to make—turns on the barrenness of dealing with people outside human relationships. The same points can be made of the lawyers and clients of rural Pennsylvania (in the fiction of James Gould Cozzens) or of Manhattan (in the fiction of Louis Auchincloss). These novelists have perceived something about the moral quality of a lawyer's professional life in America that the ethical tradition has missed. That something is an issue about ministry; it is not an issue about representation.

It is not that the novelists have missed the social significance of advocacy. Faulkner and Lee wrote about social significance as much as anything; Snow's *The Affair* is an attempt to apply the Dreyfus case to the cold war; and the other novelists were alert to notice social developments around their characters and of issues of social responsibility. My point is that the novelists saw these issues in interpersonal focus and that the ethical tradition, concerned with the same sort of lawyers and the same sort of clients, saw the issues in terms of a lawyer's loyalty to institutions. It is possible—Bloomfield shows, in fact, that it is likely—that the generations of American lawyers who lived and worked while Hoffman and Sharswood and their professional descendants debated the moral rules of the profession were more engaged with their clients than they were directly engaged with social issues, so that the novelists then were closer to writing perceptively *about* lawyers, and about the moral issues important to lawyers, than the ethical tradition was. I am arguing that the ethical tradition had done something worse than overlook a factor; I am arguing that the ethical tradition missed the main point.

How did the ethical tradition come to miss the main point? I think that it evaded the point because the tension illustrated by David Hoffman's view of the guilty and the English-barrister tradition, represented in America today in the thought of Monroe Freedman, is too great not to be resolved in superficial pragmatism. Representation is the wrong question and bound to get the wrong answer. Perhaps the revival workers of Hoffman's and Sharswood's day understood this, and understood as well the theology behind it, better than Hoffman and Sharswood did. The revival preachers were wildly naive about the society they worked in—wildly naive (but then so were enlightened intellectuals such as Thomas Jefferson) about America being God's new Israel. They did not understand, as Abraham Lincoln did, that, at best and at the highest level of hope, we Americans would only be "God's almost chosen people." But they may not have been so naive about the way the world changes for the better. Charles Grandison Finney, former lawyer and phenomenal evangelist, may not have been so naive when he said that moral change in society begins in the individual. "It is faith that purifies the heart," Finney said. Once faith could be at least tentatively assumed, he said, ministers should "inquire affectionately and particularly" into political beliefs, "whether they are cleaving to a party without regard to principles." Finney lived and preached while America was still staggering under the moral burden of slavery; he is not known as an abolitionist and did not like to be called one, but Timothy Smith's account of the revival estimates that Finney won more adherents to abolition than William Lloyd Garrison did. In any event, the novelists, and not those who drafted the rules for lawyer behavior, proved that American lawyers developed an ethics of ministry to the guilty, and performed in it, and that such a ministry is entitled to hope for results which can be seen and felt on public issues.

The issue, then, is whether a lawyer who specially adheres to the story of Israel and of Jesus can *minister* to the guilty. At first sight the answer seems obvious. Jesus saved (in both senses of the word) the woman taken in adultery; he took with him to Paradise the good thief (although he did not rescue him from his cross); he trafficked with a group of people who were probably as repulsive to their fellow citizens as Mafia dons are repulsive in America today: "When Jesus was at table in his house, many bad characters—tax-gatherers and others—were seated with him and his disciples; for there were many who followed him. Some doctors of the law who were Pharisees noticed him eating in this bad company, and said to his disciples, 'He eats with tax-gatherers and sinners!' Jesus heard it and said to them, 'It is not the healthy that need a doctor, but the sick; I did not come to invite virtuous people, but sinners' " (Mark 2:15–17). This seems to be an example of ministry to the guilty that Jesus demonstrated both as evidence of the new covenant—the idea that the tax-gatherers had already been tried and found (made) innocent—and as a consequence of traditional Judaic ethics. The self-righteous Pharisees were at fault not because they did not understand Jesus' new ideas but because they did not adhere to the moral implications of their own (and his) old ideas. There seem, though, to be some complicating issues here, as there were about the meaning of the Jesus stories on the issue of the repulsive guilty (Chapter 5). These issues are that this ministry is ironic, that it is subject to obstacles, and that it is centered in substantive morality.

Irony. I mean to use "irony" here in the sense that Reinhold Niebuhr used it. Irony follows when we realize that we make an issue of guilt in our ministry to the guilty, even though we are all guilty and even though we realize, as perhaps Hoffman's and Finney's generation did not, that the vision of a Righteous Empire in America is a delusion. We are talking about the really guilty, but the irony is that real guilt is always, in the world's terms, a failure to assimilate. This is true of Lady Mason, who had a valid complaint about the injustice of a property system in which a wealthy man could leave his wife and child penniless but who was nonetheless guilty—really guilty. It is true, in different ways, of the Mafia don, of Faulkner's and Lee's persecuted blacks, of the tax-gatherers, of the adulteress, and of the good thief. Government is doing a necessary and maybe even a righteous thing in proceeding against those who are really guilty, but government is always off target because it is always subject to the delusion of its power and of its righteousness. It is always subject to the worldly necessity to preserve and perpetuate itself, to prepare for reelection. A Christian, as Barth says, can never allow himself to be taken in by government's righteousness, even though he has also to realize that it must not be destroyed, for "there is a blessing in it."

Ministry to the guilty is not representation. Representation implies that there is something before which one represents. In ministry there is no such thing, because the community, obsessed as it must be by fear for its survival, and the government, obsessed as it must be by power, cannot provide comfort to the guilty. Government had to prosecute the woman taken in adultery and the good thief. The community had to despise the tax-gatherers. Neither the community nor the government can be expected to understand the purposes of ministry. Their failure to understand is not condemned in the Gospels; it is in fact respected. But Jesus ministers to the guilty anyway. This is irony. Irony, Niebuhr says, "depends upon an observer who is not so hostile to the victim of irony as to deny the element of virtue which must constitute a part of the ironic situation; nor yet so sympathetic as to discount the weakness, the vanity and pretension which constitute another element." The situation is almost funny, but it is also meaningful. It elicits "not merely laughter but a knowing smile," because "man ... forgets that he is not simply a creator but also a creature." Collective man, man in community and in government, on the other hand, "always tends to be morally complacent, self-righteous and lacking in a sense of humor"; people in community and as government tend to lose their "awareness of the limits, as well as the possibilities of human power and goodness." In this way ministry to the guilty is ironic, because it understands what is at stake and what is not.

Obstacles. The obstacles to a lawyer's being a minister to the guilty are centered around the lawyer's idea of himself as a lawyer. That is clear in the survival among American lawyers of the English-barrister ideal; we are not English and we are not barristers, but spokesmen as diverse as F. Lee Bailey and Warren Burger remind us that the English are better trial lawyers than we are. That message points more toward Mr. Chaffanbrass than it points toward Jesus inviting tax-gatherers into his house. It is hard to see the English barrister as a teacher of his clients; but, as William May says, much of an American lawyer's life is centered in the inquiry, understanding, openness, and sensitivity we honor in a good teacher. It is hard to see the English barrister as a bringer of comfort. When Trollope wants to present a bearer of comfort to the guilty he chooses a housewife, not a lawyer, even when his stories otherwise teem with English barristers. It is hard to see in the English barrister a faithful friend, but a minister to the guilty (a minister such as Mrs. Orme was to Lady Mason or Madame Goessler was to Phineas Finn) is a faithful friend, and he acts with scriptural warrant for being a faithful friend, for dealing with the guilty as Jesus dealt with the tax-gatherers: "The qualification we have comes from God; it is he who has qualified us to dispense his new covenant—a covenant expressed not in a written document, but in a spiritual bond; for the written law condemns to death, but the Spirit gives life.

> The law, then, engraved letter by letter upon stone, dispensed death, and yet it was inaugurated with divine splendor. That splendor, though it was soon to fade, made the face of Moses so bright that Israelites could not gaze steadily at him. But if so, must not even greater splendor rest upon the divine dispensation of the Spirit? If splendor accompanied the dispensation under which we are condemned, how much richer in splendor must that one be under which we are acquitted! Indeed, the splendor that once was is now no splendor at all; it is outshone by a splendor greater still. For if that which was soon to fade had its moment of splendor, how much greater is the splendor of that which endures! (2 Corinthians 3:5-11).

Substantive morality. One reason that American legal ethics narrowed itself to the English-barrister model is that the grand vision of the revival narrowed itself to a civil religion which has become a set of procedures. In one reading of this history (Perry Miller's), law came to replace faith because the insularity and pietism of the revival left no foundations for social ethics except the law. When the Civil War eroded the public effects of pietism, only the law was left to provide the principles around which the community could continue to cohere. In another reading (Timothy Smith's), the revival kept its social principles alive, through a period of alliance between the churches and business (and between lawyers and business), and these principles emerged as a religious witness that confronted, rather than supported, the government. In either reading, the legal enterprise in America lost the substantive morality upon which our nineteenth-century forebears supposed it to rest. Americans, taking ourselves collectively, became a bureaucracy where once we had hoped to be a Righteous Empire, God's New Israel. We are God's almost chosen people.

This history is expressed in the law, in ideas such as due process and fairness, and in what Freedman means when he says that even the guilty are entitled to "certain processes . . . which ensure the dignity of the individual." We lost something in that development; what we lost was a common understanding of what a human person is—"the noblest work of God," as James Wilson, a justice of our original Supreme Court, put it—and replaced that understanding with a set of rules. We do not have a substantive idea, held in common, of what Freedman means when he says "the dignity of the individual." What we have instead is a set of limits for a game which depends upon competition and fear. We lawyers preside over that game, and over its limits, but we preside not as ministers but as representers. The adversary ethic does not counsel ministry (although I don't think it yet forbids it). The substantive justification for ministry depends on something else; I am suggesting, for us Christians, that it can be found in the stories of Jesus among the outcasts—lepers, Samaritans, Zealots—and, more importantly for present purposes, in the stories of Jesus among the guilty.

The idea that I am advancing here is that the government, which is the accuser of the guilty, provides, for its own reasons, a license to represent the guilty. It permits, but does not require, a ministry to the guilty, and the lawyer who undertakes that ministry undertakes as well a fearful confrontation of the community (Chapter 5). Representation suggests an advocate; ministry suggests, in this context at least, a companion. An advocate takes your side when other people are against you—takes your side even when the whole world is against you—as it was against Lady Mason and Dismas, the good thief, and the taxgatherers. But, advocacy seen beyond itself, as ministry, is often an enlistment to be the only companion the client has. If the three crosses on Calvary mean anything, they mean that no one is so repulsive, or so condemned, that he is not entitled to have a companion in his misery, and that none of us—not even the Son of God—is too good to be chosen as the companion. Everyone is entitled to one last friend—even Hauptmann, Eichmann, a Mafia don, Jabez Stone, Dismas, and Lady Mason. (It was easy to be companion to Lady Mason—she was so *pleasant*—but she found none among her lawyers.)

The two issues of representation and ministry turn on a distinction, perhaps, in sources of judgment. The usual way the law-school question is put is to ask whether we may represent guilty clients—"get them off"—when they are accused justly and deserve punishment. There is no duty to the system that prevents a lawyer from representing the guilty; the same system that provides the rules and the punishment also licenses us to help our clients evade the rules and avoid the punishment.

That system—a lawyer's ability to act as advocate—is satisfied by the license to practice law. The historical process in which such professionalism and such nonaccountability have been worked out has been a tangled process, as all of history is, but its result is clear.

If there remains some duty that would *prevent* our ministry to the guilty, it does not come from the system and does not depend for justification or for survival on the system. If there remains some duty that would *require* our ministry to the guilty, it, too, comes from another source (although the government may, for the moment, and in this country, allow it). Many Jews and Christians I have talked to about this question seem at first to feel that divine justice requires civil punishment for people who have violated civil law. I understand that feeling—I feel it, too—but I find no biblical warrant for it. What I find in the Bible is a justification for cooperating with the system—for being an advocate in the system, even for the guilty—because "there is a blessing in it," provided I am willing to go beyond advocacy to ministry, provided I seek more for my client, and more from my client, than the system can provide for either of us. The scene to superimpose on the jail cells where we talk to the guilty is Jesus and the tax-gatherers. The scene to superimpose on the frightful image of my client receiving his punishment is Dismas on the cross, Dismas with an advocate and a companion hanging by his side.

CHAPTER EIGHT
The Problem of Collaboration

Thomas Furnival was able, with professionalism, to overcome the repugnance he felt in the presence of the guilty, but he was not able to overcome repugnance enough to be truthful with his client. He was able, because of the professional dynamics of fear and rivalry, to represent his client—even though Anthony Trollope could not understand a morality which allowed him to represent her. Furnival was unable to *minister* to his client, though, because he was unable to be truthful to her; Lady Mason had no comfort from any of her lawyers. I think the reason Furnival gave himself for being unable to minister to Lady Mason (Chapter 5) turned on Furnival's perception that the society in which Lady Mason lived, like the society in which we live, could not have admitted her back to respectability if she had confessed her crime and repented of it. There is a dimension to that reason not discussed in Chapters 5 through 7, though—the problem of collaboration.

Lady Mason's evil design was a continuing design. She had forged her late husband's will and lied about it in the probate proceedings following his death. She was successful in her treachery, as a result of which her son Lucius was put into possession of Orley Farm. Twenty years had gone by; Lucius was an adult and a gentleman farmer by the time Dockwrath dug up evidence of Lady Mason's original crime. Lucius's respectability depended on Lady Mason's crime, and for that reason she could not confess to the crime. If she confessed, Lucius would lose his respectability and his farm; when she confessed anyway, at the end of the novel, after her acquittal, Lucius was disgraced, dispossessed, and off to Australia. The resolution of the story is, from a social perspective, a bitter comparison of the rectitude of the law with the course of real justice—a comparison Trollope had made in *The Warden* and *The Last Chronicle of Barset,* and one he made later in *Phineas Redux.* He did not believe that law and lawyers have much to do with conscience or with the just resolution of disputes.

The difficulty, as Furnival saw it, was that he could not let his client know that he knew she was guilty. If he did that, he would feel obliged to urge her to confess her crime. Confession was an inadmissible step, from his point of view, because it would cause Lady Mason to become an outcast; there was no way he could see for her to remain respectable and restore the farm to her stepson. There was no way to be moral without causing harm. From Lady Mason's point of view, her own disgrace was a small price to pay for relief from her agony and a sense of reconciliation with God, but she could not bear the thought of Lucius's disgrace. She saw no way to be moral without causing harm to Lucius. Trollope focuses these two rather different moral tensions in the character of Edith Orme, Lady Mason's friend and neighbor. Mrs. Orme is the second person in the story to learn of Lady Mason's guilt, and the only person in the novel who is able to forgive Lady Mason. Not even Lucius can forgive her—Lucius, for whose benefit the evil design goes on. Mrs. Orme is also the only person in the novel who tells Lady Mason the truth.

Edith Orme is the widowed daughter-in-law of Sir Peregrine Orme. They live near Orley Farm, in Sir Peregrine's house, along with Edith's son Peregrine. Sir Peregrine is the first to know of Lady Mason's guilt; he learns about it because he wants to marry her, and she feels it necessary to warn him off before he becomes involved in her crime. After he knows of her guilt, he at first thinks that it is important that Lady Mason's friendship with Edith end, but Edith disagrees. The scene in which this issue is worked out between Edith and Sir Peregrine gives Trollope a chance to scoff a bit at the stern demands of the religious ethics of property, but it also makes important points about a truthful and moral way to collaborate with the guilty:

> "It is not for us to tell the story of her guilt," Sir Peregrine says, "But her guilt will remain the same, will be acted over and over again every day, while the proceeds of the property go into the hands of Lucius Mason. It is that which is so terrible, Edith;—that her conscience should have been able to bear that load for the last twenty years! A deed done,—that admits of no restitution, may admit of repentance. We may leave that to the sinner and his conscience, hoping that he stands right with his Maker. But here, with her, there has been a continual theft going on from year to year,—which is still going on. While Lucius Mason holds a sod of Orley Farm, true repentance with her must be impossible. It seems so to me." And Sir Peregrine shuddered at the doom which his own rectitude of mind and purpose forced him to pronounce.
>
> "It is not she that has it," said Mrs. Orme. "It was not done for herself."
>
> "There is no difference in that," said he sharply. "All sin is selfish, and so was her sin in this. Her object was the aggrandizement of her

own child; and when she could not accomplish that honestly, she did it by fraud, and—and—and—. Edith, my dear, you and I must look at this thing as it is. You must not let your kind heart make your eyes blind in a matter of such moment."

"No, father; nor must the truth make our hearts cruel. You talk of restitution and repentance. Repentance is not the work of a day. How are we to say by what struggles her poor heart has been torn?"

"I do not judge her."

"No, no; that is it. We may not judge her; may we? But we may assist her in her wretchedness. I have promised that I will do all I can to aid her. You will allow me to do so;—you will; will you not?" And she pressed his arm and looked up into his face, entreating him. Since first they two had known each other, he had never yet denied her a request. It was a law of his life that he would never do so. But now he hesitated, not thinking that he would refuse her, but feeling that on such an occasion it would be necessary to point out to her how far she might go without risk of bringing censure on her own name. But in this case, though the mind of Sir Peregrine might be the more logical, the purpose of his daughter-in-law was the stronger. She had resolved that such communication with crime would not stain her, and she already knew to what length she would go in her charity.

The length to which Edith went was to assist Lady Mason through the trial—that is, to stay by her side and to convince Sir Peregrine to stay by Lady Mason's side and to help secure the acquittal; then to counsel confession of the crime to Lucius and to assist with that even more difficult step; and then, after the trial, to see to the restoration of the farm to Joseph Mason. All of this happened in the story; Edith's resolution of the problem became Lady Mason's. I notice several things about this solution:

It was *personally risky*; when Edith resolves that she can escape stain, she means moral stain rather than the disapproval of her neighbors. But both she and Sir Peregrine suffer at the hands of their neighbors.

It was *morally risky*, since she became part of a plot to frustrate justice in the governmental sense. Sir Peregrine supposes, during the interview with Edith, that "he himself would be guilty of some outrage against the law by aiding a criminal in her escape. He had heard of misprison of felony; but nevertheless, he allowed his daughter-in-law to prevail." It is important to understand the risk involved in the moral life—the risk of offending the norms of the community, of offending the law, and of violating professional convention. I believe it is possible to undertake this risk and still to hope that I can do right without doing *wrong,* but it is not possible, in my view, to undertake counseling, sharing in, and bearing tragic moral choices without the risk of doing *harm* to myself and to others. There is a fair amount of misleading moral guidance available on what the word "trust" means in this respect; an example is in Nena and George O'Neill's book *Open Marriage*—"Trust is the feeling that no matter what you do or say you are not going to be criticized." That seems fatuous to me; Mrs. Orme did not suppose she could trust and be trusted without risking criticism. Even Lady Mason, in her banishment in Germany, might well have come to despise her.

It was *truthful.* Edith is the only character in the story who tells Lady Mason the truth that she is guilty and the truth that she must repent of her guilt and restore the farm to Joseph Mason.

It was *tragic.* Edith Orme is also the only character in the story—although Lady Mason comes to join her in this—who sees clearly that there is no moral alternative that will not cause pain to Lady Mason, to Lucius, and to herself. The solution Edith works out, and Lady Mason adopts, exactly fits Stanley Hauerwas's definition of the tragic moral choice—restoring the farm, with all of the pain and dispossession that act causes, but done despite the toils of the law, represents the triumph of meaning over power.

It was *loving:*

And Mrs. Orme did forgive her. Many will think that she was wrong to do so, and I fear it must be acknowledged that she was not strong minded. By forgiving her I do not mean that she pronounced absolution for the sin of past years, or that she endeavoured to make the sinner think she was not worse for her sin. Mrs. Orme was a good churchwoman but not strong, individually, in points of doctrine. All that she left mainly to the woman's conscience and her own dealings with her Saviour,—merely saying a word of salutary counsel as to a certain spiritual pastor who might be of aid. But Mrs. Orme forgave her,—as regarded herself. She had already, while all this was unknown, taken this woman to her heart as pure and good. It now appeared that the woman had not been pure, had not been good!—and then she took her to her heart again! Criminal as the woman was, disgraced and debased, subject almost to the heaviest penalties of outraged law and justice, a felon against whom the actual hands of the law's myrmidons would probably soon prevail, a creature doomed to bear the scorn of the lowest of her fellow-creatures,—such as she was, this other woman, pure and high, so shielded from the world's impurity that nothing ignoble might touch her,—this lady took her to her heart again and promised in her ear with low sweet words of consolation that they should still be friends.

The question for us lawyers is whether such an office of comfort was possible for Lady Mason's lawyers, given the fact that Lady Mason was not only guilty but proposed to continue in her evil design. It is important to notice that Lady Mason proposed to continue in her evil design out of a sort of inevitability. She proposed to continue in her evil design because she saw no alternative. It was when she gained a counselor who loved her that she began to see an alternative and her design began to be other than evil.

And if such an office was possible to Lady Mason's lawyers, how is it that they failed to perform it? My answers to these questions are that it is possible for a lawyer to remain, as Mrs. Orme did, in the presence of an evil design, if the lawyer is willing, as she was, to exercise moral influence against the design. The reason lawyers fail at this work or are uneasy in their success at it—the reason the issue is seen as one of collaboration rather than as one of counsel—is more difficult. One suggestion that has occurred to me is that we stumble over our own narrow definition of our relationship with guilty clients; another is that we are afraid.

There is an assumption in discussions of the issue of collaboration that a lawyer, once he agrees to represent a client's interests in the situation at hand, is bound to do what the client wants done (leaving aside an area of reserved professional decision on issues of tactics and etiquette). This is explicit in Monroe Freedman's argument against Richard Wasserstrom:

> Wasserstrom suggests that a lawyer should refuse to advise a wealthy client of a tax loophole provided by the legislature for only a few wealthy taxpayers. If that case is to be generalized, it seems to mean that the legal profession can properly regard itself as an oligarchy whose duty is to nullify decisions made by the people's duly elected representatives. That is, if the lawyers believe that particular clients (wealthy or poor) should not have been given certain rights, the lawyers are morally bound to circumvent the legislative process and to forestall the judicial process by the simple device of keeping their clients in ignorance of tempting rights.
>
> Nor is this a caricature of Wasserstrom's position. The role-differentiated amorality of the lawyer is valid, he says, "only if the enormous degree of trust and confidence in the institutions themselves (that is, the legislative and judicial processes) is itself justified." And we are today, he asserts, "certainly entitled to be quite skeptical both of the fairness and of the capacity for self-corruption of our larger institutional mechanisms, including the legal system." If that is so, is it not a non sequitur to suggest that we are justified in placing that same trust and confidence in the morality of lawyers, individually or collectively?

Freedman's is an ethic of role (Chapter 1); Wasserstrom's is an ethic of isolation (Chapter 2). Freedman accuses Wasserstrom of aristocracy; Wasserstrom would probably say that he must trust his conscience more than the legislature. The twain may meet, but the difficulties in their meeting on common moral ground are formidable. What I am interested in is a smaller point, and that is Freedman's position that once a lawyer enters upon the lawyer-client relationship he has given up his moral right of conscientious objection, a right Freedman otherwise acknowledges as making it possible to be a lawyer and a good person:

> In order to exercise . . . responsibility and initiative, each person is entitled to know his or her rights against society and against other individuals, and to decide whether to seek fulfillment of those rights through due process of law.
> The lawyer, by virtue of his or her training and skills, has a legal and practical monopoly with respect to access to the legal system and knowledge about the law. . . .
> Accordingly, the attorney acts both professionally and morally in advising clients candidly and fully regarding the client's legal rights and moral responsibilities as the lawyer perceives them, and by assisting clients to carry out their lawful decisions. Further, the attorney acts unprofessionally and immorally by depriving clients of their autonomy, that is, by denying them information regarding their legal rights, by otherwise pre-empting their moral decisions, or by depriving them of the ability to carry out their lawful decisions.

I understand that last phrase to mean that a lawyer acts immorally and unprofessionally if, once he has agreed to act for his client, he claims conscientious objection from the client's lawful purposes.

Freedman's position may be generalized as one view of a lawyer's duty to be *loyal* to his client. The *Code* invokes that duty in terms of a lawyer's loyalty to his client's interests; it forbids "divided loyalties"; it says a lawyer must "insure loyalty unimpaired by . . . conflicting interests" or by "compromising influences and loyalties." The *Code* and other sources of professional guidance encourage "undivided" loyalty, "complete" loyalty, and an "obligation to loyalty" which, however, "applies only to . . . discharge of professional duties." The *Code* discourages "diluted" loyalty, "questioned" loyalty, and "divided" loyalty. The *Code* does not go as far as Freedman goes in nullifying a right of conscientious objection, once the lawyer is employed, but it can fairly be read to say that moral decisions should be, by and large, left up to the client. It was this point in the *Code* that Harry Jones and Murray Schwartz found to be a departure from the 1956 Joint Commission report on professional ethics, which departure both of them regret and propose to amend.

Another way to look at this question would be to focus on the lawyer's *fidelity* (or faithfulness) to his client, rather than upon his *loyalty* to the client. I think the distinction has semantic difficulty but that it is not, finally, a semantic distinction only. For example, I am faithful to my friends but do not necessarily try to be loyal to them. One difference may be that I do not believe friendship requires me to hate the people my friend hates. I can be *faithful* to my friend without that; perhaps—or so some of my friends may think—I cannot be *loyal* to my friend unless I hate the people he hates.

The *Code* often uses the two words as if they had different connotations. It speaks of the fidelity of counsel, of the client's reliance upon his lawyer's honor and fidelity, of the lawyer's most valuable professional possession being his "well merited reputation for professional capacity and fidelity to trust." It warns lawyers not to engage in behavior which endangers their fidelity, speaks of "a most scrupulous fidelity," and says that "fidelity to trust ... cannot be forced.... [It is the] outcome of character and conduct." The word *fidelity* is associated with words such as reputation, good faith, counsel, character, and trust, rather than with words such as interests, influences, dilutions, questions, and division.

The difference is emphasized, I think, in three situations the *Code* uses to illustrate a lawyer's faithfulness. In one example (E.C. 5-13), a corporate lawyer (that is, a lawyer who is a full-time employee of a corporate employer) is told that there is no rule against his joining a union made up of the corporation's employees, provided he maintains his fidelity, as a lawyer, to his employer. This suggests to me that this person, as an employee, may risk disloyalty and join the union when his employer does not want him to do that, but that he cannot, as a lawyer, do anything in the union which would risk his faithfulness, as a lawyer, to his employer; the person can join the union, but not the lawyer. (That distinction poses moral and psychological problems not relevant on the present point.)

In another example, the professional literature speaks of a lawyer's reputation for "fidelity to private trust" as being a valuable possession for him, his clients, and the profession. This is used in such a way as to be synonymous with (and in one case is tied to the phrase) "reputation as an honest person"—that is, a person of truthfulness, of character. A third example is the literature's use of fidelity as permitting the lawyer to perform two duties that may appear inconsistent—so that a lawyer is counseled to maintain fidelity to his client, but not to lie to the court; to maintain the "highest fidelity" to both client and court; and to maintain "fidelity both to private trust and to public duty." It is possible for a person of character to work out the conflicts.

The literature does not talk about a *reputation for loyalty,* although such a thing is possible. Trollope likened the loyalty of Mr. Chaffanbrass to that of an Irish bandit. It does not talk—nor do we talk in ordinary discourse—of loyalty to each of two demands that appear to be in conflict. One can be loyal to a demand, but one cannot be faithful to it; in what I suppose to be the accurate sense of the word, a person can only be faithful to persons, as the God of Israel is faithful to his chosen people, or as Jesus is faithful when he keeps his promise to be with us until the end of time. When a public servant swears, as he takes office, to faithfully protect the Constitution, his duty of faithfulness runs to his fellow citizens; he promises to be faithful to them, in the terms stated in a consensus statement on the purposes and conduct of the government.

Fidelity is, as William May has put it, an ethical word which has to do with a *mutual* human undertaking. Our Jewish and Christian tradition has often used the word "covenant" to express the undertaking itself. Covenant (and faithfulness) suggest a tradition in which one performs for others freely, even gratuitously. Professional traditions—the legal profession's, the medical profession's, the clergy's—suggest that a professional performs the services needed because they are needed and not primarily to be paid. Fidelity, pursuant to covenant, is not purchased; it is spontaneous and in some sense gratuitous. It arises from ethical principle and dedication; it implies trust; it aims at a *relationship.*

Loyalty, as I perceive the word to be used in professional discourse, is narrower and more pragmatic. The *Code* assumes that one cannot be loyal to his client and at the same time serve interests other than his client's; but, because such a duty cannot possibly be carried out by its terms, the *Code* specifies what a lawyer cannot do (e.g., be paid by someone other than the client, acquire an interest adverse to his client's, represent conflicting interests). The *Code* must limit loyalty to "the discharge of professional duties." There is a tendency, when the word "loyalty" is used, to define obligations in terms of minimal duty rather than in terms of ethical principle, generosity, or spontaneity. One way to read the rules on loyalty is in terms of the means lawyers can use to protect themselves from criticism, by, for instance, entering into specific agreements on what they will do for their clients, and then by obeying the letter of what they have agreed to do. Many lawyers find such specification of duty to be repugnant, and the *Code* condemns some forms of it. In a general sense, one who heeds his loyalties tends to think of duty as located in codes and contracts; his behavior suggests obedience and role. He tends to think of his client as dependent on him. One who heeds his fidelity (and here it may be possible to use the singular) thinks more in terms of dedication, of teaching and learning from his client rather than obeying him, and of a relationship of trust rather than dependence.

My thought is that fidelity rests in a relation (Chapter 3) and loyalty rests in a role (Chapter 1). Fidelity is more the result of covenant than of contract; loyalty is more the result of contract than of covenant. The Jewish and Christian traditions use the word *covenant* to express a mutual undertaking between God and his people, but it would be blasphemous to suppose this was a contract, a *deal* between God and his creatures. The Christian tradition, particularly in some of its Calvinist specifications, extended the idea of covenant to a covenant among God's people (which established a community) and a covenant between God's people and their rulers (which established a state). The duties imposed by these human covenants could not be explicated, though; they rested on trust–on character, if you like. In the covenant idea, God will be faithful to his people because he said he would; his people will be faithful to one another, and *they know what that means.*

The idea of contract is different. The western ethical tradition has never been sure of how to treat the moral duty to keep a bare promise. It has never been sure what to do with contracts. Alan Donagan, generalizing from the tradition, says that the duty to keep a promise derives from the duty to tell the truth (the duty not to lie), which derives from various cultural expressions of what Jews and Christians alike call the Golden Rule. The idea of keeping promises has difficulties, though. One is that a promise always includes tacit conditions. For example, your promise to come to my house for dinner is not broken when an emergency keeps you away. Another difficulty is the problem of heavier responsibilities. It is not a violation of your promise to come for dinner for you to decide it is more important for you to stay with your sick child; your responsibility to your child is, in the circumstances, heavier than your responsibility to me. A third example is the problem of the coerced promise; in order to avoid a duty to obey such a promise I have to decide that the coercer and promisee somehow, as Donagan puts it, "forfeits his right as a rational creature."

The idea of faithfulness induced by a covenant would, I think, treat these problems differently. In the cases of tacit conditions and heavier responsibility, it is possible for you to be faithful both to your sick child and to me. There is sense in which we can both be seen to have a responsibility to your sick child because we are faithful to one another. The health of your child, because I am faithful to you, is a matter not of your heavier responsibility but of our mutual responsibility. We have a common undertaking, we two who are faithful to one another, and this matter of your sick child is not merely a condition on your promise to me, but it is a matter we share. Turning the coerced promise question into a coerced covenant question would be absurd on its face. No one can coerce my faithfulness; no one can, as I am using the word, coerce a covenant. As the ABA Ethics Committee once put it, "fidelity to trust cannot be forced." It is a matter of character.

The ideas of free choice, of gratuitous undertaking, and of spontaneity, are fundamental to a covenant of faithfulness, but they are not fundamental to a contract for loyalty. The difference is that covenant and faithfulness do not rest on a *quid pro quo,* but contract and loyalty do. Faithfulness does not, as we lawyers say it, depend on consideration. The professional ideal of gratuitous service is the ideal that a professional will meet a need when he perceives it and that in meeting that need he will render faithful service to his client.

Is it helpful, then, to think of the professional relation as resting on a covenant and on faithfulness, rather than as resting on contract and a duty of loyalty? It seems to me that it is, because it is then possible to think of my serving both goodness and my client—or, to put that a better way, as serving goodness through my client and my client through goodness—or to put that in an even better way, as serving the goodness of my client. That is the service, the faithful service, that Edith Orme rendered to Lady Mason. I would prefer to say that the problem is not whether I should be loyal to my client's interests; it is whether I should be faithful to my client as I contemplate the fact that my client is an infinitely valuable and inscrutable person who unfortunately seems to want me to help him continue doing evil. I should not be loyal to his evil purpose and, in that sense, cannot be loyal to him. But I can be faithful to him despite his evil purpose.

This idea of faithfulness does—to return to Freedman's charge against Wasserstrom—endorse an oligarchy, but it is an oligarchy of character, not an oligarchy of professionalism. I do not argue that lawyers automatically have character, but I do argue that the problem of *Orley Farm*—the problem of being faithful to Lady Mason but at the same time not collaborating in her evil purpose—rests on character and not on a role-determined concept of loyalty. Philip Rhinelander, who, in 1977, came from his retirement as a philosophy professor at Stanford to assist journalists in pondering their moral dilemmas, put this better than I can; but he does not deny, nor can I, that the morality of character depends on the judgment and behavior of less than all of the people in a society:

> Ethical standards apply to human character or human conduct. When we make ethical judgments about persons we generally use terms like *good* and *bad* in the sense of virtuous or vicious. When speaking of acts or behavior, we generally use terms like *right* or *wrong* in the sense of praiseworthy or blameworthy. But there is one difference worth noting. Whereas terms like "good" and "bad" have comparatives (better, best and worse, worst), terms like "right" and "wrong" do not. This may be

a linguistic accident, but I would suggest that it points up a difference between two approaches to ethics. The great classical writers considered that character was fundamental. Consequently they stressed the importance of developing virtues, or dispositions of character, such as courage, wisdom, temperance and the like. For them rules about particular kinds of conduct were secondary and derivative. By contrast, a legalistic approach to ethics begins with rules about particular kinds of conduct and makes virtues secondary. Under this sort of view, virtue tends to be reduced to obedience to moral rules. The first approach tends to be more flexible. It puts more weight upon the judgment of the individual. It also emphasizes the need for practice and training because acquiring a virtue is like acquiring any other skill. The legalistic approach tends in the other direction. You live by the book. This makes (theoretically) for more precision, but also for more rigidity and for a kind of delusive exactness, since (as Aristotle noted) it is virtually impossible to lay down hard and fast rules for all cases.

I prefer the older view. I note the difference because when people rebel against the tyranny of rules, they often forget that there is an alternative. Under the alternative view, you can have rules for common situations reflecting what the virtuous person would habitually do, but in special situations the virtuous person would take special action. Here the ultimate standard is the model of the virtuous person: what he or she would do is the test of what is right.

Rhinelander's solution to the problem of deciding what to do about the tension between my faithfulness to my client and the client's evil purposes is a classic, Aristotelian solution. I find it helpful in explaining three things: how Edith Orme could be a counselor and companion without being a collaborator (because her character guided her in negotiating the channel between care and stain); how she could do this when Lady Mason's lawyers could not (their ethic was a role-determined ethic of loyalty where hers was an ethic of faithfulness that finally depended on character); and how the sort of moral witness she undertook is a witness that rests in the ability to love, to counsel, and to bear tragic choices.

CHAPTER NINE
An Example on the Problem of Collaboration

Should a lawyer continue to minister to a client charged with crime after the client states to the lawyer that the client intends to commit perjury in his testimony at the trial?

(Lady Mason did not tell the truth to her lawyer about her forgery and perjury, but she did tell the truth to Mrs. Orme, a confidante who represents in the story the ministry her lawyer should have provided. The present issue can be given a narrative context by supposing that Lady Mason proposed to testify in her own defense and to repeat the lies which she had been using for twenty years to keep her son in possession of the farm.)

The ethics of care in lawyer-client relationships is, depending on how you look at it, either circumscribed by or defined to include personal moral limits: A moral person who is also a lawyer cannot be loyal to his client if his loyalty violates his own conscience; he should stop short of complicity in his client's evil design; he should not be a collaborator in his client's wrong. The reason for this limit, or specification, is stated in the virtually universal principle of morality that Jews and Christians call the Golden Rule. In Leviticus 19:18, "You shall love your neighbor as a man like yourself." Or, "You shall treat your neighbor lovingly, for he is like yourself." According to Rabbi Hillel, "Do not do to your fellow man what you would hate to have done to you." According to Jesus, "Always treat others as you would like them to treat you" (Matthew 7:12). And, according to Immanuel Kant's "second formulation of the fundamental principle of morality" (in Alan Donagan's rendering), "Act so that you treat humanity, whether in your own person or in that of another, always as an end, and never as a means only." I therefore cannot lie to another person—judge, juror, prosecutor, or whomever.

Selective ignorance. I assume, first, that a lawyer should not avoid the truth of what his client intends. A lawyer should not take refuge in what Monroe Freedman calls "selective ignorance." Selective ignorance is an untruthful solution; it supposes that the moral life can be lived by looking the other way; it fails to honor an implied, preliminary requirement of the Golden Rule, that a person should treat himself lovingly (or, if you like, as an end and not a means). It is also a corrupting delusion that—viewed from the perspective of the ethics of character—makes the moral life either impossible or more difficult than it would be if the lawyer told himself the truth. Most moral authorities condemn selective ignorance, although some are self-righteous in doing so.

Abandonment. I argue that a lawyer should not abandon his "perjurious" client. His client is dependent on him, in the dependence of one who has been treated, or should have been treated, as one who is loved or as the lawyer would like to be treated if he were in the client's shoes, or as an end and not as a means. The lawyer has promised, either expressly, by implication, or by the fact of holding himself out as a member of the profession, to be faithful to his client. Another reason why lawyers should not abandon such clients is that the lawyer-client relation—the relationship itself—is a means to service to persons who are to be treated in the way prescribed by the Golden Rule. Some moralists (Martin Buber, for example) would say that the relation is an end in itself; it does not need the Golden Rule, or any rule, to justify it. It is something that should not be destroyed, for reasons both ontological (i.e., it is in relationships that we come to be) and moral (and come to be good).

Because a lawyer should not abandon his client, so long as it is possible to remain faithful both to his client and to the truth, he should not abandon him spiritually by deciding prematurely that his client will lie. The lawyer should not abandon his client when his client tells him that he (the client) *intends* to commit perjury in testimony at his trial. No moral dilemma requiring abandonment has then been presented. The client who proposes to commit perjury is in need of more talk with his lawyer, not less. The essence of the position is that the lawyer will, in faithfulness to his client, counsel the client against lying. He cannot counsel his client if he abandons him, and he cannot counsel in a convincing way unless he remains faithful to his client. He cannot, for example, counsel in a convincing way if he is convinced that his client will be impervious to moral argument. The virtue of hope is required. Monroe Freedman says that the lawyer should "advise the client that the proposed testimony is unlawful." I mean much more than that when I say "counsel." I intend to invoke the practice of care.

No lie will be told in the case until the client speaks the words from the witness stand. Even if traditional morality would say that the lawyer participates in the lie when it is told from the witness stand, he does not participate in the lie until it is told. The moral reasons why the lawyer should not abandon his client are, first, that the lawyer-client relation is necessary to treating the client in a loving way (since you cannot be loving to someone you do not know), or necessary to treating the client as the lawyer would himself like to be treated, or necessary to treating the client as an end and not as a means; and, second, that the lawyer should not abandon his undertaking unless it would be wrong to continue it. The second argument is a matter of keeping promises or of faithfulness. A *third* way to put this would be to say that the lawyer should not manipulate his client for his own (the lawyer's) purposes. If he abandons his client only because of his client's statement, what he says about himself is that the client is merely a means to the lawyer's end (fee, fame, or whatever)—a means that can be abandoned when it appears that the client may prove unreliable.

Threat. The third argument may be important on a subsidiary question—whether the lawyer may use the *threat* of abandonment as a counseling technique. Threatening abandonment might be consistent with, and might even support, the position that the lawyer should not abandon the client, because (as many criminal defense lawyers say) such a threat is a potent argument for convincing the client he should tell the truth. It is, in a crude sense, a form of moral witness. An argument the other way might rely on the third reason against abandoning the client—that abandonment demonstrates that the lawyer is manipulating his client. Threat manipulates the client, too, although toward a different end—the end that the client tell the truth. This argument might be that manipulating another person is always and self-evidently wrong, or it might be that manipulating a person, to the extent it is untruthful and because the Golden Rule requires that the lawyer tell the truth to his client, is wrong because it is deceitful. It may be possible to reason that a threat is neither a lie nor a statement of intention, because the threatener harbors what we used to call "a mental reservation" (even though I threaten to quit, I probably won't). The mental-reservation argument sounds contrived, but it is not unusual. It seems to be the argument allowing our national leaders to point nuclear missiles at potential enemies while at the same time agreeing (as some of them do) that the *use* of nuclear missiles would be immoral. I am not convinced by the mental-reservation argument. I think it is wrong to threaten abandonment of the client unless I mean what I say, and say what I mean, that I intend to abandon the client if and when he lies on the witness stand.*

---

*The position of the ABA *Code* may be that the lawyer would be justified in abandoning the client at that point, or even before that point, since the lawyer is forbidden to "use" perjured testimony. The *Code* is consistent with my position to the extent that it would not *require* abandonment. An additional consideration in my position on threatening abandonment is that it may indicate moral arrogance in the lawyer; it may not be the "conditional advice" that is necessary in the ethics of care.

Moral influence. An important factor supports this position against abandonment. The fact is that lawyers have moral influence on their clients. Criminal-defense lawyers say that most clients who at first propose to commit perjury give up their proposals after their lawyers urge them to tell the truth. This fact is not offered as a basis for my moral position. My position is a reasoned position based on the Golden Rule; it does not depend on results. The fact of lawyer influence demonstrates, though, that my assumption that moral counseling is a worthwhile enterprise for a lawyer—that it is not something that will leave a lawyer weeping and gnashing his teeth—is a defensible assumption. If there were *no* chance of success in counseling, I would still argue that a lawyer should not abandon his client, but I might not want to be a lawyer.

My reason for not abandoning the client is based on the person of the client. Some other arguments for remaining faithful to the client are not acceptable. One such argument says that the lawyer should not abandon the client because the law gives the client a right to testify and a right to the assistance of counsel in doing so. If a lawyer accepts this argument, he accepts also the proposition that his observance of the Golden Rule is conditioned on the needs of the government. He seems to believe that he may treat another lovingly only when the Supreme Court says that it is all right to do so. In Kant's terms, he treats himself and his client as means to the government's ends. In the terms stated by Hillel and Jesus, he seems to say that he would like to be treated lovingly but only if loving treatment is required by due process of law. (The Golden Rule, as Hillel and Jesus stated it, requires this resort to what the actor would like.) I should probably be content to let this argument stand as self-evidently ridiculous. But I won't. Suppose there is a lawyer somewhere who finds it not ridiculous; he says that he does not want to be treated lovingly unless due process of law requires loving treatment. This raises an old argument against the Golden Rule as a norm—that it causes a person to reason from his own selfish preferences to a supposition about the selfish preferences of the other. My answer to the argument, in this example, is that one who defines his destiny as dependent on the government's definition is idolatrous. The Golden Rule implies that one define his own destiny in a nonidolatrous way.

Serving goodness. My argument is that the lawyer should refuse to abandon his client *and* that he should attempt to convince his client not to lie. The reason he should attempt to convince his client not to lie is because loving treatment of the other—faithfulness to the other—means helping the other to become a good person. This goal of counseling is implicit in the Golden Rule, although goodness (or good person) can be defined variously as meaning the good life in an Aristotelian sense, or as meaning conversion to faith, or even as meaning such a formal goodness as autonomy. It is probably not necessary, in this context, to be more specific about what goodness (or a good life) means, since almost any answer to that question would include or imply a life in which one lives truthfully. The idea will, though, need to be elaborated in other contexts.*

Arguments for abandonment. Arguments stating that a lawyer should not continue to represent his client if circumstances make the lawyer *appear* to be telling lies, or assisting his client in doing so, depend on the assertion that a lawyer is "an officer of the court," or a member of an honorable profession. Because of the public or fraternal office, a lawyer should not *appear* to be doing wrong. A lawyer should not bring the courts or the profession into disrepute. To the extent that these arguments depend on the consideration of appearances, and not on acts which are wrong, they are not, in my opinion, moral arguments. One could even say that such positions use the lawyer and his clients as means to the ends of the government or of the profession and therefore are, in Kant's terms, arguments for immoral behavior. To the extent that these arguments turn on the act of lying or helping another to lie (as, for example, in the prediction that lawyers will coach their lying clients, so that the perjury is more effective), they are appropriate only if the lawyer does not seek to serve his client's goodness in the counseling phases of his employment. Aside from that, the arguments for abandonment are inappropriate on the issue presented when the client says he plans to lie. No lie has been told; part of the lawyer's purpose, in the moral enterprise of being his client's companion and counselor, is that the client not lie. There may be some danger of scandal, of course, to those who observe the lawyer from outside. But if those people knew all of the facts about the moral enterprise of the lawyer's being a companion and a counselor they would find the lawyer's faithfulness edifying – or they should find it edifying. The lawyer's enterprise as minister is scandalous only to those who do not know the facts or who are making conclusions from faulty moral principles.

The constitutional law argument. One reply to the "officer of the court" position is that the client's perjury is really not a lie, or at least that it is a lie the lawyer can do nothing about and therefore is, so far as the lawyer is concerned, not morally significant. The most common version of this answer depends on a prediction about the constitutional law of the future: The client has a constitutional right to testify (even if he proposes to lie). The proposed *Rules of Professional Conduct,* in their 1980 draft, provided that "A lawyer for a defendant in a criminal case

---

*In reference to James Edwin Horton (Chapter 14), Thomas More (Chapters 18 and 19), and Franz Jagerstatter (Chapter 20).

... may offer evidence, regardless of belief as to whether it is false or fabricated, if required to do so by law." The drafters of these proposed *Rules* adopt the position of the *Code*—that a lawyer may not use perjured evidence—and say that the old rule "should apply to defense counsel in criminal cases, as well as in other instances." They then add, "Ultimately, however, *the definition of the lawyer's ethical duty* in such a situation *is determined by the law's definition* of due process and the right to counsel in criminal cases" (emphasis added). The duty not to lie is here held waived if the government says it may be waived. The *Rules'* proposition is suspect because it appears to depend on the government's requiring a lawyer to tell the truth and not on a more fundamental and dependable source of morals. The duty not to lie is an administrative convenience which may be taken away when the rules of procedure are changed by the courts. The standard becomes, "Do not lie except when the government says you must in order to carry out your function as a lawyer."

Monroe Freedman, who may be the source of this position, is candid in defending a lawyer's complicity in perjury when the Constitution is thought to require complicity: "What that means—necessarily, it seems to me—is that the criminal defense attorney, however unwillingly in terms of personal morality, has a professional responsibility as an advocate in an adversary system to examine the perjurious client in the ordinary way and to argue to the jury, as evidence in the case, the testimony presented by the defendant." The drafters of the *Rules* adopt Freedman's position but limit it to cases of legal right.*

Freedman's argument is that it is useful that the ability to testify and to have the assistance of counsel be insured, even in liars and perjurers, because the adversary system would collapse or the civil liberties of truth tellers would be imperilled or both things would happen if liars and perjurers were not assisted. Freedman's argument is an argument both as to what the law ought to be (but is not yet) and a moral argument. The drafters of the *Rules* take no position on what the law ought to be but say that, if the law turns out to be as Freedman wants, the law should then settle the moral question. The drafters of the *Rules* seem to me to say either that the law should be the source of morals or, if it is not, only the immoral should practice law. Neither position talks, typically, about the conversion of those who propose to lie and perjure themselves. Both are, in that regard and depending on how you look at it, cynical or naive or both.

The drafters of the proposed *Rules* do not argue from moral bases, but their position (and Freedman's) seems to depend on either or both

---

*Thus the dispensation would not be available in a civil case or with respect to a witness other than the defendant.

of two faulty moral assumptions. Perhaps lawyers are to be excused from complicity in perjury because the lawyer's participation can be treated as a sort of legal fiction—like one of our forebears' pleading in detinue that his client had lost his horse, when what had happened was that the defendant stole it. But that reasoning will not work in the perjury context because, in perjury, people are in fact being deceived and are therefore not being treated lovingly, or as the lawyer would like to be treated, or as ends in themselves. Perhaps, and more likely, the implicit argument is that the Constitution, as construed, can be depended upon as a source of moral guidance on difficult questions. But the position that the government can be depended upon to say what is truth, or what truth is important, is a disastrous moral position.

Disastrous or not, the argument that moral rules for lawyers should follow the law is prominent, in this context and in others, in the profession's moral reasoning. Virtually every authority that has raised the perjurious-client problem in the discussion within the American Bar Association has depended to some extent on the once and future state of constitutional law—so that the position of the Supreme Court on the constitutional right to testify or to the assistance of counsel is determinative on the moral issue of complicity in perjury, as if perjury is perjury only when the government says so. At considerable risk of incivility, I have argued that this moral position is indistinguishable from Eichmann's saying that the orders of the Third Reich decided, for him, what he should do with his Jewish prisoners. The prevalence of the constitutional argument does not prove, of course, that the lawyers, judges, and professors who labor over this issue for the profession can be duped into enormous crimes; but it does evidence how pervasive the profession's drift into positivism has been since the days of David Hoffman. It demonstrates too, I think, that the issue of "right to counsel" cannot be resolved morally without a theory of representation that includes an interest in the *client's* being a good person.

The testimony itself. The question becomes more difficult when it is considered in reference to consequences. Traditional moral reasoning (or at least some of it) would say that moral judgments cannot be made in reference to consequences; one reason they cannot is that no one knows what the consequences of an action will be. Here, for instance, if I remain in communication with my client, the consequence will probably be (or so criminal-defense lawyers say) that he will not lie, despite what he tells me now. But he may lie, despite our relation and despite my witness for truthfulness, and then I may or may not have participated in his lie. I will have asked in court the questions which he answered falsely.

Will I have then participated in a lie to the court and jury? I would argue that I will not have, since, if my reasoning is valid on the lawyer's behavior prior to the lie, the outcome of my efforts to counsel truthfulness cannot determine the moral quality of the efforts themselves, or of the lawyer-client relation and my efforts to preserve it. It is not that wrong has come about because of my efforts but that wrong has come about despite my efforts to prevent it. I assume that the questions a lawyer asks in direct examination can be formed so as to encourage the client to tell the truth. For example, I should not ask my client a question the answer to which either will be a lie or will harm his case. Here it is important to notice that my position against abandoning the client does not depend on results. It does seem to support my position that most lawyers who have experience in this situation say that their clients decide, after counseling, not to lie. (Clients decide either not to testify at all or to testify truthfully.) But, I suppose, if the last thing the client says to his lawyer, as they go to the witness stand, is that he intends to lie, the lawyer is naive to suppose that the client will change his mind when questions are put to him. My position is that the client should not be abandoned, even in the face of such apparent determination to lie, because the morality of my counseling efforts still—even then—does not depend on results—not on predicted results and not on actual results. My position is that the lawyer's hope that the client will not lie (and I assume that this hope has been put into practice in counseling) is justified by the truth about human beings that underlies the Golden Rule (that they are children of God, infinitely valuable, more valuable than any government or all governments); and that, in this hope, the lawyer's being his client's companion, even to the witness stand, does not become the use of perjured testimony when it turns out that the client lies. My position would, then, reject the position, taken by the Criminal Justice Section of the ABA in 1970 and abandoned by the Section in 1978, that the lawyer in this situation should put his client on the stand but refuse to ask him questions.

Revealing the lie. Must I reveal this lie to the court, now that I have heard it? The answer here is no, on conventional and traditional principles that turn on my promise to my client not to reveal confidences. Even if this promise is implicitly limited to statements regarding the past—and not to the statement he made, before he testified, that he intended to lie—it still binds here because this conduct is now past conduct. This is the reasoning behind 1974 amendments to the *Code*; and it appears to me to be sound, not on utilitarian grounds, but on the ground that confidentiality was consistent with my faithfulness to my client before he lied and is consistent with counseling after the lie. The proposed new *Rules* reach this result, too, but only when the law requires it; otherwise the new *Rules* would require the lawyer to disclose the lie in his client's testimony.

Using the lie in summarizing the evidence. Must I avoid the lie when I summarize the evidence to the jury? There are two aspects to this question: First, reference to the lie as if it were the truth. That is not a problem in the legal profession, where lawyers are forbidden to treat any testimony as if they vouched for its truth. This first moral question therefore does not arise. Second, reference to this testimony as if it were entitled to be believed—that is, as if it were the same as other testimony—when I know that it is not entitled to be believed. It is possible to make an argument on this aspect that resembles the argument I made on the first aspect: When I argue to the jury, I do not vouch for the truth of the testimony on which my argument is based. I compare inferences and the logic of facts, and I construct the set of inferences and the pattern of logic that will benefit my client. The drafting committee in the Criminal Justice Section argued in this way for the 1978 Section draft on this point. In fact, the committee said, silence on my client's testimony amounts to a statement that I do not believe it: "[A] lawyer's silence regarding his client's testimony amounts to an expression of personal opinion regarding such testimony."

I have two difficulties with the committee's argument here. The first is that it is not convincing. It seems to me that I would be misleading the jurors if I let them think that, to my knowledge, my client's lie was as believable as other testimony in the case. I would not be treating them lovingly, as I would like to be treated if I had been appointed and sworn to find the truth. The second difficulty is that the committee limits its argument to the testimony of the defendant, and then only when the Constitution requires that it be presented. The committee would require the lawyer, in summation, to avoid mentioning the lies of other witnesses (and to avoid mentioning lies in civil cases) and, in those situations, would allow lawyers to make indirect expressions of belief in the truth of the testimony. If the committee's moral argument is an acceptable argument, it is acceptable generally or it is not acceptable at all. It will not do to say that a moral argument is valid only if the Supreme Court says it is.

The better position on the second question having to do with jury summation is that the lawyer, once he knows his client has lied and has not corrected the effects of the lie, should avoid further reference to the false testimony. This is, in part, the position taken by the Criminal Justice Section in its 1970 Standards; that position, and my argument, assume that the lawyer will endeavor not to violate his client's confidences as he argues to the jury. He will use his advocate's art and will not tell the jury that his client has lied. The task—which will not often be required, or so I am told—requires a lawyer to be faithful both to his client and to the truth.

The position I argue for would permit the lawyer to remain his client's counselor and to conduct the direct examination of his client in court, on the reasoning that no lie occurs until the client speaks the lie from the witness stand. The same reasoning would not extend to jury summation and would not always extend to false physical evidence or the testimony of third persons, since the counseling relation cannot always put truth into physical evidence and does not always extend to third persons. I can find no argument that would justify the position the Criminal Justice Section took in 1978, that the lawyer should, after the client lies in court, "treat his client's [false] testimony as any other evidence." I reject the argument that the Constitution or the adversary function requires that treatment, since a moral person cannot allow either the government or the profession to decide what is truth and what is not. The principle on which I base the lawyer's moral ability both to counsel and to examine is the principle that the client should be served by the trust and faithfulness of his lawyer; he is, in Kant's terms, an end that justifies and may even require faithfulness, despite what the profession has come to call "the appearance of impropriety." However:

It is not possible to live the moral life without causing harm. I have wondered why it is that arguments, such as mine, from traditional moral premises, are prominent in nineteenth-century American writers on legal ethics (Hoffman and Sharswood for two examples) but have been replaced in the last decades by arguments assuming that the beginning and end of professional morality can be found in the law. I suspect the reason is, in part, that lawyers are people who like to have things come out well; we like to suppose that our lives and our systems can avoid doing harm. But the aspiration to avoid harm is a delusion; moral life is impossible without causing harm. My client's telling the truth may bring him, his family, his business, and even me, to disaster; if it will, and I still counsel him to tell the truth, I may—and, even more, he may—discover something about the morality of the Golden Rule: The God of Abraham, Isaac, and Jacob, the God of the Cross (the God, too, of Immanuel Kant) is also the God of Job. Our moral tradition is not a tradition that promises happiness. It is a tradition that shows how meaning triumphs over power.

So, for example, the solution to the problem of the client who proposes to commit perjury is not solved by my withdrawing from the case. That solution, which is perhaps implied in the *Code,* requires the lawyer to refuse to proceed with a client who proposes to commit perjury. The principal argument for that solution is that it saves the lawyer and the profession from the appearance of evil—which means that it *uses* the client to serve the ends of the lawyer and the lawyer's professional colleagues. The solution is sometimes defended by saying that the first lawyer's withdrawal will cause the client to go to a second lawyer, who will not know about the proposed perjury (even if he cooperates in it) and will therefore have a clear conscience and will preserve the integrity of the profession and of the court. That aspect of the solution is wrong, too, not only because it cheats the judicial system (which it does), but because it *uses* the second lawyer and initiates a professional relation based on falsehood. It was not a mistake for the client to be candid with his first lawyer; it was a *good* thing, as his telling the truth in court would be a *good* thing. What is wrong is to suppose that the result of good choices is security and prosperity. The God of Job is more interesting than that.

The ethics of care in counseling. If you look on the lawyer as someone who does what his client wants, or serves as an instrument of the government, you define the lawyer's morality according to the standards of civil service. If you look on the lawyer as an isolated moral agent, you define the lawyer's morality as if it were constantly threatened by clients. If, for a third option, you look on the lawyer as one of two people in the valuable relation Martin Buber defined as the "I-Thou" relation, you define the lawyer's morality and the client's morality as interdependent. The two people learn, morally, from one another. You affirm that moral choices in the lawyer-client relation have to be worked out. The last orientation—what I call the ethics of care—gives this "perjurious client" problem a different perspective. The most hopeful thing I see in the 1978 approach of the Criminal Justice Section to this problem is the experience of criminal lawyers in working with their clients, and particularly the testimony of these lawyers that clients do, as a result, decide not to lie. The Section's 1978 draft repeats twice the importance of the counseling phase of the relation and then adopts a rule that will protect the counseling relation. I think it goes wrong after that, but, because of its beginning point, it maintains an emphasis different from the emphasis of the proposed *Rules*.

The differences are these: One system assumes that the lawyer-client relation is a means to a governmental end; the other implies that the relation is a means to serve the client in the way in which people are to be served under the Golden Rule. Thus the relation is conceived of as a matter of ministry in one way of thinking and as a matter of service to the adversary system of justice in the other. In one system, it is enough for the lawyer to "advise the client that the proposed testimony is unlawful" (Freedman), but in the other the burden of the enterprise comes to be focused on what the lawyer and client say to one another, on the experienced fact that the result of the conversation is, usually, that the client decides not to lie. In one system, lawyers talk about building a solid lawyer-client relationship because trust is important for the client and fidelity is important for the lawyer; in the other system, confidentiality is explained by the system's need, and therefore the lawyer's, to gather facts for the courtroom.

The moral choice may be to abandon the client. I don't deny that there may be circumstances in which a lawyer's ministry must be denied by the lawyer. I don't argue that circumstances justify the lawyer's committing wrong or deluding himself about his own behavior. It may be necessary to refuse to be my client's companion, because my view of what truth requires will not let me go with him. The enterprise I am recommending is one of ethical risk—and other kinds of risk, too—and that means that it may not work out to serve the goodness of the client, or, even if it does, it may demand too high a moral price for me. Often, I think, this is a decision in which principles are not helpful. Thomas More decided to resign his chancellorship at a time when resignation was not logical and seemed not to be required by any principle. He decided to refuse the Oath of Supremacy and go to the block at a time when virtually every other Christian in England decided the other way. Thomas More even refused to say that objective moral logic required either of his decisions. Much the same point could be made of the rare *Christian* martyrs of Nazi Germany (Jagerstatter, Bonhoeffer), or of Judge James Edwin Horton in the *Scottsboro* case. The social side of such choices is that decisions that change society are individual and even eccentric. They are decisions taken by one who, in James Burtchaell's phrase, "cannot expect society around him to be virtuous, so that his integrity may come easily." Robert Bolt said of More that he was "a man with an adamantine sense of his own self." And of those who, in a modern context, decline the opportunity to be modern examples, he said: "We fly from the idea of an individual to the professional scribes, the classifiers, the men with categories. . . . Both socially and individually it is with us as it is with our cities—an accelerating flight to the periphery, leaving a center which is empty when the hours of business are over." At the extremities, I think, we tend to choose better when we choose personally and with advertence, but to choose more poorly—to choose poorer professional lives—when we choose by not choosing.

PART TWO
Advocacy

Introduction

There is a romantic tradition in our profession that the office of advocate began in English law with the office of champion in medieval trials by battle. The tradition may owe more to Sir Walter Scott than to history, but the image of an able defender appearing to stand up for the embattled litigant is inspiring and, when it is put into historical context, instructive.

Here is a report from The Rolls of the Justices in Eyre for Yorkshire, 1218–19:

> Henry of Shelley seeks against Lalger le Vavasur 3½ carucates of land with appurtenances in Sharleston. Malger came and vouched to warranty therein Robert his brother, who came and warranted him. The same Henry seeks that land against this Robert as his right, and as that whereof Hawisa his great-grandmother was seized in the time of king Henry the elder, the grandfather of king John, as of fee and right, etc., taking explees therefrom to the value etc., and from this Hawisa the right in that land descended to Liolf her eldest son, and from this Liolf to Robert his son, father of that Henry, and from Robert to this Henry as his son and heir. That that land is his right and inheritance and descends to him by hereditary right, he offers to prove by the body of a certain free man of his, Robert son of Thomas, who speaks from the sight and command of his father.

The champion appeared in faithfulness—to God, to his client, and to his father. He came at risk and he came gratuitously. The fiction that he had sworn to his father (on his father's deathbed, by some accounts) to stand up for his client apparently began with the fact that the champion was a witness who was permitted to testify that, although he had not seen his client's ancestors in possession of the land, his (the champion's) father had seen them.

The statement came to mean that the champion acted for his client because he had promised his father that he would. One form of the client's pleading was, "I am ready to prove by my free-man ... to whom his father, when on his death-bed, injoined by the faith which a son owes to his father, that if he ever heard a claim concerning that land, he should prove this as that which his father saw and heard." That later idea—which also became a fiction—was that there was a faithfulness in the champion's act that had nothing to do with the client but that rested on the memory of the champion's father as an honest man. This was a detached faithfulness, corollary perhaps to a need in the client, who was not allowed to be his own witness.

The purpose of the battle was to arrive at the truth. The idea was that God, in his faithfulness, would not permit a perjured claim to prevail. The champion for the client who was telling the truth would win the battle. The important thing was not the risk the champion took in the battle, but the result of the battle. Champions did not fight to the death, did not usually even fight until one of them was injured. Champions used weapons which were not lethal, and the trial was over as soon as one of them seemed, with these weapons, to prevail. The personal risk for the champion appeared at the end of the battle. The common law took him almost literally when he said that he was there to prove the truth of a fact by his body. If he lost the battle he lost his reputation, his property, and, on the Continent, his hand.

Champions were not permitted to take fees. The punishment for being a hireling was worse than that of battle or the punishment which followed a lost battle. Bracton mentions a hireling named Elias Piggun who, in 1220, was found to have taken a fee to appear as champion in a lawsuit over a stolen horse. Piggun was put to trial, was found guilty of fraud, had his foot and his fist cut off, and was told that he should be thankful that the punishment was not worse. What was forbidden was a connection between the champion's service and his prosperity.

This is, even if romantic, not a bad image for the efforts of an advocate. There is something to be said for a profession that aspires in such an image to be faithful to its clients, to the truth, to one another, and to God, and that says that it can maintain this diverse faithfulness—not only says it can, but pledges the welfare of its individual members in the hope that it can.

The system of trial by battle rested on a faith that seems superstitious to a modern mind. But behind it lay a faith that reconciliation in human affairs was possible—that there was such a thing as the truth and that there was a divine justice in which people, individually and in their governments, could be reconciled. In a sense which can accept that faith—a faith many of us still have—the image of the champion is an image of reconciliation for the community and within the community. It is an image of what we have come to call "the administration of justice" which distinguishes the judges whom government sends to

Introduction 109

keep the peace from the other agencies of power. The image of the champion says, and we lawyers still say, that there is a difference between what judges do and what clerks in the drivers-license office do.

I see five issues in this derived idea of the champion as a reconciler. The first has to do with the reconciler as faithful to the truth (Chapter 10); the second with reconciler as faithful to his client (Chapter 11); and the third with the reconciler as faithful to the community (Chapter 12). The fourth issue (Chapter 13) is whether there is a difference between the justice government administers and the justice it cannot administer. The fifth (Chapter 14) seeks to understand the situation of the reconciler who appears to have no reason to suppose that his action can be successful.

CHAPTER TEN
The Practice of Reconciliation

The freedom in which, in his distress, every man stands before God must not be disturbed. If, therefore, he is persuaded to overthrow the results of his reckoning without being first persuaded of the wrongness of his manner of reckoning; if his earnest determination be deprived of its objects without first being provided with its proper object; if he is made superficial and careless and muddleheaded where he had previously been strict and precise; then he is simply disturbed and led astray and hardened, and stumbling blocks and occasions of falling are piled up in his path. What he needs, however, is to be persuaded to break through, with the same earnestness and with the same determination to the place where – to the pure all things are pure.

Karl Barth

Advocacy is in tension in a lawyer's life, a tension similar to that between being a public servant and a companion for one's client (Part One). Our professional tradition, nourished by images of the champion, invites lawyers to consider their advocacy as a form of private warfare – a crusade for rights, perhaps, or, laconically, as an alternative to chaos, and, in either case, a valuable social function. "Lawyers, as guardians of the law, play a vital role in the preservation of society," the *Code* says.

Advocacy is largely, in fact, the practice of reconciliation. Most litigation turns out to be appropriately conciliatory; ninety percent of civil lawsuits are settled, more than two-thirds of criminal charges are resolved in plea bargaining, and most disputes between citizens never even reach the stage where lawyers file papers in courts. Those who explain these facts from the top down – as if courtroom battle were the model – see the advocate as *avoiding litigation*. Those who explain these facts from the bottom up – as if peaceful life in groups were the model – speak of advocacy as a form of reconciliation. Advocacy, thus, and first, reconciles the advocate with those whose champion he proposes to be; that is the insight in the fictional claim that the champion came to assist his "client" because he promised to do so at the deathbed of his father. Advocacy then reconciles the advocate with his hearers. It reconciles the person whose cause is advocated with the persons who hear advocacy. And it reconciles people who are, seen from the top down, at war with one another.

Seen from the bottom up, advocacy brings to communities a new sense of those the community neglects. Seen from the bottom up, advocacy seeks to make things better and is therefore a form of moral discourse. This chapter will look at advocacy as reconciliation in an institutional focus— that is, as a form of moral witness that takes place within an institution, conducted in the name of justice (or of the welfare of some people in the community). This sort of advocacy is sometimes called "public interest advocacy," although, in my view, it involves goodness more than interests, and it invokes interpersonal harmony more than what "the public" wants. Chapter 11 will attempt to carry the idea of advocacy as reconciliation into a broader context, into forums which are presided over by the government (that is, by judges) and in which the advocate appeals for a particular client. Chapter 12 will seek to draw some conclusions.

After King David took Bathsheba, the wife of Uriah the Hittite, and arranged the murder of Uriah, God sent his prophet Nathan to the king. Nathan was sent to decry the injustice David had done to Uriah. "The sword shall never depart from your house," Nathan said to David. God, Nathan said, would "raise up evil against you out of your own house . . . take your wives before your eyes, and give them to your neighbor. . . . Because by this deed you have utterly scorned the Lord, the child that is born to you shall die." But before Nathan spoke in this judicial fashion, he engaged the conscience of David. He told him a story: "There were two men in a certain city, the one rich and the other poor. The rich had very many flocks and herds; but the poor man had nothing but one little ewe lamb, which he had bought. And he brought it up, and it grew up with him and with his children; it used to eat of his morsel, and drink from his cup, and lie in his bosom, and it was like a daughter to him.

"Now there came a traveler to the rich man, and he was unwilling to take one of his own flock or herd to prepare for the wayfarer who had come to him, but he took the poor man's lamb and prepared it."

When King David heard Nathan's story, he was angered at the injustice done by the rich man; David condemned the rich man, and then Nathan said, "You are the man. . . . [God] anointed you king over Israel, and . . . delivered you out of the hand of Saul; and . . . gave you your master's house, and your master's wives into your bosom, and gave you the house of Israel and of Judah; and if this were too little ... would add to you as much more. Why have you despised the word of the Lord, to do what is evil in his sight?" The result of Nathan's advocacy was that David condemned himself. He prayed for relief from the Lord's judgment, and when the judgment came anyway he acknowledged the justice of it. In the end, David was reconciled, "and," the scriptures say, "the Lord loved him." Bathsheba bore him a second son, Solomon, whose name means peace (2 Samuel 12).

The greatest advocates of our century—people such as Martin Luther King, Jr., or Mohandas Gandhi—have been Nathans. What made these advocates unique was their concern with goodness. They insisted on being concerned with the goodness even of the power brokers to whom they appealed. They based their advocacy on the goodness in those who were their clients. They appealed not to power but to conscience. Their advocacy tended to reconcile people rather than defeat them, as David was reconciled rather than defeated. Appeals to power—that is, to authority, to profit, and to secondary values such as order—are effective or not without regard to the conscience of the decision maker. Appeals to conscience are concerned with primary values. They are concerned with the conversion of the decision maker—with his goodness. I understand goodness to mean "the place where—to the pure all things are pure," that is, at least, as Paul put it (in the passage to which Barth's comment is addressed), "the things that make for peace and build up the common life" (Romans 14:19). One result of living in that place, and pursuing those things, is that one is reconciled to those he has, or might have, wronged. Nathan, King, and Gandhi understood that; they were practitioners of reconciliation.

A friend, an academic philosopher, related two experiences. First, he was employed to set up and, as they say, coordinate a series of community discussions of morals in banking, with particular emphasis on the distribution of capital by banks so that the poor get a share. Second, he spoke, by invitation, to a group of executives from a manufacturing company on the subject of moral reasoning in business. In the first case he noticed that the most coherent moral challenge to the banks came from an articulate young legal-services lawyer. The philosopher was impressed by the lawyer but was dismayed to report that the lawyer's challenge had been ineffective. The bankers who heard the challenge were not influenced by it. In the second case, the philosopher had a similar experience himself; his coherent presentation of ethical insight was not heard by the business executives who had employed him to give it.

This sort of advocacy is common in America. It has occurred recently in a massive civil rights movement, in resistance to the Vietnam War, and in argument for better treatment of the poor, the mentally retarded and disturbed, prisoners, the handicapped, women, and even animals, mountains, rivers, and trees. Several observations about the nature of this advocacy are important:

It is almost always moral advocacy. The claims it makes are moral claims. If one were to state these claims in terms of principles, the principles would be moral. So, for example, the advocate argues from fairness, equality (an almost unquestioned moral value in America), the plight of the disadvantaged (no man is an island), the welfare of future generations, or the idea that people are the stewards of nature. These claims are often legal as well as moral, but their force in law is consequential to their moral force; their legal character is consequent on the tendency of moral problems in America (slavery, contraception, abortion, racial discrimination, experimentation on live fetuses) to become legal problems.

It seems prophetic. The advocate is making a moral claim; he is calling upon bankers to think of the poor and upon business people to think of the employees and customers in their enterprises as their most important asset. In both cases, as is perhaps more typical of law-reform lawyers and philosophers than of lawyers in private practice, the advocates have decided not to use appeals to gain, even though other advocates of the same objectives use appeals to gain. Thus, while one could argue that concern for the poor is "good banking" in the profit-and-loss sense, or that sound human-relation programs in business produce profits, it is more characteristic of a prophet to disdain such argument and argue instead in terms of goodness. These advocates also seem to be prophetic in that they do not mind being irritators. They have decided to take the risk of irritation. A characteristic of the prophet is that he puts himself at this risk.

The prophets in the Old Testament were at risk; they were confrontive, uncivil, and direct. They seemed less to persuade than to invoke the wrath of God. Nathan engaged the conscience of the king—a persuasive device—but he also said boldly, "*You* are the man." In an Old Testament way, Gandhi told the English judges who sat on cases in which he was accused that they had only one choice—to send him to jail or to come down from the bench and join him in his cause. King defied unjust law by breaking it and inviting his accusers to defend the law by imposing it on him. He sought to illustrate injustice by challenging his persecutors—the persecutors of his clients, American black people—to stand up for unjust law. Prophets are not merely irritating but are uncivil and are at risk.*

---

*Robert E. Rodes, Jr., helped me understand this; he mentioned the Pharisees and how Jesus treated them, William Lloyd Garrison, the Vietnam War protestors, and those bearing witness against the old regime in Rhodesia. "There are," he said, "cases where you cannot be taken seriously unless you show that your claim transcends civility."

However, the legal-services lawyer and the philosopher were also *unlike* Old Testament prophets. For one thing they seem not to have called on a transcendent morality. The Old Testament prophets put themselves at risk *in the light of* transcendent morality. As Father Vawter puts it, the prophets invoked "the fearless revelation of the moral will of Yahweh." The words of the prophet are greater than the prophet; "the prophetic word lives a life of its own," even though the prophet "was personally involved in the word ... lived for it and was prepared to die for it." This transcendent morality was also a shared morality, and it was advertently religious. Though prophets were rarely religious leaders, "they inculcated a known morality or at least one that should have been known." It may be possible for modern democratic prophets–Gandhi may be an example–to call on some "transcendent" political truth, but that way of looking at the prophetic seems to me watered down; it seems a pale notion when put up against Dr. King, kneeling with his followers in Selma, Alabama, and praying to the God whose truth he was invoking with his body.

This difference between the legal-services lawyer and philosopher and the Old Testament prophets has two aspects that should be noticed here. One aspect is that it is difficult in modern America to appeal to any transcendent morality known, or that should be known, to all hearers; it is difficult to find the common moral ground on which Nathan and David stood, or even on which Dr. King and his Bible-believing racist persecutors stood. This difficulty can disappear, though, as the group to which moral witness is made becomes smaller. There are common moralities, including biblical moralities, alive and well in groups in America, even if we Americans no longer share a common national morality. In other words, the groups to which the legal-services lawyer and the philosopher spoke might have been open to transcendent truth, despite the probable disappearance of a transcendent truth for all of America. The failure of prophetic witness might not have been in the advocacy so much as in the advocates and in the substance of the appeal they made.

The other aspect of the difference between these two sets of prophets is a matter of closeness. The Old Testament prophet operated within an intimate circle. "It would be impossible to find a non-Israelite court prophet who would speak to his king as Nathan did to David," Vawter says. Nathan was able to speak as he did because of a shared transcendent morality *and* because he was personally significant to David. There is an irony in the idea of Old Testament prophecy, an irony appearing also, in some slight way, in the prophecy of King and Gandhi and not appearing so clearly in the prophecy of the legal-services lawyer and the philosopher; that irony is that when they invoked the transcendent they invoked it *at home*.

It is ineffective. Perhaps the legal-services lawyer and the philosopher were ineffective because they did not, as Nathan did, first engage conscience. They seem not to have known how conscience is addressed when decision makers act in groups—as they usually act when the issue is a public issue and the moral claims are made in the name of the community. My reaction to my friend's stories was an image:

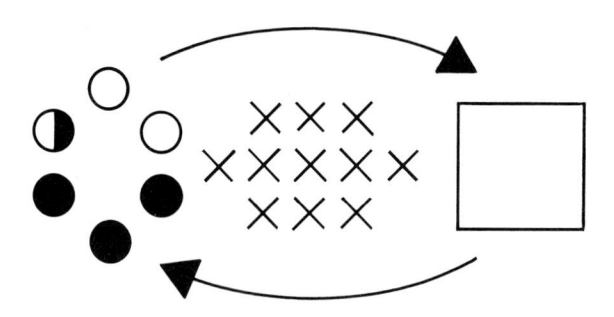

The image represents a moral encounter that involves social justice. The arrows suggest apparent communication from the advocate (the square or block or bloc) to the decision makers (the circles) and back again, with the public (cross marks) turning its attention one way and then the other, as if they were watching a tennis game. This is the way a public moral debate looks when one reads about it in the newspapers: The lawyer accuses the banks of denying loans to the poor; the banks answer with economic and social data, or with folk wisdom. The philosopher tells the corporate managers about Aristotle and Aquinas and the moral shallowness of utilitarian argument. And they, if they reply at all, tell about income statements and the barbarity of competition. Neither side appears to convince the other; neither appears to bring the other to pause or reflection. This is a debate; it does not seem possible that those who are accused will stop and say, "Gee, maybe you're right." They are, in Barth's phrase, being disturbed, led astray, and hardened.

It seems even less likely that the accuser will stop and say, "Gee, maybe *I'm* mistaken." This is an important point. It seems necessary to moral discourse that the advocate himself be willing to be persuaded. When Thomas Aquinas talks about "fraternal correction," or Karl Barth about "conditional advice," each of them emphasizes this quality of openness in the advocate. Barth says, "He who takes the risk of counseling must be prepared to be counseled in turn by his brother if there is need of it."

(I am tempted to say that the risk of counseling—that is, of being persuaded—is somehow corollary to the risk the prophet takes when he speaks boldly and risks his life. There is a sense in which the resemblance is appealing—a poetic sense, perhaps. But the possibility of a resemblance needs to be tempered by noticing that there is a difference between conditional advice and moral compromise. The prophet might have been willing to pause and listen to see if he had it right, but he would have done so only on the assumption that the discussion would be governed by truth. He would not have been willing to bracket his convictions and listen to others if the mutual assumption about his doing so was that the result would be governed by power. That is the difference between conditional advice and compromise.)

The uncolored figures (little uncolored circles in the big circle, and the square on the right) are people who are or might be irritators; they might even become prophets. The difference between those in the circle and the square (the advocate) is the difference between being involved with power and being alienated from power (and it is important to remember the ironic fact that the Old Testament prophet was involved with power, not alienated from it). The square is alien here in two senses of the word. He is excluded by the group, and he chooses to be excluded. He is perhaps a deviant, in Kai Erikson's analysis of deviance—as Ann Hutchinson was in colonial Massachusetts, to use one of Erikson's cases, or as many of the early abolitionists were toward the American commercial enterprise that nurtured slavery. The suggestion of deviance is useful here because there seems to be a connection between being alienated from the decision makers and being ineffective in making moral claims on the decision makers. The square, which represents the legal-services lawyer in the banking story and the philosopher in the corporation story, is an irritator and a maker of moral claims, but he is ineffective—ineffective but visible, visible and sad. He is *ineffective* because the circle is impervious to his moral claim on it. He is *sad* in that preparation, good intention, and even rightness ought to have influence on those who wield power, but they do not. Examples are sometimes tragic (Jesus before the resurrection, Socrates) and sometimes pathetic (the character representing William Jennings Bryan in *Inherit the Wind*). The result is personally sad, too, because the most admirable effort is often also the most intense effort; effort approaches tragedy as it becomes intense and nonetheless fails. Finally, he is *visible,* which is important because private failure seems more like frustration than like tragedy. This ineffectiveness is hard work made visible but come to naught.

The colored figures are the people who exercise power. They are among the circle of those who decide, but they are more influenced than influencing. In relatively organic groups (for example, some academic faculties), these are the elders. In boards of directors, they are the insiders. In business there may be only one such person; but usually, even when the corporation appears to be an autocracy, decisions are made in a group. In academic power groups, these exercisers of power are a minority of those who hold authority collectively. In some informal groups they are transient in membership but stable in their loyalty to a coherent tradition. While this group may sometimes be referred to as an "inner circle," the existence of a core of power in such groups is more circumstantial than organizational. When it is a group rather than an individual, it is not chosen by anyone, not even itself; its authority is not usually planned. Its power is not formal, not negotiated. It does not show up on an organization chart. Such a group is not nearly as active as naive people suppose it to be; it often does not, for example, *meet* at all. It does not expressly decide, let alone articulate its decision, even when everybody knows what it will do. Its power, which is always real, is sensed by its own members most of all, and sensed to a lesser extent by social scientists and investigative reporters.

There is a distinction between the colored circles and the uncolored ones, but a person who is one can informally become the other. Change from one status to the other is probably the most common transience in groups that exercise power and is at the heart of their closed politics. (C. P. Snow's novel *The Masters* is about such transitions.) What is distinctive about the uncolored circles is that they are eligible to be irritators and are therefore potential prophets. In business, they are the people who are chosen as targets by those who want to influence, change, or coerce corporate behavior. The Securities and Exchange Commission thus makes demands regarded as drastic on "outside" corporate directors or on independent auditors or on lawyers retained to advise corporations.

Professional groups, and those who think of themselves as articulators of the public interest, make similar demands on those members of the circle who think of themselves as professionals. Lawyers and accountants are clear examples. There are transitions toward professionalism by other members of the circle. An example is the public-relations professional, who is more clearly dominated by managers than lawyers and accountants are but who is beginning to insist upon an extracorporate professional (and moral) identity. In my image, the uncolored circles might be an accountant and a lawyer and the half-colored circle a public-relations officer.

The uncolored circles are, of all the positions suggested in my image, the most likely to become prophets. That is, (1) they can speak to the colored circles from a shared morality, even if this morality is only a tentative group consensus; (2) they can use arguments that are self-evidently valid, because they know the moral language of the decision-making group; (3) they can identify personally with their moral claims (something that lawyers, as lawyers, are not even supposed to do);

(4) they can be close to power without necessarily being political;* (5) they can speak *for* someone who is not in the group rather better than the real power-wielders, the colored circles, can;** and (6) they are, by the nature of things, at risk. These uncolored circles are not only those on whom moral demands from outside are made; they are also those who are, ex officio, eligible to make these moral demands on themselves, and, through themselves, on the organization. (The "through themselves" is what gives the position its risk.) They are potential moral irritators who can be effective. They are the focal point for the fact that a ruling group is necessary if any organization of people is to control selfishness enough to make an organizational effort possible; *and* they are the focal point for another fact—that all ruling groups tend to canonize themselves after a while and therefore need prophets to control their collective selfishness.

The outside world—the S.E.C., bar associations, and investigative reporters—puts moral demands on the uncolored circles because moral discourse is more likely to take place *within* the circle than between the circle and the square. Irritators from outside might better aim at initiating this moral discourse and nourishing it with thought and concern than at making moral demands on the organization as if the organization were monolithic. The organization is not monolithic. It in fact contains within itself the machinery for moral discourse and a way to conduct or discourage moral challenges that it has not yet considered. Moral arguments are heard there; more of them would be heard, and heard more carefully, if those who make moral demands on organizations understood the way moral discourse works in organizations. For examples:

The moral demand that women should have more status, pay, and responsibility is, in the political society, an argument from constitutional principles relating more or less to historical ideas about distributive justice. The moral discourse within the organization is more likely to be in terms of injuries to particular people and in terms of resources lost to the organization because of these injuries. At its most effective this argument turns on making partners of people who are otherwise dependents. The legal or philosophical demand, which is a demand from principle, makes decision makers defensive. It pulls the colored circles and the uncolored circles together in opposition to the demand. It tends to resolve itself, if at all, in coercion—often in a lawsuit. The personal demand sounds and feels more like a wrong. If one thinks of himself as an advocate for women who should be advanced,

---

*Academic faculties always have such members—people who are for the most part "above" politics. Snow's *The Masters* has several examples.

**Louis Eliot's role in Snow's *The Affair* is an example.

he will do better to argue for *them* than for their *cause*. The uncolored circles tend to understand this; the square appears not to understand. An experienced trial lawyer would understand this point better than the young legal-services lawyer or the philosopher did.*

The moral demand that corporate lawyers should call for independence from the chief executive officers who are their employers is a demand in principle. It turns on an idea about what corporate lawyers are; it turns, that is, on a role (Chapter 1). Proponents of that view might better ask what it is they want to accomplish (for example, more honesty in disclosure statements) and let the lawyer decide where best to initiate moral discourse. The lawyer, when he acts, might act more as business colleague, coreligionist, or friend than as lawyer.

Moral claims about environmental pollution or exploitation of the poor are least effective when irritators argue about the welfare of society and most effective when prophets make the argument, which is like Nathan's, that says to the decision maker, "*What* are you doing?" Nathan's argument is more effective, but—and this is the main point I want to make about it—it is also more like moral discourse. By this I mean it is more likely to cause the decision maker to choose to do the good and therefore to choose his own growth toward goodness, toward the place where, to the pure, all things are pure. These results occur in prophetic advocacy because prophetic advocacy makes evil personal and personally discoverable. All of this suggests that advocacy, seen as moral discourse rather than as warfare, seen from the bottom up rather than from the top down, is different. It is different tactically and dynamically. It is relatively private, even intimate sometimes, and much more personal. It turns less on principles than on the character of the individual or the story of the enterprise on whom moral claims are made.

---

*It is ironic, and less than truthful, that, when the experienced trial lawyer comes to draft "ethical" rules for lawyers, he talks about legal or philosophical principles.

CHAPTER ELEVEN
Advocacy of the Person

In April 1976 Joseph Saikewicz was found to have terminal leukemia. He was 67 years old and had been for 53 of those years a resident in Massachusetts state institutions for the mentally retarded. He had an intelligence quotient of ten and a mental age of three. The prognosis was that the leukemia would soon kill him but that chemotherapy might prolong his life by as much as a year. The chances of even that limited success were less than half, but most people who are in this situation and who are able to choose between chemotherapy and death without it choose chemotherapy.

The treatment is unpleasant but does not produce unusual side effects; Saikewicz had probably endured all of the probable side effects. The usual side effects are nausea, vomiting, bladder irritation, numbness, and a tingling sensation in the hands and fingers. Because the drugs are administered intravenously, and because Saikewicz would remember the side effects between treatments, the doctors expected resistance from him and planned to strap him to a hospital bed. A doctor who knew him said, "When you approach him, he flails at you and there is no way of communicating with him, and he is quite strong; so he will have to be restrained and that increases the chance of pneumonia." However, pneumonia was only a slight risk; the other risks were not unlike those parents choose every day when they offer up their children for hospital treatment.

The alternative was, as the medical ethicists tend to put it, to "let him die." The superintendent of the Belchertown State School, where Saikewicz had lived since 1928, decided, probably from parental as well as medical premises (he is a physician), to give Saikewicz chemotherapy. He also decided, probably after talking to the school's lawyer, to seek a court order to that effect.

The probate judge appointed a lawyer to represent Saikewicz. The lawyer at first assumed that this was a case for arguing "the right to treatment," an idea new in the law, as health care for the retarded is new in medicine. At this point, Saikewicz had the benefit of the aspirations of both professions. His advocates sought for him both prolonged life and the same care that moneyed, nonretarded people can obtain.

But Saikewicz's lawyer found that there were physicians in Belchertown who were against treating Saikewicz. Under their influence, the lawyer abandoned the "right to treatment" argument (even though the judge at first agreed with it) and argued instead that his client should be allowed to die. This lawyer said that Saikewicz would not be able to understand the discomfort and side effects of chemotherapy. Saikewicz himself, to the slight extent he could be consulted, would obviously resist treatment. This lawyer and the doctors on his side tried to decide what Saikewicz would want and then tried to follow his "decision." That is also what the courts did. The probate judge and the justices of the Supreme Judicial Court of Massachusetts decided that Saikewicz should not have chemotherapy. The local judge remarked that if he had been Saikewicz he would have preferred to die without treatment.

The advocacy used in the Saikewicz case began with a consideration of what the client wanted—not what was best for him, but what he wanted. And it proceeded in a moral discourse between lawyer and physicians, discourse that disregarded the professional ideals of prolonged life and the right to treatment. The opposing argument, made by the attorney general of Massachusetts, was that the interests of the state required chemotherapy for Saikewicz.

Saikewicz died in September 1976. It is not possible to know if his death was painless, but the physicians had predicted that it would be; the probate judge had ordered, in innocent but ironic evidence of the delusions of power, that Saikewicz be allowed to die "peacefully and comfortably." The order of the Supreme Judicial Court had been entered in July, but its opinion was delayed until the end of November, nearly three months after Saikewicz's death, so that the court could receive briefs on the issues and prepare an opinion that spoke to the difficult public policies involved. Either because of the memory of what they thought in July or out of judicial habit, their opinion is an example of moral discourse in appellate literature: The judges were reconciled to their suitor; they had become advocates.

The court's opinion is a remarkable and positive example of moral argument. It is revealing in the way advocates and judges attempted to understand Saikewicz and in their assertion of the minimum worth of a human being. It also reveals, curiously enough, a lot about the results of lawyer-dependent moral decisions by showing how the medical and legal professions make moral judgments for their clients when clients are able to speak for themselves, as Saikewicz was not.

The main argument these lawyers, doctors, and judges used was Saikewicz himself; they refused to argue from an egalitarian category (all people are alike), which here would have led to chemotherapy since most people with Saikewicz's disease choose chemotherapy. The court talked at some length about the *Quinlan* case and found that case less difficult because the New Jersey judges had had the benefit of the testimony of Miss Quinlan's father, who spoke from "many years of what was apparently a close and affectionate relationship with her." The *Saikewicz* court struggled in an obviously sincere way to provide for itself a substitute for Mr. Quinlan's testimony without surrendering to "objective criteria." That means that the court had to attempt to explicate reasons, personal to Saikewicz, against choosing a longer life. The court said that the value of life carried the same weight for Saikewicz as for any other person, but Saikewicz was different in that he would not understand the pain of treatment and could not therefore *choose to suffer*. That bit of human nobility had been denied him. He could not cooperate with his doctors and therefore giving and receiving comfort was denied him. "He ... would experience fear without the understanding from which other patients draw strength," the judges said. "The inability to anticipate and prepare ... leaves room only for confusion and disorientation."

The judges, because, I think, they approached the case in this personal manner rather than from the standpoint either of principles or of equality, demonstrated remarkable sensitivity on the issues of suffering and pain. They understood, as Stanley Hauerwas argues, that "what distinguishes suffering from pain is its personal quality.... [I]t may be that the function of medicine is to relieve that painful suffering which makes it impossible for us to claim suffering as our own. [W]e do not experience suffering until we know how to name it and we must be taught how to do that."

The judges did not accept, as many in both professions have, arguments about "quality of life." The probate judge had premised his decision in part on "the quality of life possible for [Saikewicz] even if the treatment does bring about remission." The Supreme Judicial Court refused that reason "to the extent that this formulation equates the value of life with any measure of the quality of life," but it suggested that the judge may only have intended to take "special care ... to respect the dignity and worth of Saikewicz's life precisely because of his vulnerable position." People might be equal before the law, but they are never equal before one another, and professionals in the law had best take account of the fact that some of us are aggressive and many are victims. When advocacy argues from the person of its client, rather than from his interests or his cause, it can take account of his vulnerability.

"Quality of life" is a fatuous notion, and the Massachusetts judges treated it as such. Arguments from professionalism were, as they usually are, more formidable; this is because arguments from professionalism are arguments from power, and arguments from power are often successful for reasons having nothing to do with the arguments themselves.* Professional arguments are also paternalistic, which tends to disguise the fact that they are centered in power. The examples in *Saikewicz* were the (medical) argument that Saikewicz had a "right" to have his life prolonged and the (legal) argument that he had a "right" to be treated. Both arguments are professional, paternalistic, power centered, and relatively heedless of the person. Here they were also rather different from one another. The argument for prolongation of life was made from egalitarian premises—apparently for Saikewicz's benefit, but without regard to who he was. The argument for right to treatment was that the integrity of the medical profession required treatment in his case. The judges said, first, that the state cannot require a person to bear "the traumatic cost of [the] prolongation" of life unless he chooses to do so. "The value of life ... is lessened not by a decision to refuse treatment, but by the failure to allow a competent human being the right of choice." The "right of choice" belongs, too, to an incompetent person, "because the value of human dignity extends to both."

On the right-to-treatment point, and its argument from the integrity of the medical profession, the judges noted that the prevailing ethical practice in medicine seems to recognize that the dying are more in need of comfort than of treatment. As some medical ethicists put it, they are more in need of care than of cure. It was not necessary, the court said, "to deny a right of self-determination to a patient in order to recognize the interests of doctors." If it ever becomes necessary, the law should come down on the side of patients. Those of us who disagree, on moral grounds, with the Supreme Court's decision in the abortion cases notice that similar reasoning was not applied there to unborn children, because the court did not extend the definition of "person" to the unborn child, and that those cases therefore turn on the judges' view of the integrity of the medical profession.

The *Saikewicz* case is an example of the reconciliation of the person whose cause is advocated with those who listen to advocacy. Reconciliation in his case was both easier and harder than it is in more usual cases—easier because the Massachusetts judges' view of the "substituted judgment" doctrine required it to look as deeply as it could at the personality before it, and harder because this sort of case tempts judges to

---

*Examples abound in selective-service cases of the period 1968–72.

the comfort of egalitarian solutions. Some other examples of what I mean by egalitarian solutions are:
1. Cases that construe "good moral character" in the immigration laws, which have tended, even with such judicial giants as the late Learned Hand, to be construed by reference to public opinion
2. Cases that construe the "interest" of a person before the court on the positivist assumption of maximum selfishness, such as in the Kentucky case involving kidney donation between twin boys
3. Cases that are governed by the narrowest sort of professionalism, such as the Supreme Court's decision in the Indiana case involving judicial immunity from suit for having ordered an involuntary sterilization for a retarded girl
4. Cases that find it impossible to adjust the governmental system to the perceptions and abilities of unusual citizens, so that, for example, a moderately retarded person, though capable of working and raising a family, cannot be a suitor before the courts and must either be put in an institution or left, and therefore licensed, irresponsible.

The remarkable nature of the *Saikewicz* case is that these egalitarian solutions were avoided by turning, on every issue, to the human person the court had to consider—had to consider even in his weakness and, finally, in his immortality. Conscience is at work in such cases; you can tell that it is when you review incidental facts about the case that show how vulnerable conditional advice is in practice: Saikewicz's lawyer first argued from the right to treatment—a fashionable argument these days, one only recently established in the Supreme Court and one that demonstrates, if nothing else, that a lawyer is current on his constitutional law. But he changed his mind after moral discourse with doctors in Belchertown, doctors who were themselves turning from the medical profession's narrow devotion to the ideal of prolongation of life. The probate judge in the case first decided to order treatment, then, after considering the changed views of Saikewicz's lawyer and his unconventional medical advisers, changed his order. In the Supreme Judicial Court, newspaper reports on the original judicial order in the case—entered before Saikewicz's death, and entered without opinion—noted dissenting votes. But when the final opinion was published, after these judges had talked among themselves about the case, the opinion was unanimous.

CHAPTER TWELVE
Moral Discourse and the Community

Advocacy as moral discourse reconciles advocate to client, advocate to those who listen to advocacy, and those who hear advocacy to the client. It reconciles those otherwise seen to be at war. It does this, as the *Saikewicz* case illustrates, by exalting care over professionalism, through arguing to the consciences of those it addresses, and through arguing from the persons of those whose cause is advocated. Advocacy as moral discourse also radiates into the community, into consideration of social justice, because of four features that distinguish moral discourse from adversary discourse: Moral discourse is interpersonal; moral discourse argues from the person of the client; moral discourse is addressed to the conscience of those who hear it; moral discourse, because it is a form of reconciliation, binds the community together.

Interpersonal. The *Saikewicz* case was unusual in method as well as in substance. It was different in medicine because some of the physicians involved argued against medical treatment. It was different for law because ordinary legal methodologies did not suit the case. The court pointed beyond ideas of health, or ideas of right, to Joseph Saikewicz himself. The judges decided he would be better off if our professions left him alone. What the poor man needed, as he ended more than half a century in a "school" for the retarded, was a friend as he died. The court could not explain his needs in terms either of health or of rights. It had to explain them in reference to Saikewicz himself.

Advocacy as moral discourse begins in the person of the client. The advocate has to cultivate an examination of conscience in which he asks himself where his advocacy does *not* begin: The first question is whether I have violated professional consensus. If what I am doing would be generally approved by my professional colleagues, it may be wrong—it may be more professional than personal. We lawyers have had some of our best moments when we were made uncomfortable by renegades such as William Kunstler and Michael Tigar. Maybe doctors have their best when they are challenged by renegades such as Thomas

Szasz and the physicians at Belchertown who thought that the frail dignity of Joseph Saikewicz was more important than medical expertise. Advocacy as moral discourse seems to require humility, and the least likely humility is humility in a professional group. (This fact is a bitter irony, since the sort of humility primary in the Jewish and Christian traditions is the humility of service.)

Another question is whether we annoy our governors. When the community says we are overstepping our bounds—that it is not a doctor's job to advocate, nor a lawyer's job to say what should be done for the sick—we are probably doing something right. We professionals have franchise and power, but we pay a price for it: We are expected to subordinate our personal sense of good to our expertise. The world needs to keep its experts in their place. Experts, as someone said, are supposed to be kept on tap, not on top. When we are on tap we are easy to predict. We annoy the world when we become unpredictable.

This is not to say, of course, that violation of professional consensus and social convention is some sort of *test* of the quality of moral discourse; but these are two important questions, if only because it is so easy to forget to ask them. People as members of professional groups enjoy strength and vantage for the practice of moral discourse—Chapter 10 attempts to make that point—but they are more vulnerable to self-deception than people taken one at a time. The moral life, as Barth put it, is a hard life in such circumstances: "We stand in need, not of patience, but of the impatience of the prophets, not of well-mannered pleasantry, but of a grim assault, not of the historian's balanced judgment ... but of a love of truth which hacks its way through the very backbone of the matter, and then dares to bring an accusation of unrighteousness against every upright man."

The person whose cause is advocated. Advocacy should find its mission in the unique personality of the client and then hold that unique personality up as its strongest argument. An advocate who sees the task in these terms advocates a person more than a cause. Professionalism gets in the way here, too. It shows up in the legal profession in the nearly universal tendency to let adversary ethics, rather than the persons of clients, control advocacy. We lawyers use the adversary system to avoid moral discourse. We use it to hide all our great moral questions—the problem of the guilty client, the problem of assisting evil people to advance evil designs, and the ultimate problem of whether lawyers are of value either to their clients or to the community. We are rarely caught in our evasion because we are attracted to it as a competitive game and we become good at the game. We come to think that it has validity. Stephen Wexler gives this example from a courtroom exchange several years ago:

[The case involved] a soldier who wanted to get out of the Army for religious reasons. His petition for *habeas corpus* was denied, and his attorney asked the court to prohibit the Army from transferring him to Vietnam pending the filing of an appeal. The Assistant United States Attorney on the case looked, for all the world, like an ordinary human being; yet, when the soldier's attorney asked for the stay of transfer orders . . . the Assistant United States Attorney said "I'm afraid we'd have to oppose that."

No one even checked with the Army to see if it would cause a problem. The delay was opposed because within the lawyer's game it could be opposed. One little piece on the board was the U.S. Army, the other was the soldier; and the soldier's lawyer had just drawn a card which said: "ON HIS NEXT TURN THE OTHER PLAYER MAY MOVE YOUR PIECE TO VIETNAM."

One reason this sort of thing happens in the legal profession is the phenomenon of imputed competence. A client is not really allowed to think about the competence of his lawyer. He is to assume it. The professional is the one who knows how to move the pieces. This idea persists despite persuasive evidence (Douglas Rosenthal's, for example) that it is morally and fiscally untrue.

Our profession sometimes grows ashamed of its arrogance, but when it does it attempts to apportion power to clients, to turn them into bureaucrats, instead of going back and looking at them as the reasons for the enterprise. In the legal world Wexler wrote about—poverty law—the profession at first decided that the solution to professional arrogance was to require the participation of the poor—not in their own cases, but in the supervision of law offices. The clients were to become powers in the bureaucracy. Art Buchwald reports an interview he was inspired to give after the government and the legal profession made this decision. He finally located a man who would admit he was poor:

> I asked him if he thought he would like to serve on a committee to see what could be done about poverty.
> "Mister, if I had any ideas what to do about poverty, I wouldn't be poor."
> "But there is a school of thought in Washington that poor people are the only ones who know the real problems of the poor, and they should be strongly involved in the program to formulate and implement antipoverty programs."
> "I wouldn't serve on a board unless they paid me," he said.
> "Oh, I'm sure they would pay you. If they agreed to pay you, what is the first thing you would do?"
> "I'd move out of the neighborhood."
> "But if you did that, you would lose contact with poor people and you would no longer be able to speak for them."

"Exactly. Poor people don't want to be spoken for. They just want to get the hell out of the neighborhood."

Participation by the poor didn't work. Poverty in America is a moral question, as well as a political question. The advocacy that poor people need includes advocacy which requires the rest of us to look at poor persons, and to think about each of them, and to feel ashamed of ourselves for allowing such misery in the midst of plenty. Buchwald's point was that it will not do to tell the poor to take our money and go do something about themselves. What we should have learned was something about ourselves: We don't want to help the poor unless they fit our definitions.

The conscience of the hearer. The greatest example in Christian literature of advocacy to conscience is the story of Jesus and the woman taken in adultery. Some law professors brought the woman to Jesus, hoping to confound him and establish his disregard for the law. In the process they proposed to give the woman her just deserts. " 'Teacher,' they said to Jesus, 'this woman was caught in the very act of committing adultery. In our Law Moses gave a commandment that such a woman must be stoned to death. Now, what do you say?' " John reports that Jesus wrote on the ground with his finger for a while, and then said, "Whichever one of you has committed no sin may throw the first stone at her." He returned to his writing and the law professors left. The woman stayed behind and held moral discourse with the founder of Christianity (John 8:1–11).

The story illustrates how group consensus is an obstacle both to advocacy and to justice. There was no doubt about the rightness of a rule against adultery; Jesus, who was himself a teacher of Mosaic law, did not argue about that. He did not even argue about the sanction. But the rule and the sanction had hidden the reason for the enterprise, which was the goodness of people like that woman. Sometimes one has to bear witness against the rules in order to give purpose to the rules.

Larry Churchill, a medical ethicist, argues this way with reference to ethical rules in the medical profession: Professional ethics become accountable when they include within them "the capacity for self-restriction and self-criticism" on grounds other than those which currently undergird the profession. "The absence of such a self-critical principle makes all questions raised by the public seem to be an attack and makes the healer's mantle an aegis from the variety of values held by his patients. It makes the physician an adversary of his patient instead of an advocate." Churchill argues that doctors should develop a morality of self-accepted moral principles and move beyond a morality of conformity. "The transition ... is blocked when there is confusion between group loyalty and the validity of the moral principles the group holds." The same argument applies to the law, and especially to the adversary ethic. The idea, as Churchill puts it, is "awareness of oneself as an autonomous agent, able to judge the morals of his group for himself." Theories of health and theories of human rights would be enriched by that sort of moral enterprise. The enterprise becomes moral advocacy when we translate it into discourse outside the professional group. When moral advocacy begins, we will discover that we have become committed to something greater than our professions.

Moral discourse reconciles: It binds together the hearer, the advocated, and the advocate. Three of the four heroes recommended in these chapters (Gandhi, King, and Nathan) were not lawyers, and the behavior of the fourth (Saikewicz's lawyer) was not traditional lawyer behavior. These facts suggest that there is a difference between advocacy as moral discourse and adversary discourse as it is traditionally described by the legal profession and as it is distilled into principles, aspirations, and regulation in the *Code*:

1. Adversary discourse involves ideals of dignity, image, influence, and survival in the professional group, the legal profession. Moral discourse tends more to the development of a compassionate community, to "the things that make for peace and build up the common life" (Romans 14:19). It tends to look beyond the group, and even beyond the state. Both forms of discourse are advocacy; that is, each is addressed to decision makers and wielders of power. King, Nathan, and Gandhi addressed power as much as modern American lawyers do; Saikewicz's lawyer addressed power both as lawyers do and as King, Nathan, and Gandhi did. The difference seems to inhere in the self-images—the roles, if you like—that members of professional groups have.

2. Adversary discourse emphasizes uprightness, respectability, and moral independence in individual practitioners; moral discourse emphasizes the moral claims of clients, and, more than is true in adversary discourse, first negotiates and then identifies with the moral claims of clients. Moral discourse makes this identification with clients advertently, but it does not necessarily lose its identification with power groups as it does so: Saikewicz's lawyer did not surrender his status at the bar; King steadily gained influence among powerful groups in America; Nathan, as prophet, both confronted the king and was a member of the king's court. (The career of Charles Morgan is another contemporary example.)

3. Adversary discourse seems to concentrate on loyalty to the client as its governing ethical principle; it exalts loyalty rather than faithfulness as a virtue (Chapter 8). Moral discourse is based less on loyalty to the client than on the goodness of the client. King's leading the civil rights movement in prayer for its oppressors is an example of that—if

one believes, as King did, that a believer seeks to rise to the aspirations of his prayers.

4. Adversary discourse, in the *Code*'s explication of loyalty as a virtue, justifies its goal in terms of service to the government. The reason for loyalty, as the *Code* explains it, is that loyalty will lead to more acceptable service to the judicial system (that is, to the government). Moral advocacy explains itself more in terms of service to the person; it radiates into the community because it is interpersonal, because it argues from the person of the client, because it is addressed to the conscience, and because it seeks reconciliation rather than victory. As Paul Tillich said: "[T]he ambiguities of competition ... work continuously for inequality in the encounters of people in daily life, in the stratification of society, and in the political self-creation of life. The very attempt to apply the principle of equality, as contained unambiguously in the acknowledgement of the person as person, can have destructive consequences for the realization of justice." The heroes of moral discourse are heroes of reconciliation, and that means that moral discourse does not serve power; it does not seek to justify itself in terms of power.

The *Code* tends to celebrate advocacy in the service of power. This is, to be sure, only a tendency. The *Code* is not palpably hostile to the sort of advocacy discussed in these chapters, but it neglects it. The tendency and the neglect might be illustrated with two texts from the *Code*. One, under Canon 7 ("A Lawyer Should Represent A Client Zealously Within The Bounds Of The Law"), deals with the situation in which Joseph Saikewicz's lawyer found himself:

> If the client is capable of understanding the matter in question or of contributing to the advancement of his interests, regardless of whether he is legally disqualified from performing certain acts, the lawyer should obtain from him all possible aid. If the disability of a client and the lack of a legal representative compel the lawyer to make decisions for his client, the lawyer should consider all circumstances then prevailing and act with care to safeguard and advance the interests of his client.

That aspiration, by turning more on the *interests* of the client than on the *person* of the client, tends toward argument for such things as the right to treatment and against arguments that are based on a compassionate view of the client's situation. In *Saikewicz,* it was the proponents of chemotherapy who argued from Saikewicz's *interests*; the lawyer who argued for Saikewicz himself, and, ultimately, the judges in the case, grounded their decisions in something more human than interests.

A broader example is the final, summary ethical aspiration in the *Code,* under Canon 9 ("A Lawyer Should Avoid Even The Appearance

Of Professional Impropriety"). It illustrates that the *Code*'s governing moral principles are loyalty to clients and service to power:

> Every lawyer owes a solemn duty to uphold the integrity and honor of his profession; to encourage respect for the law and for the courts and judges thereof; to observe the Code of Professional Responsibility; to act as a member of a learned profession, one dedicated to public service; to cooperate with his brother [*sic*] lawyers in supporting the organized bar through the devoting of his time, efforts, and financial support as his professional standing and ability reasonably permit; to conduct himself so as to reflect credit on the legal profession and to inspire the confidence, respect, and trust of his clients and of the public; and to strive to avoid not only professional impropriety but also the appearance of impropriety.

By contrast, the examples used here as ideals share a tendency to reconciliation and disdain a tendency to support for power, professional honor, and protected membership in a protected group. Martin Luther King's earliest public advocacy, in the bus boycott in Birmingham, started with his knowing the black people in the back of the bus. It proceeded with his holding up those people until white citizens were ashamed of themselves. It ended with people being brought back together—the advocates, the advocated, and the decision makers. That was King's usual procedure. In the heat and turmoil and cruelty of Selma, King gathered his followers together and prayed *for the police.* He talked to his followers about redemptive love—*for the police.* His was like the procedure Gandhi used when he told the English judges that they had a choice—to uphold unjust laws and send him and his followers to prison, or to come down from their benches and join him in his witness against injustice. That is moral discourse—an interpersonal thing—a thing grounded in the person of the client, a plea to conscience, and a form of reconciliation.*

---

*One is tempted, in such dramatic cases as King's and Gandhi's, to see an opposition between love and justice; the opposition is useful in thinking about King's social witness. King might have admitted, though, that in the final analysis he sought a just order between the police and the people of Alabama: "[The] basic ontological order is love, then justice; but in terms of the gradual achievement of order, the order may be [but was not in Selma] justice, then love. . . . That love is indeed great—that considers whatever is here and now obstructive to one's neighbor and the community as no longer a right at all, demonstrative legal title and honest acquisition to the contrary notwithstanding. For love there is a clear distinction between abstract right and the actual need for that right. . . . Before God, the duties of love are no less binding than the duties of justice. . . . [T]he duties of love are measured by the progress of the person in good" (Bernard Häring). This question is implicit throughout the next chapter.

CHAPTER THIRTEEN
The Administration of Justice

What do we mean when we say "the administration of justice"? Is that phrase a slogan, or is it an idea that tells us something about our view of America, of our profession, of our clients, and of ourselves? Is it possible to talk about "the administration of justice" as an idea?

To talk about the administration of justice may be a way to talk about justice itself. Or it may be a way to reduce justice to manageable (administrable) terms—and, if that is what it is, we have to ask what price we pay for simplicity. One risk in equating "justice" and "the administration of justice" is that we may not be accounting for what the administration of justice is up to. Another risk is that talking only about the administration of justice leaves out of account much of what people mean, and what they mean to do, when they talk about justice itself.

A million contracts are performed for every contract taken to the government for enforcement. Some of the contracts performed without benefit of government would not be enforceable if they were taken to the government (those which do not conform to the Statute of Frauds, for example). A thousand dispositions of property are given effect without incident for every disposition of property that becomes the subject of governmental administration. These examples are part of the daily occurrence of justice as it is experienced by practicing lawyers. Examples beyond the ken of the profession are even more common. Airline passengers, for example, appear to have a right to tip their cramped tourist seats back as far as they were made to go—and thus into the jugular veins of the passengers riding behind them—but they rarely take advantage of this right.

Perhaps when we say "administration of justice" we mean to refer to the government, and especially that part of the government that wears judicial robes. Government acts in judicial robes in order to keep the peace or to vindicate the freedom of choice of citizens who repair to the government with vindication in view. We talk about government in its judicial robes in this way—that is, as "the administration of justice"—when we seek to make government more efficient, so that the disputes it adjudicates can be resolved quickly, at low cost, quietly, and without disruption in the community—or, failing that, at least without disruption in the courthouse.

When we citizens call on the government to "administer" justice we call upon the tools of fear. We ask the government to frighten somebody into behaving himself. The tools of government, and especially the tools of government in its judicial robes, are the tools of fear. That seems an ugly way to talk about the law, but I think it is useful to be ugly, at first. One reason it is useful to be ugly at first is that it helps us see that we are inclined to ignore the ugly by talking about "the administration of justice" as if it were not fearful. We talk about government under law, for example, or about the history of American democracy, and we appeal to the sort of patriotism invoked by our leaders when they established Law Day as an antidote to the poison of communist totalitarianism.

When "the administration of justice" is talked about with patriotic connotations, it is helpful to remember (if only as a listener) that our government maintains itself by fear as much as communist totalitarianism does; and it is helpful to notice that "the administration of justice" in a Law Day talk does not mean what the phrase means in a discussion of the mechanics of court administration. Reporting that appellate dockets are short—which is what the chief justice in my state does every year when he talks to the house of delegates of the state bar association—indicates a view of "the administration of justice" which is not the same as the view taken in Law Day talks. Such a report may or may not indicate a limited view of what justice itself is, but most of us would agree that the docket report is less about justice than the Law Day talk is. It might keep concepts clearer to agree that we should not talk in the same phrase about clear dockets and the ideals of the American experiment any more than we should talk in the same phrase of democratic government and the status of litter.

I mean to suggest that there may be a delusion in our profession's thinking about "the administration of justice." Perhaps the delusion is a matter of too quickly identifying "the administration of justice" with justice itself. The danger in that identification is the assumption that government (which administers things) is a source of justice and therefore a source of goodness. But if government is a source of goodness, then goodness can be obtained through fear.

The SS colonel in "The Holocaust" thought that goodness could be obtained through fear. He did not set out, as an idealistic young Nazi, to do evil. He did not choose murder, torture, genocide, and terror. He came to the place where he thought those things were necessary incidents of his culture's search for goodness. He came to that sorry place because he thought that goodness could be obtained through fear. His problem was not a conscious choice of evil; his problem was a delusion. He did not tell himself the truth. His bad idea was bad because it was not truthful; it was evil because it was untruthful. The delusion that government is a source of goodness makes that much difference.

There are alternative ways to think about justice. There are ways to think about justice as something other than "administration," in order to see if "the administration of justice" has anything to do with justice itself and in order to understand how it is that we come to talk about "the administration of justice" in the first place. An issue which would combine these objectives would be this issue: Can justice be administered? That issue is really two issues: (1) Is "the administration of justice" a sound idea? (And by "sound" I mean to ask if it is a truthful use of the word "justice"); and (2) Is the idea of justice itself an adequate idea for virtue in communities? What we might learn in talking about those issues is to be modest about the justice that can be administered and about the administration that can be just.

Justice as love. One alternative idea of justice is what is described in the second article of the Apostles' Creed: Justice is how we describe loving relationships, and the model for loving relationships is the love of God for his people. That is a Jewish and Christian idea. To Christians the idea is embodied in the man Jesus Christ. Justice thought of as loving relationship comes almost to the embodiment of all virtue; it comes to be coextensive with love, and love, according to Jewish and Christian theology, summarizes the moral law. The biblical idea of the "just man" is not an idea about law or only about giving to others their due. To Jews the just person is one who lives a virtuous life and who therefore stands *justified* before God. In the Christian (Pauline) idea the just person is a person who has died and been resurrected with Jesus, the Christ, and who proposes to follow him. He is *justified* at the Cross.

Justice as avoiding harm. Another idea of justice would be one that considers the harm done by imposing judgment. Oliver Wendell Holmes, Jr., said that the imposition of criminal punishment as educative and deterrent, and therefore appropriate for a democratic republic, was a morally deficient idea. If that idea were truthful, he said, we should hang every thousandth thief. He implied that a better idea would be the idea that force is imposed only where force is deserved. This second alternative idea about justice is a common one among lawyers and judges and it causes us difficulty because we don't know when force is deserved and what force is appropriate. A divorce-court judge said on the Public Broadcasting System series on conflict resolution that American judges had godlike powers. He said this as if the thought humbled him; Holmes would say that he is right to be humble.

The idea that justice is a matter of appropriate harm is a consequence of the collective attempt by people in the twentieth century to control their existence. Through the lens of the Jewish and Christian tradition the attempt is futile and even blasphemous. The tradition of Israel and of Jesus claims that God is Lord of all and that he is among his people. He is at work in the world. It is pretentious to suppose that human beings can act without causing harm. We cannot appropriate God's power in the world; we can only witness to it. We can only be suffering servants before his Lordship. Walter Kaufmann's observation on the disasters predicted by the Hebrew prophets makes just this point; they sought to *prevent* what they foretold. "Jeremiah did not gloat when Jerusalem was destroyed; he was grieved by his failure."

We cannot act morally without causing pain; the tradition of Israel and of the Cross is a tradition of pain. Justice involves pain and it is not adequate (not truthful) to suppose that the just man is the man who prevents the infliction of pain. This doesn't mean that Holmes's idea is one that should not be held at all, but only that it is not truthful to hold that idea of justice and at the same time to ignore the delusions of power. There needs to be a warning made about an idea of justice that relies on happy endings; it is a warning sounded by the religious tradition that brought Puritan suspicion of power to these shores and that tends to be lost when the religious tradition of the Puritans is forgotten.

Justice as interpersonal debt. Another alternative way of looking at justice would be to see it as a way for people to live together. This is like the first alternative idea—the idea that justice is the exercise of virtue—but it differs because it makes an attempt to explicate obligations. Law fits this third alternative idea, if law is seen as a way to work out the interpersonal claims we make on one another. It recognizes the lordship of God but claims that God allows his people to exercise some of his lordship. Our working out of our claims on one another is a participation in God's lordship. Law is, as Stanley Hauerwas puts it, the space God gives us to work things out. The power is not ours, which helps mitigate the delusions of power; but power is not something God keeps to himself. This idea rests somewhere in almost all Jewish and Christian theologies of government, and in the older American jurisprudence.

Justice, in this view, is a matter of interpersonal debt, but there are two ideas of justice as interpersonal debt, and the distinction between them may be important. It might be helpful (if overly simple) to call one of these Greek and the other Jewish. The Greek idea of justice as interpersonal debt calls upon me to exercise the particular virtue of rendering to other people what is due them. The Jewish idea of justice as interpersonal debt calls upon me to live a just life in the sight of God (who is my judge). The Jewish idea is very broad; it calls upon me to be the person I was created to become. Its interpersonal implications cover most, if not all, of what it means to live a moral life. The Greek idea is narrower; it deals with rights and duties. The Jewish idea sees our indebtedness to one another as infinite, as supporting or illustrating what Jesus talks about when he censures anger, urges his followers to turn the other cheek and walk the second mile, and says that the *meek* shall inherit the earth. The Jewish idea is that justice requires more than what we (or the Greeks) think of as being just.

The Jewish idea occasionally appears in formal American law—in the "rescue doctrine" in tort, for example; but it more often appears where people gather together without the law—in companies, on airplanes, in families, and, sometimes, in churches. The question is not what you are entitled to demand from me, but how we are to live together.

The idea of justice I am calling Jewish also implies a reluctance to invoke fear—to invoke what Paul calls the power and dominion (Ephesians 1:21). One who is just in this sense of justice might repair to the force of the state, but he would do that reluctantly—in Richard Neuhaus's phrase, as a pacifist might go to war. Resort to fear is resort taken when one cannot suffer any more and is then taken without revenge. An example here is the way Paul sought help from the Roman army when the Sanhedrin threatened to kill him (Act 25-28). The reluctance to resort to fear suggests the Jewish and Christian admonitions not to go to court for the solution of disputes. It supports secular and religious—even Marxist—efforts toward forums of mediation and settlement that refuse the coercive power of government. It calls on impulses to cooperation and friendship and not on impulses to assert rights, demand duties, and threaten force.*

---

*I am, and intend to be, at odds with a reading of American history that sees us as grimly economic bands of immigrants. My claim is to religious traditions that had what I see as communal force among the Puritans, in the revivals of the eighteenth and nineteenth centuries, and in periodic bursts of effective Christian witness in American life. What I am at odds with is expressed in Professor James Q. Wilson's review of Ann Strick's book, *Injustice for All*:

> The United States is an adversary culture. It was created by persons preoccupied with the assertion and maintenance of individual rights. Not only government, but our fellow man, was to be checked and limited so as to leave personal liberty intact. The task of the government was not to govern, but to supply those few things that citizens could not supply by themselves. Institutions, including government, had neither divine nor historical sanction, but only such license as might be provided by their utility. Throughout a century and more of mass immigration, the country grew by the addition to it of

The Jewish idea of justice as interpersonal debt also includes the idea that justice is a process. But the process is not dispute resolution; it is the hope that we can give substance to justice as we work together. We seek to do justice as we talk about justice. Justice seen in this interpersonal perspective is loving community—not a crazy or utopian idea at all, but an idea that has been behind most of the spiritual history of America. This idea of justice as something *to do* sees people—citizens—in fealty to the lordship of God over all things and therefore not pretentious or optimistic about their power. It is a conversation about the claims we make on one another and the infrequent use of fear as a way to realize on our claims. Justice, seen this way, is a gift people give to one another. It is not something we have from the government. Justice can be administered, because the idea of justice cannot be separated from the process of administering justice; but those in administration must be modest about the claim that their work involves justice in a specialized way. There are no experts in justice. The lawyer, as a just person seeking to be faithful to his client, candid to the court, and fair to third persons, is doing justice no less than the court that pronounces judgment or the litigants who seek either to avoid the necessity of judgment or to live with judgment in peace.

This idea makes it possible to talk about the administration of justice as a small part of something vast and grander—and as something truthful. "If the law goes against truth, then it's worse than useless," said Joyce Cary's character, Capt. James Latter. "It is an evil thing because it brings fair dealing and decent conduct into disgust. It brings in the worst corruption because the people give up all idea of fair dealing and think only of every man looking out for himself. It turns everything into trickery and bluff."

The Jewish idea of justice as interpersonal debt, which makes it possible to talk, but only modestly, about the administration of justice and which makes justice an adequate basis for community, is a good idea because it is a truthful idea—and, given the Jewish and Christian roots from which the idea comes in our culture, it is a hopeful idea, too. The idea that justice comes from the government, that it can be managed as the issuance of drivers' licenses can be managed, is untruthful. It is false because goodness is not the result of fear. It is a bad idea because it suggests that justice deals with what a person should claim, rather than with what a person should give. It is a bad idea because it implies that

---

people who, distrustful of government and suspicious of power, came to this country in order to claim their rights and seek their advantage.

Not only do I find that view to be *nunc pro tunc* history—compare, for example, M. Marty's *Righteous Empire*—but I think it reduces the idea of justice to a trivial notion unworthy of either a book or a book review.

the justice of rights and duties is a model for relationships. It endorses the moral bankruptcy of a culture that conceives of the good of a person only in terms of procedures—of freedom of choice, for example—and that is without the hope necessary to begin talking about a good life.

If the administration of justice, as an idea, depends on the notion that goodness can be produced by fear, it would aid discourse to call it something else—"the administration of civic peace," perhaps, or "the administration of coexistence." If those who talk about the administration of justice in this untruthful way cannot be persuaded to adopt a new word, those of us who trust to an older and more American idea of what justice is need to find a different word to express the hopeful idea we have about community in our country.

CHAPTER FOURTEEN
On Being Effective

Hear, you who have ears to hear! Whoever is to be made prisoner, a prisoner he shall be. Whoever takes the sword to kill, by the sword he is bound to be killed. This is where the fortitude and faithfulness of God's people have their place.

Revelation 13:9–10

John is here saying, not as an inscrutable paradox but as a meaningful affirmation, that the cross and not the sword, suffering and not brute power determines the meaning of history. The key to the obedience of God's people is not their effectiveness but their patience. . . . [T]he triumph of the right, although it is assured, is sure because of the power of the resurrection and not because of any calculation of causes and effects, nor because of the inherently greater strength of the good guys. The relationship between the obedience of God's people and the triumph of God's cause is not a relationship of cause and effect but one of cross and resurrection. . . . [T]his position is nothing more than a logical unfolding of the meaning of the work of Jesus Christ himself, whose choice of suffering servanthood rather than violent lordship, of love to the point of death rather than righteousness backed by power, was itself the fundamental direction of his life. . . . The cross is not a recipe for resurrection. Suffering is not a tool to make people come around, nor a good in itself. But the kind of faithfulness that is willing to accept defeat rather than complicity with evil is, by virtue of what happens to God when he works among men, aligned with the ultimate triumph of the Lamb.

John Howard Yoder

The Scottsboro trials, in rural Alabama in the early 1930s, were a sign that America was losing its delusion of innocence. They were a symbol of what finally happened to the Righteous Empire that the nineteenth-century revival claimed for us and to the optimistic social gospel of the turn of the century. The loss of innocence those trials underline made way both for the chastened Christian moral theology of the Niebuhrs and Paul Tillich and the American discovery of Karl Barth and for the utilitarian power politics which could justify Hiroshima, Dresden, and Vietnam—not a politics that could *commit* those atrocities (*any* politics can do that) but a politics to justify them by arguing that the moral use of power is impossible. Scottsboro proved that America was no longer, in Reinhold Niebuhr's phrase, "a society in which the morally embarrassing factor of power [was] pushed under the rug."

Scottsboro had its heroes—not in its black victims (who were more pathetic than heroic) nor in its "outside agitators" (who were cynical), but in lawyers, and most especially in the character and conduct of one of its judges, James Edwin Horton, the judge who presided over the fifth trial in the series, the second capital rape prosecution of Haywood Patterson.

Horton's story is more complicated than a dramatic rendition of it (such as the 1976 network television program "Judge Horton and the Scottsboro Boys") suggests. He is an aristocratic Southern lawyer—wealthy, well known, from an old and respected family. He is relatively well educated, one of a minority of Alabama lawyers of his generation who went to law school. He is both a gentleman and a gentle man. When Patterson's case came up for trial, Horton had been a state senator and an equity judge and had served most of two terms as circuit judge. When he ran for reelection in 1929, he was not opposed. He was also a "good judge" in the sense in which lawyers commonly say that—calm, thoughtful, firm but kind. He was relatively progressive in his attitudes about black people; he befriended the two black journalists who were assigned to the Patterson trial, for example, and even shook hands with them when they arrived for court. He accepted the view of Patterson's lawyers that the two prosecutors in the trial should use courtesy titles in addressing black witnesses. He appeared to be open to evidence that the defendant was innocent, and he reflected that openness in his rulings from the bench, although he began the trial assuming Patterson was guilty. (No one involved in the case doubted that the defendant would have to be proved innocent; no one doubted, at least so far as the jury was concerned, that the burden of proof was on the defendant. Even Judge Horton's opinion on the motion for new trial speaks of the evidence "preponderating" for the defense.)

Patterson's was the fifth of the Scottsboro trials; it was held in March and April, 1933, not in Scottsboro but on a change of venue, sought by the defendant, to Morgan County, Alabama. The trial was in the courthouse in the county seat, Decatur. James Edwin Horton, whose home is in Athens, Alabama, and who was the elected circuit judge for the Thirty-eighth Judicial District, presided over the trial, heard a verdict of guilty and the sentence of death from an all-male, all-white jury, pronounced the sentence on Patterson, and then set the verdict aside and ordered a new trial.

Horton's action on the motion for new trial was courageous and futile. Patterson was put to trial in the fall, before a different judge. He and the eight other "Scottsboro Boys" were all found guilty, all sentenced to death. The motion for new trial in Patterson's third case was not granted; all of the judgments, on all of the defendants, were upheld by the Supreme Court of Alabama. Although the Supreme Court of the United States again interfered in the case, there was nothing in the history of the country, or of the federal courts since the tacit national settlement of the Southern racial question in the 1870s, and there was little in judicial precedent, to suggest that further appeals to the federal courts would be successful. In any event, Judge Horton's action on the motion, which ended Patterson's second case, had nothing directly to do with further federal interference. If he had wanted to provoke that interference, he should have overruled Patterson's motion. Federal interference never set Patterson free; Patterson got out of prison by escape, in 1948, 15 years after his trial in Decatur.

Judge Horton knew that his ruling would end his judicial career. His plan, as he decided to grant a new trial, was not to stand for reelection. He did, finally, stand for reelection, at the urging of the local bar association, but he was defeated. Horton knew, I think, that his ruling and his careful defense of it would not affect the dominant opinion in Alabama, and he knew that the prosecutions would go forward, despite his ruling, to their predictable conclusions. I believe he knew that Patterson was not going to be saved by Horton's ruling on the motion for new trial: If Horton granted the motion, Patterson would be tried again; if he denied it, the Supreme Court of Alabama would agree with him and affirm the conviction and sentence.

There were defensible reasons for denying the motion and saving his career. The popular view seems now to be that the evidence for guilt in the trials—and notably in Haywood Patterson's second trial—was fabricated. That view seems to me to be anachronistic and, more importantly, to hide a significant moral quality in the case. The state had witnesses, including at least one of the "victims" and several bystanders, black and white, who supported its theory of the case. Their testimony was weakened as the trials went along; Judge Horton said, after he had heard all of the evidence against Patterson, that the state's key witnesses were not worthy of belief. But it misstates history to contend that prosecutors, police, and witnesses for the state simply concocted the state's evidence. The fact is that many decent people in Alabama were ready to believe that nine black men raped two white women in broad daylight on a moving freight train. People were afraid, really afraid, that just such a thing might happen. And they were ready to use power if such a thing happened. It is very important to see these people as, to this extent, *innocent,* because it was the peculiar innocence and fear of that racist culture Judge Horton rejected when he granted Patterson's motion for a new trial.* What he rejected was the white fear that made the evidence against Patterson plausible, and this allowed him to disbelieve the evidence even though he was prepared to believe the rape had happened and to use power to punish rape when it happened.

The common white folk of Alabama were as ready to believe in gang rape by blacks as Northerners, particularly Northerners who were inflamed against social injustice in America, were ready to believe that Alabama had set out to lynch nine innocent black men. The view that Alabama conducted its judicial processes by lynching is correlative to the view that the defenders of the Scottsboro boys were New York Jewish communists. The Scottsboro story is explained by the politics created by these deluded views of what was happening in Decatur and in America. The reasonable claim of "outsiders" that Alabama accord due process of law to black people was seen as an assault upon the reasonable claim of Alabamans that they be allowed to conduct their judicial business without the influences of foreign revolutionaries and liberal Northern bankers.

Thirty-five years later, in an interview for Dan Carter's book on the Scottsboro cases, Judge Horton said that he ruled as he did in the Patterson case because of a hundred-year tradition that had been observed in his family; he said he had learned, "as a child," the Latin maxim *fiat justitia ruat coelum*—let justice be done though the heavens may fall. It seems that the issue was not so clear to him at the time, though. He allowed outrageous, bigoted histrionics by the prosecution's lawyers—slurs on black people and on Jews, prejudicial behavior for the benefit of the jury, a system of jury selection that excluded all qualified black citizens, and intimidation in court of black witnesses for the defense. He failed to act when a pure hero, a hero out of fiction, might have acted—if he could have understood what was going on and if he saw that *fiat justitia* was the governing principle.

---

*"Innocence" here is collective naivete; I use it as Reinhold Niebuhr did in his interpretation of American history—as masking a collective delusion and a corrupt social ethic.

The state had used two medical witnesses in the trials prior to Patterson's. The witnesses had testified on the physical and emotional condition of the "victims" immediately after the incidents at issue and had stated their conclusions in such a way that the rapes might have occurred. Both medical witnesses were scheduled to appear in the second Patterson trial, but the prosecution asked that the second doctor be excused from testifying on the ground that his testimony would be cumulative. Judge Horton excused the second doctor. The doctor then asked if he could talk to the judge alone, and Horton talked to him privately. The doctor was a young man. He had a private practice in Scottsboro. He told Judge Horton that he was convinced that neither of the "victims" had been raped, and that would be his testimony if he testified, but he did not dare to testify because his telling the truth would ruin his career. Judge Horton allowed the doctor to leave without testifying.

Fiat justitia does not justify that conclusion. It is, first of all, an indefensible conclusion, given what happened later and what an experienced judge in Alabama must at least have been afraid might happen. After all, Patterson's life was at stake; if the judge guessed that the jury might acquit, *fiat justitia* would have required him to demand that the jury have the benefit of the young doctor's testimony—even if the heavens fell and the young doctor's career was ruined. It piles delusion upon delusion to suppose that justice could have been done in Patterson's case without causing harm to innocent people. And if Horton believed that the doctor's conclusions, taken with everything else, proved Patterson's innocence—and Carter suggests that Horton did believe this—he should have used every weapon in the trial judge's formidable arsenal to see to it that the doctor testified.

I say all of this only to show that Judge Horton, like any of us, and—more to the point—like any person of his time and place, walked fearfully in a dark night. As most of us would have, he wondered what he should do and, as lawyers and judges always do, he assumed more righteousness in the system than the system had. Like any of us, he did not see clearly, and he did not always do the right thing. The significant fact is that he came to see *fiat justitia* as applicable in the case; he came to see that overruling the motion for new trial would be complicity with evil. He came to this conclusion both *despite* his time and place and *because* of his time and place. The hundred-year tradition he spoke about explains both the delusion of innocence that caused his mistakes and the reflection, seen in a glass darkly, that caused him to see *fiat justitia* as the appropriate maxim. Horton is not a hero out of a spy thriller; he is a real hero.

The trial was surrounded by furor. On the day Judge Horton ordered the National Guard to protect the prisoners (Patterson and the other eight, all of whom were in jail in Decatur) and to do so "so long as we have a piece of ammunition or a man alive," the *Daily Worker* labelled him "a lyncher in sheep's clothing." The defense was conducted by lawyers hired by the International Labor Defense, widely thought—and with some plausibility—to be a communist organization. (It is probably important to recall that many respectable left-wingers in America were, in those days, communists—but also important to notice that their rhetoric was the rhetoric of revolution and their interest in truth only occasional.) The NAACP, which later bore most of the expense of the defense, lamented that, on top of everything else, the defendants were laboring "under the additional burden of communism."

The popular press in Alabama regularly referred to defense counsel as "New York Jews" and suggested that their tactics and their financing were coming from Russia. Even the attorney general, who restrained his vituperation against blacks, used anti-Semitic innuendo in court and out of court, and the jury summation of his co-counsel sounds like a speech by Adolf Hitler. After the trial was over, but before Judge Horton ruled on the defense motion, it was apparently a general view in the North that the motion would be denied; the leading defense lawyer became a popular hero in New York, the text of his speeches always being that Alabama was a nest of lynchers and bigots. (In fact, although he lost the next election, Judge Horton was supported in his ruling by leading Alabama lawyers and others in the state, including some newspapers in Alabama, and was able, after he left the bench, to sustain a busy law practice in his home town.) This was the climate in which the judge acted; it is hard, in that climate, to do justice and let the heavens fall, and it diminishes the lesson to be learned from his experience to accept his saying that his moral behavior was as consistent as that.

Judge Horton ruled on the defense motion in an oral opinion delivered in court without first hearing oral argument. Carter says that the defense lawyers were prepared to argue but expected to lose the motion. Horton's opinion was mostly an analysis of the evidence, but he began it by saying that "social order is based on law and its perpetuity on its fair and impartial administration"—this by way of locating the issue on the question of prejudice in the jury. He then talked about the consequences of corrupted justice. "The teachings of Christianity and the uniform lessons of history," he said, "illustrate without exception that its perpetrators not only pay the penalty themselves, but their children through endless generations." He invoked the judicial traditions of Alabama, of the rest of America, and of England in support of his judicial power to overturn a prejudiced verdict, then analyzed the evidence, which, he said, "greatly preponderates in favor of the defendant," and granted the motion. He told Carter, in 1966, that he had hoped his thoroughness would convince the state to drop the case against Patterson, and all of the other cases as well. But he must have had his doubts, even then. He had suggested, before ruling on the motion, that the attorney general drop the case. He had then been visited privately by a representative of the attorney general; the representative told him that his granting the motion would end his judicial career. "What does that have to do with the case?" Horton asked. "I told 'em you'd say that," was the reply. The attorney general, who had prosecuted the case, promptly announced that he would re-try Patterson. He announced at about the same time that he was a candidate for lieutenant governor. He won the election; Horton lost his attempt at reelection to the bench, even though his local bar association supported him; the Patterson case, and the others, were assigned for trial to other judges.

The word for this is *irony*—the irony of a society that was proud, and in many respects justifiably so, of its long tradition of judicial excellence; the irony of a nation that came so late to consider what it had done to black people, and then began to come to its senses with such vindictive narrowness; the irony even of a judge who could tell himself that all that was involved was fealty to a Latin maxim. Horton's action was an ironic rejection of an ironic fact—that all sides in the Scottsboro case were so sure of themselves, so sure of the innocence of their God-blessed culture. It is as Reinhold Niebuhr said would be the case if America were to fall to communism: "The primary cause would be that the strength of a giant nation was directed by eyes too blind to see all the hazards of the struggle; and the blindness would be induced not by some accident of nature or history but by hatred and vainglory." Horton's taking the ineffective step of granting Patterson's motion was an ironic action, not in the sense that it was also deluded, but in the opposite sense; it was a comment on the struggles of power—of hatred and vainglory—that were going on around him, and, as such, it was a supremely individual, human thing to do. It was not the exercise of power so much as it was a comment—not a judicial act so much as an act of prophecy. Horton's heroism consisted in his telling the truth.

What is interesting to me, and what I try to describe by reference to Reinhold Niebuhr's view of American history, is the fact that Judge Horton ordered a new trial even though his action was ineffective. One can say that he acted as he did because it was the right thing to do, but that is the point at which ethical inquiry begins. One can say that his action was a rejection of the delusion of innocence and that he made the Scottsboro case a symbol of what happened to America after the revival; but that point, too, needs to be translated ethically. One way of attempting the inquiry and the translation would be to say that Horton chose a relative good; another would be to say that he chose an indicated good, even though it should have been clear to him that the indicated good was a futile and impossible choice; and one might say that he chose a hoped-for good, a good that was not impossible, even though it was unlikely and even though it appeared futile.

There are differences among these three interpretations. All three of them are attempts to explain how a good person comes to do something both courageous and futile. The differences here attempt to explain how power and hope might have been involved. If Horton's decision is explained as the choice of a relative good, it is seen as an exercise of power, but not the exercise of all possible power and therefore not the exercise of hope. One explains such choices by talking about "the art of the possible" or something like that. This would be a way of explaining how it was that Horton gave Patterson a new trial but did not force the young physician to testify. The second alternative explanation, the choice of an impossible good, is not an exercise of power at all; it is a gesture. The third possibility, the choice of a hoped-for good, involves both the exercise of power and a trust in the truth that the powers of racism and class hatred do not decide ultimate questions. Both the second and third explanations are consistent with the view that Horton's was an act of witness of the fortitude and faithfulness of God's people; the difference between the second and third is that the choice of the hoped-for good is more than a gesture.

Relative good. A Jew or Christian can believe, as Yoder says, that "suffering and not brute power determines the course of history" but believe also that it is impossible to act in the world without doing wrong. There is a tradition in Christian moral reasoning, an ancient tradition that traces through Martin Luther back to the Old Testament, that says that any decision to act in the world is an acceptance of the fact that the actor will fail to be moral. Karl Barth called this "the syndrome of the two kingdoms." Barth did not agree with Luther's view; he would probably have agreed with Stanley Hauerwas that it *is* possible to avoid wrong but not possible to avoid harm. An example is the reaction to the private disclosures of the young doctor. Forcing him to testify would have been harmful; it would have destroyed the doctor's medical career. Not forcing him to testify might be (and I think it was) wrong—wrong resulting (depending on how you look at it) either from the delusion that it is possible to use power morally without causing harm, or from the belief that it is impossible to use power morally. In any event, the tradition that sees moral choices in the exercise of worldly power as a matter of relative good (and therefore of relative evil) has a theory to explain how it was that Horton chose to let the doctor go. This view would say that Horton decided it was better in the circumstances to minimize harm. He chose this way even though the price of the choice might have been (and was) conviction and a sentence of death, a price Patterson would have to pay. He also chose minimum disruption in his court, even though brave black leaders in Alabama had to suffer continued exclusion from juries and repeated humiliation when they appeared as witnesses in the Scottsboro trials. This theory of relative good, in other words, can be used to cover the facts of what Horton did and reconcile his lamentable choices with his admirable choices. He might have done better and he certainly could have done worse, but he could not have acted without guilt.

The impossible good. In choosing to grant the motion for new trial, Horton chose something that could not be effective. If he had not seen this fact earlier in the trial, he must have known it at the time he ruled on the motion. But he granted the motion anyway. As a Jew or Christian might put it, and as Horton, a Christian, might well have put it to himself, he *bore witness.* He exercised "the faithfulness of God's people" at the price of his own judicial career, even though his witness did not have a chance of being effective. This is a choice that can fairly be called prophetic; it is not a judicial (i.e., governmental) act so much as it is a proclamation of conscience. It is on the individual side of the distinction Niebuhr makes when he says that "all nations, unlike some individuals, lack the capacity to prefer a noble death to a morally ambiguous survival." If the word is given enough respect, it might even be called a gesture, "the kind of faith that is willing to accept defeat rather than complicity with evil" (Yoder). It puts me in mind of a scene in Orwell's *1984*:

> He would have liked to continue talking about his mother. He did not suppose, from what he could remember of her, that she had been an unusual woman, still less an intelligent one; and yet she had possessed a kind of nobility, a kind of purity, simply because the standards that she obeyed were private ones.... It would not have occurred to her that an action which is ineffectual thereby becomes meaningless. If you loved someone, you loved him, and when you had nothing else to give, you still gave him love. When the last of the chocolate was gone, his mother had clasped the child in her arms. It was no use, it changed nothing, it did not produce more chocolate, it did not avert the child's death or her own.... The refugee woman in the boat had also covered the little boy with her arm, which was no more use against the bullets than a sheet of paper. The terrible thing that the Party had done was to persuade you that mere impulses, mere feelings, were of no account, while at the same time robbing you of all power over the material world.... What you did or refrained from doing made literally no difference. Whatever happened you vanished, and neither you nor your actions were ever heard of again. You were lifted clean out of the stream of history. And yet to the people of two generations ago, this would not have seemed all-important, because they were not attempting to alter history. They were governed by private loyalties which they did not question ... a completely helpless gesture, an embrace, a tear, a word spoken to a dying man, could have value in itself.

The hoped-for good. Neither the idea that Horton chose a relative good nor the idea that he chose an impossible good seems to me the most instructive interpretation of what happened in Decatur in April, 1933. Neither seems to me to best explain Horton's action in reference to the "faithfulness of God's people," in John's phrase or the interpretation given that phrase by John Howard Yoder. The instructive way to interpret Horton's story, I think, is to see his action as one that obeyed conscience, that saw the result in terms of "the ultimate triumph of the Lamb," and that therefore *did* alter history. That way of looking at the story does not see Horton as accepting a relatively minor complicity with evil; nor does it see him as making a tragic gesture, however nobly described. It sees him as doing something hopeful—and by that I mean that his action was optimistic (as it in fact was), but also that it was both truthful *and* political. That is, he realized that his action was ineffective, but his action says that "suffering and not brute power determines the meaning of history."* His act was not a (mere) gesture; it was a *political* act.

This view, too, would see Horton as transcending the *function* of being a judge—the role. He acted from function, from role, when he let the attorney general intimidate black witnesses; that was wrong, but it was not inevitable. He acted from function, from role, when he did not do something about the young doctor's unpresented testimony; that was wrong, but it was not inevitable. Finally, he could have acted from function, from role, and overruled the motion for new trial. There was, after all, evidence of guilt; the jury had apparently believed it and had voted, unanimously, to convict, after five minutes of deliberation. Virtually every other judge who considered records in the Scottsboro cases acted from function. We say now that they chose evil; they were deluded; they let the law take its course. But Horton's action, in transcending his function, was more than a gesture, an impulse, or a feeling. It can be seen as a statement of belief about the real Ruler of the world and the ultimate triumph of His rule. It was, as I prefer to think of it, both "faithfulness that is willing to accept defeat rather than complicity with evil" *and,* "by virtue of what happens to God when he works among men, aligned with the ultimate triumph of the Lamb."

---

*Karl Barth's image is the visit of the pregnant Virgin Mary to the house of Zechariah and his wife, her cousin, Elizabeth (Luke 1:39–40): "Can God's promise be a mere word? Yes, surely, one has to *wait*; fulfillment lies wholly in the future; there is *promise* and 'only' promise. To have faith and only to have faith is what matters. But wherever there is waiting for *God* and for the fulfillment of *his* word, wherever *he* is the future and the promise, there the word 'only' can mean no restriction. There 'only' does not mean any lack. For particularly where 'only' the promise of God is believed, there God is *present*!" I am not talking here about a cargo cult.

PART THREE
Lawyer Culture

We respond to these events in accordance with our interpretation. Such interpretation, it need scarcely be added, is not an affair of our conscious, and rational, mind but also of the deep memories that are buried within us, of feelings and intuitions that are only partly under our immediate control.

* * *

To say the self is social is not to say that it finds itself in need of fellow men in order to achieve its purposes, but that it is born in the womb of society as a sentient, thinking, needful being with certain definitions of its needs and with the possibility of experience of a common world. It is born in society as mind and as moral being, but above all it is born in society as a self. . . . The picture of the radical doubter who sits down before natural events like a little child to be freshly taught by them could be painted only by a generation which had made no study of little children.

H. Richard Niebuhr

The Abbot ought always to remember what he is and what he is called; and that from him to whom much is given much shall likewise be required. Let him consider how difficult and arduous a task he has undertaken—namely, that of ruling souls, and of adapting himself to the dispositions of many. Let him so accommodate and suit himself to all according to the character and intelligence of each one, winning some by kindness, others by reproof, others again by persuasion, that he may not only suffer no loss in the flock committed to him, but may even have cause to rejoice in the increase of a virtuous flock.

Above all, let him not, while disregarding or undervaluing the salvation of the souls committed to him, be oversolicitous in regard to things transitory, earthly, and perishable; let him always bear in mind that he has taken upon himself the government of souls, of whom he must one day render an account. And lest he should plead in excuse his want of temporal things, let him remember that it is written: "Seek first the kingdom of God and His justice, and all these things shall be given to you besides"; and again, "There is no want to them that fear Him."

And let him know that he who has undertaken the government of souls must prepare himself to render an account. And no matter how large the number of brethren that he has under his care may be, let him be absolutely certain that on the day of judgment he is to render an account to the Lord of all these souls, and without doubt likewise of his own. And thus being ever fearful of the coming judgment of the shepherd concerning the sheep committed to him, whilst he is careful of the accounts of others, he becomes solicitous also of his own. And whilst he ministers by his admonitions toward the betterment of others, he himself becomes freed of his own defects.

Saint Benedict

CHAPTER FIFTEEN
A Theology of Lawyer Culture

> *The Christian life is always only a beginning yet none the less a definite kind of life.*
>
> Stanley Hauerwas

I belong to the post–Korean War generation of law students. I was one of many who came to law school with a spouse and (three) children, and left with (the same) spouse and (two more) children. My young sons began to get into fights over things they found in the common play area at Vetville (the Notre Dame married student housing complex) at about the time I began to get into fights over *Moses v. Macferlan* and problems about the possession of animals *ferrae naturae*. These two kinds of fights, both entering our family at about the same time, coincided when I, who was a patriarch at the age of 25, was called upon to resolve disputes among my children.

Say, for example, that my son Tom (then about three and a half) found an abandoned steam shovel in the Vetville sandbox and brought it into our apartment, where my son Francis (then about two) picked it up and began to play with it, and that Tom wanted the steam shovel back. Tom asserted the claim of an owner, Francis asserted the claim of a possessor, and there was a dispute which was brought before the first-year law student who held court in that apartment. I managed the dispute, with principles penciled into my law-school notebook, as follows:

1. One must consider, first, the rights of the owner. Tom, your first duty is to find out which of the neighborhood children left the steam shovel in the sandbox. (Answer: I tried to find out but have not found out yet. I will keep trying.)
2. Well, then, Francis, one must apply the proposition that the right to personal property which is found rests in the finder, as against all of the world except the owner. (Tom's answer: Right! Francis's answer: But Tom has had *his* turn.)

3. Exclusive use is the essence of ownership and, in this case, of possession. (Answer: Uproar.)

This analysis, despite its slender success, has a certain appeal at first—and to this law student it had an appeal that lasted too long. It lasted until I realized that one reason we have parents in the home is that we cannot abide judges there.

But even if I no longer use the law to rule my household—no longer try very hard to rule it at all, really—I still enjoy talking about such things as the rights of the finder of personalty and telling people (students, my wife, older children, clients) about the ancient, enduring principles of the law of property; and I retain a wary faith that the talk will resolve disputes among my fellow citizens even if it did not resolve disputes among my children. (What happens to children is that they grow up as the rest of us grow childish.) I am a lawyer, you see, and I rejoice in the culture of lawyers because it is fun and because it is important. This lawyer culture of ours is like a penny-ante poker game; we lawyers have enough investment in it to keep the seriousness that makes the thing seem important and therefore *really* fun.

It is possible (but not for me) to look upon lawyer culture as a delusion, as something that leads lawyers to live out of roles instead of real selves; this book has to this point amply described that point of view. It is possible (but not for me, not any more) to look upon lawyer culture as an ennobling thing, as Justice Holmes and many nineteenth-century American lawyers did, so that the study of law is something that makes people better and lawyers come to have an acquired claim to aristocracy. That point of view underlies and supports one theory of our professional brotherhood (and that is what it is thought of—as "brotherhood"—so that we have had certain difficulties assimilating women into the profession); this leads us to an ethic of intra-professional faithfulness, to protectiveness toward one another, to a love for shop talk, and to such things as the honored maxim that lawyers are good people to drink with. The idea that just *being* a lawyer ennobles a person, or that it should, or that it can, leads to sentimental nonsense at bar-association meetings, but it also gives us comfort and implies an optimism that seems to me not altogether false.

Most of us lawyers righteously bridle at a third way of looking at lawyer culture—a way that sees our professionalism as corrupting. The third point of view is illustrated in some of the quizzical literature about "Watergate"—literature on the corruption of lawyers, and corruption of others by lawyers, in the presidential administration of Richard M. Nixon. This quizzical literature provokes defensive rejoinders that point out such things as the fact that few of the Watergate lawyers were acting *as* lawyers (which proves too much) or the fact that the heroes of the Watergate story (Cox, Richardson, Jaworski, Jenner, Sirica) were also lawyers, and they were acting as lawyers.

The subject of lawyer culture needs a perspective that can be amused at its pretensions, serious about its truth, and hopeful for the people who take professional culture seriously. It needs a point of view that shows more concern for clients than professional culture just naturally shows. And it needs a theory that can, as a matter of moral education, preserve whatever lawyer culture has that is simple and clear and not corrupting. It isn't that my way of deciding the sandbox cases was mistaken, but that the judiciary in those cases took itself too seriously. We sandbox judges need to think about ourselves and smile anyway.

Perspective. The most helpful perspective I have found for this comes from the reflections after debate of the great English Christian C. S. Lewis. He got into a relatively noisy public argument on whether culture was a good thing or not. By "culture" the debaters meant the things that English esthetes value most, and, in Lewis's own case, especially poetry and good language. Lewis had at first thought he had to argue with those of his colleagues who claimed real goodness for culture—who contended, probably from Aristotelian metaphysics, that there was such a thing as the goodness of something that was just good at being what it was. "The Christian knows from the outset," Lewis said, "that the salvation of a single soul is more important than the production or preservation of all the epics and tragedies in the world: and as for superiority, he knows that the vulgar since they include most of the poor probably include most of his superiors."

When he reflected on this argument, after the debate, Lewis decided he had been too strident. He was misled by his denial of his own strong esthetics. "A man is never so proud as when striking an attitude of humility," he said. He decided that the culture of academic literature is, in itself, at least innocent. "I cannot see," though, he said, "that we are encouraged to think it is important." He did not agree with Cardinal Newman's idea that good taste was a virtue. He did not agree that a good painting or a good piece of music is good just because it is good at being what it is.

In fairness, Newman had said that most of what happens in a university—that was the site of his culture and of Lewis's—produces gentlemen and not necessarily Christians. Lewis admitted that Newman "will not for an instant allow that it makes men better." It merely gives them style—law school does that, certainly, and still does it, even in America—and style may be a way to endure, although it is not especially related to becoming good while one endures. "Well brought up people have always regarded the tumbril and the scaffold as places for one's best clothes," Lewis said.

Lewis decided that culture is not good in itself, not even a little bit, but he found some things to say about intellectual craftsmanship and creative insight, after it has been purged of pride and distraction, which allowed him to think that culture can at least be innocent. First, he said, for most of us, our culture is how we earn a living. It is a good thing—even on scriptural premises—to get to work on whatever it is that a person does for a living. "The need for money is . . . an innocent, though by no means a splendid, motive for any occupation," he said. We should not be ashamed of our need to earn bread, although we cannot suppose the need to be a virtue. It is probably a better thing for us to consider the need with relative candor—as our modern lawyers' code of ethics and bar association programs do—than to perpetuate the fiction that the profession is made up of those who never need to think about survival. The days of disdain for the hireling champion are long past.

Lewis thought, second, that most activities can become better when believers participate in them. In a Christian perspective, "bearing witness" is primarily a matter of obedience: We do it because we are told to do it—and we are told in no uncertain terms! The results of our obedience, which probably include conversions, include other things, cultural things, as well. Ultimately, I suppose, "bearing witness" is a way God chooses to be among plumbers and retail-sales clerks, English teachers, poets, prison guards, and lawyers. It may help prevent the abuse of what is otherwise an innocent way for a person to spend time. It is easier for me to imagine Jesus as a plumber or an English teacher than as a lawyer, but, as Lewis said, "to believe in the Incarnation at all is to believe that every mode of human excellence is implicit in his historical human character." He thought that "the mere presence of Christians in the ranks . . . will inevitably produce an antidote" to the abuse of the culture of employment.

Lewis's third point, that the pursuit of culture is a pleasant way to bring pleasure to others, is a more relaxed point than the point about bearing witness. It is comforting to a lawyer who enjoys—as most of us lawyers do—talking shop, arguing about legal principles, chopping bits of logic, and finding obscurities that our companions overlooked. We lawyers enjoy that pedantry in one another; sometimes our clients enjoy it, too. The point here is that lawyer culture takes on a value beyond itself when it becomes, and simply because it becomes, interpersonal. Lewis did not say so, but I think he would agree—looking back on his hours in an academic common room—that joining in this sort of professional fellowship is an act of love. It is a way for us to learn—especially for us law teachers, who need so much to learn this—how not to use our lawyer culture to hurt people. We teachers can learn this in the common room or the bar association because in those places we cannot always get away with pulling rank.

Fourth, professionalism may be a better thing (a "sub-good," Lewis called it) than a lot of other things we could be doing or teaching others to do. Official values and legal values, even though they are always partial, often pretentious, and sometimes false, point beyond themselves to fuller and unpretentious values. They are—at least the best of them are—parables. Lewis was critical of the notion of honor, which is a prominent sub-good in the culture of lawyers. "To the perfected Christian the ideal of honour is simply a temptation. His courage has a better root, and, being learned in Gethsemane, may have no honour about it." But—in his reflective mood, after the debate and with the debater's humility—he admitted that the road out of Jerusalem also leads into Jerusalem: "[T]o the man coming up from below, the ideal of knighthood may prove a schoolmaster to the idea of martyrdom."

He made the same point about justice: "Apparently the way to advance from our imperfect apprehension of justice to the absolute justice is *not* to throw our imperfect apprehensions aside but boldly to go on applying them. Just as the pupil advances to more perfect arithmetic not by throwing his multiplication table away but by marking it for all it is worth." That idea translates, too, into a lawyer's consideration of the old American civil religion. It could make something of the pompous phrases we hear in Law Day speeches about patriotism and a government of laws and not of men. We American lawyers ought to try to make something of those ideas, if only because we give so much effort to proclaiming them. While patriotism is not really a virtue, at least not to a radical Jew or Christian in the latter half of the twentieth century, it is not necessarily a bad thing; it may be something that, like imperfect justice, could lead to virtue. It may be a parable—sometimes. "If all the cultural values, on the way up to Christianity, were dim antepasts and ectypes of the truth, we can recognize them as such still. And since we must rest and play, where can we do so better than here—in the suburbs of Jerusalem."

Concern for clients. Lewis would say to modern American lawyers that the important thing is not to be fooled. Our civil religion contains more history and pragmatism and sophistry than wisdom. Our clients and less sophisticated fellow citizens may know that better than we do, and may therefore be less likely than we are to go the wrong way on the road that leads to and from Jerusalem. The untutored, as Lewis said it, "expects a certain amount of meaningless nonsense—which expectation, though very regrettable from the cultural point of view, largely protects him from the consequences of which we, in our sophisticated naivety, are afraid." The law—our civil religion—has, as the Bible says, "but a shadow of good things to come" (Hebrews 10:1).

Steven Wexler made Lewis's point about the untutored close to home when he wrote several years ago about his experience as an advocate for the poor. The poor, Wexler noticed, know more about their lives in and under the law than lawyers do. "Poor people are always bumping into sharp legal things," he said. "The law-school model of personal legal problems, of solving them and returning the client to the smooth and orderly world in television commercials, doesn't apply to poor people." Lawyers, he said, tend to think of problems rather than of people. We tend, even in thinking of problems, to think of them as abstracted from their fuzzy human context, as if they were stated in a law-school examination or lined up, one-to-a-client, in the waiting room. Wexler argued that these ideas, which are part of our lawyer culture, are harmful to the poor because the poor have too many problems and too few lawyers and a history of failing to act together. They need strength more than they need solutions.

"Lawyers are taught to believe, and have a three-year investment in believing, that what they have learned in law school was hard to learn, and that they are somehow special for having learned it. It is difficult for a lawyer to commit himself to believing that poor people can learn the law and be effective advocates; but until he believes that, a lawyer will create dependency instead of strength for his clients, and add to rather than reduce their plight." Wexler's argument was radical; what he was saying was that lawyers should pass their culture along to their clients. Also, he said, "The poses that the ... lawyer adopts in order to be able to talk to his clients are called his professional bearing or manner; it is very important that a poor people's lawyer drop that professional bearing. He must realize that what makes him a lawyer are accidents of birth and interest, and those accidents have not made him something special; they have only given him the opportunity to help someone else."

My law practice was among the rich. I noticed in that world that lawyers tend to become like their clients. Wexler noticed no similar danger when one practices among the poor. Lawyers for the rich become like the rich; lawyers for the poor become like lawyers. That is backward, in both cases. Christians are called to become poor, not rich; to become humble of spirit, not like lawyers. But—and this is Wexler's point, and it is true as well of the point Jesus makes in the Sermon on the Mount about becoming poor—humility in a professional culture means the humility of suffering servanthood. It means the service of a servant in doing what we do as professionals. It means applying a radical idea of servanthood to what Wexler called "the affirmative techniques of practice."

The "affirmative techniques of practice" are a part of our lawyer culture that is innocent, but innocent as raw materials are innocent. Techniques—everything from the way we write letters and furnish the waiting room to the way we talk to people and listen to what they say—are capable either of serving the goodness in us lawyers and our clients or of being a moat between people who ought—*ought*—to be drawing closer together. The special self-deception of these affirmative techniques in professional life is the idea that *the lawyer knows best*. This bit of our culture—or this distortion of our culture, if you like—hides from our eyes the truth and grace that comes from other people. "He who wants to bring about change," Henri Nouwen says, "has first of all to learn to be changed by those whom he wants to help." Nouwen's point—which was being made to pastors—is like the one Lewis argued to teachers, in reply to a literary critic who said that critics were able to detect "the falsity of the values of contemporary culture." Lewis thought not; he distinguished between identifying an implicit value (which is like identifying the reasoning behind a legal argument or the origins of a legal rule) and deciding whether the implicit value is any good:

"Now I for my part have no objection to our doing both ... but I think it is very important to keep the two operations distinct. In the discovery of the latent belief we ... speak as experts; in the judgment of the beliefs, once they have been discovered, we humbly hope that we are being trained, like everyone else, by reason and ripening experience, under the guidance of the Holy Ghost, as long as we live, but we speak on them simply as men, on a level with all our even-Christians [and not-even-Christians], and indeed with less authority than any illiterate man who happens to be older, wiser, and purer, than we." My lawyer culture gives me a rule about things found in a sandbox, but it doesn't tell me what to do with the rule.

Lewis recalled that when he was a boy he was inclined to like a new playmate less after he found that the playmate liked prunes. "Even for adults it is 'sweet, sweet, sweet poison' to be able to imply 'thus said the Lord' at the end of every expression of our pet aversion." We lawyers, being sophisticated people, may be good at distinguishing things, at saying what things are, but we are likely to be weaker than our clients are at saying what things are worth. Our keenness is a strength; our relative inability to feel value is a weakness. Both strength and weakness are assets in ministry.

A theory for preservation. The professional culture of lawyers is characterized especially by vocational concern for justice. We are supposed to be experts in the principle that every person is entitled to his due. This culture of justice is worth preserving from corruption, but it can be preserved from corruption only if the professional culture reaches beyond itself to something better and more elementary than justice. The difficulty with justice as a professional culture is that it defines human relationships in so limited a way that it excludes the virtues which are needed in the interpersonal lives of lawyers and clients. The trouble with my sandbox justice was that my law-school notes did not remind me that the suitors in my court were grander than the claims they made on my expertise.

The professional allure here is also, perhaps, the source of professional corruption in the delusion of expertise. (That's what the sandbox judge had to get rid of.) If the university decides that there is an issue on the idea of justice that should be studied or mauled by an academic committee, there has to be someone from the law school on the committee. The local bar association, which takes special responsibility for Law Day programs every May, builds its program on the social virtues suggested by the idea of justice. I have been asked to talk to community Law Day celebrations at which the honored guests were new citizens, admitted to citizenship on that very day by the federal district judge. The implication of these occasions is that instruction about justice as a social virtue is a good way to launch these guests on their careers as American citizens. That is an innocent supposition, I suppose—in Lewis's sense of innocence (there is not necessarily harm in it) and Reinhold Niebuhr's more ironic sense of innocence as a delusion inviting sympathy more than wrath. It is, though, more important that new citizens of the United States think about compassion and hope, as they begin to live as Americans among Americans; talk of justice can do that for them only if justice is described as something that reaches beyond itself.

The moral sensitivity of lawyers themselves is limited, too much, by the professional culture of justice. Justice as a professional aspiration is corrupting to the extent that the culture of justice finds it hard to say that a lawyer's life is ministry and that that ministry aims beyond justice to compassion and hope. Compassion is the heart of counseling, and counseling is what lawyers do most of the time. Lawyers do not, most of the time, "dispense" or "administer" or serve justice; they serve people who know and who want to know how to live together. The professional culture's proclaimed concern with justice, because justice is often irrelevant to this enterprise, makes compassion more rather than less difficult, and, therefore, the professional culture makes things worse. The practice of hope in a lawyer's professional life involves the use of knowledge and intellectual skill as an expression of truth; but exclusive concern with justice in the professional culture often comes out expressing itself in terms of coercion, rather than truth, and in that way, too, professional culture makes things worse. Justice is an important professional virtue, no doubt, but it is not an adequate aspiration for the life the average lawyer leads.

Those who are exclusively concerned with justice as (if you like) a professional story thus overlook the importance of compassion (which means the virtue of "suffering with" and can usually be translated "love") and hope. Exclusive concern with justice leads instead to reliance on the government—that is, on "the administration of justice," rather than on the justice clients bring with them into law offices. The government's justice diminishes compassion and hope; the client's justice exalts compassion and hope. The reliance on government that justice, seen as "the administration of justice," implies is always open to the collective notion that government has real power. That reliance is, finally, a delusion, however you look at it—whether you look at power as a believer, who says that only God is Lord, or as a garden-variety American democrat, who says that the people have the power. Those who come to believe that power is the source of goodness in society come to be oriented by tyranny. They become either tyrants or the collaborators of tyrants.

Our American professional culture has perhaps not yet led us to tyranny, but it has led us to what we call the adversary ethic, which is nearly as bad. The adversary ethic is the most cherished and the most vulnerable of the consequences of our profession's seeing itself as a guild specializing in justice. The adversary ethic announces that justice is the goal of professional activity and that the means to justice is zealous loyalty to the interests of one's client. It seems unable to entertain an ideal of professional service involving faithfulness rather than loyalty—one difference being that faithfulness aims at goodness rather than the realization of interests. There are not always clear differences between loyalty and faithfulness, or even between a client's interests and his goodness; but there are some differences, and the adversary ethic is inadequate to the extent that it does not provide us with ways for seeing the differences when they are there. The adversary ethic has, no doubt, and perhaps often, produced sound results. It has proved itself most useful in those episodes in our national life when what we needed most was a coerced alternative to chaos. (There is something to be said, particularly in a crisis, for the authority that quiets things down and gets them evened up.) But the adversary ethic is an inadequate aspiration for a community, and it is a pernicious moral principle. As an idea about power in the community, it depends not on goodness but on force and therefore reaches only the small, desperate residues of the community's life. As a moral principle it depends on the idea that one person should be able to buy the loyalty of another and often poisons the hope that people can grow together.

Power and loyalty are the ideas on which the adversary ethic rests. Neither power nor loyalty are virtues; they are, taken together, the aspiration Dr. Johnson found to be the last refuge of a scoundrel.

Virtues—by which I mean an old-fashioned idea, good habits—have names such as compassion (love), hope, and even faith. The lawyer's professional culture is innocent to begin with and, to the extent that it reaches beyond itself, can encourage the development of these good habits among those the profession serves. We lawyers are fond of our hero stories—Gavin Stevens and Atticus Finch with their persecuted black clients, Daniel Webster defending the students and teachers of Dartmouth College, Thurgood Marshall representing a schoolchild from Topeka. We might usefully try to realize that those stories, and the formation of a lawyer's life as it comes from stories such as those, rest more on faithfulness to persons than on loyalty and power.

CHAPTER SIXTEEN
Moral Moments in Law School

After considerable empirical research, Robert Redmount and I found that law school is like a poker game: "One leaves it a little poorer (or a little richer), having enjoyed the experience and not been touched by it, having liked it or found it boring. The difference may be that law students would decline an opportunity to return." We found that a common impression among poets and educators—that legal education causes students to become callous or pompous—is not borne out by an examination of the process and the effects of the process.

Law school is also like reading Heidegger; it can be a massive intellectual experience, but one's character, whatever it is, tends to survive. Students are narrowed, but only temporarily; when they leave law school they have recaptured most of whatever breadth of vision they had when they came. Their most interesting complaints about law school are that it does *not* change them and that it gives them no skills for carrying out the altruism they came with.

All of this is according to plan. The late Professor Karl Llewellyn, a giant in legal education and in law reform (he was, among other things, the drafter of the Uniform Commercial Code), gave introductory lectures to law students at the University of Chicago. These were later published in a little volume, a classic in the what-to-expect-in-law-school genre, called *The Bramble Bush*. Llewellyn told students that they were welcome to their morals but that their morals had little to do with the culture of lawyers. "The hardest job of the first year," he said, "is to top off your common sense, to knock your ethics into temporary anesthesia. Your view of social policy, your sense of justice—to knock these out of you along with woozy thinking." His point is one that is celebrated in American legal culture. It was elevated into legal philosophy by the American legal positivists. For most American lawyers, the point is at least an analytical one: It is necessary, in working with law, to set morals aside. This is not to say that morals are not important. It is not even to say that law and morals are *really* distinct.

It is a matter of form, a habit useful to analysis and therefore to professional skill. "If you want to hit a bird on the wing," Justice Holmes told the Boston Bar Association, "you must have all your will in a focus. You must not be thinking about your neighbor." In legal education, whether this doctrine is a matter of philosophy or merely an educational device, morals are considered irrelevant. The result of this view is that morals *become* irrelevant.

Methods for dealing with moral sensitivity in legal education—avoidance. There is a legend law teachers tell that has a first-year professor (probably someone like Kingsfield in the television show "Paper Chase") grilling a student about an appellate opinion. After no small amount of battering, the professor finally gets the student to state accurately what the result in the case was. After a pause, the student adds, "But that's not *just!*" And the professor answers, "If you wanted to study justice you should have gone to divinity school." Redmount and I, in recording and analyzing classes in five law schools, found the legend revived in an evidence class on an ordinary Wednesday morning:

Professor: Brown, what's a trial?
Brown: An adversary proceeding.
Professor: For what purpose?
Brown: To discover the truth. (There is silence in the class for five seconds, then laughter.)
Professor (after waiting just long enough for the laughter to help him make his point): Who cares what truth is?
Brown: I care. (Loud laughter.)
Professor: Well, in your conversations with God, you can take those questions further. (Pause. Then, to another student:) Smith, what's the purpose of a trial?

We found that sort of experience to be frequent in legal education and we believe it to be universal. Llewellyn emphasized it in his talks to lawyers and in his legal thought. It survives in the nostalgia of alumni. It occurs, as nearly as I can tell, in every American law school. It has everything to do with the way a lawyer learns about morals in his professional life.

The moment itself is usually more subtle than it was in the evidence class; Redmount and I were lucky to find such a clear example. It is also not usually so much a moment as an insinuation. It is often announced by mentors in the law more with a whimper than with a bang. It is primarily an educational device. It involves a road taken and a road less traveled by. In Frost's poem the road less traveled by is the road taken, but here the choice is more conventional. Sophisticated law in America, like sophisticated American political life, prefers to pretend that morals have nothing to do with the enterprise. The road less traveled by, the road not often taken in law school, is the road on which the analysis and exploration of moral propositions become an intellectually important part of professional education.

The road taken is the road on which there is no time to think about one's neighbor, on which thoughts about one's neighbor are scorned as woozy thinking. A student of mine at the University of Virginia said, "One of my greatest frustrations at this law school has been the lack of person-centered law. After a while one would come to think that there isn't any such thing." Even if there is such a thing as "person-centered law," one is expected to proceed as if there were no such thing. "Person-centered law" is the road not taken. The fork in the road is no different, and the choice of roads no different, at law schools which profess a religious heritage or which trace their origins to churches. Since the choice is not *against morals,* but only against regarding morals as having intellectual importance, the road is open both to believers and to nonbelievers.

The choice and the moment of avoidance usually involve both process and content. In the example from the evidence class, the *content* of the exchange involves an assertion about the relation between truth and justice. It is a respectable philosophical position, certainly, to maintain that there is a difference between the two. Gavin Stevens, Faulkner's lawyer, said he had been forgiven in advance for preferring justice over truth. That preference is arguably necessary to human judicial processes, since there is always a point where truth cannot be found or where, if truth can be found, the search will be too expensive. It is defensible, even, to say that the end of trials (and trials are the subject of an evidence course) is keeping the peace, a function that aspires to justice but may not be able to demand truth—at least not always and everywhere. In other words, the apparent issue presented in the dialogue is an interesting intellectual issue. The content of the student's proposition is relevant. However, the proposition was ruled out of order. The lesson was taught, and taught quickly: Truth has nothing to do with the law of evidence. It is not clear that justice has anything to do with the law of evidence. In losing truth, maybe trial law loses justice too. Many laypeople suspect as much. Joyce Cary's Gulley Jimson put it well in a dispute over the value of one of his pictures:

> I nearly got in a state in that case, because of all the nonsense they talked, and all the lies they told about poor old Hickie. Not knowing anything about art or pictures or Hickie or me, and what was worse, not caring. I was just going to start on to tell that chap what I thought of him, and twice I tried to put some sense into the court and make it understand that a picture wasn't a bag of flour. . . .
>
> But when I saw them all so serious and reverent, and the police with their hats off as if ready for prayer, I said to myself: Don't be a fool, Gulley, they're doing their best and they couldn't do any better. They

know it isn't justice and they know there can't be any such thing in this world, but they've got to do their job which is to keep the handles turning on the old sausage machine, and where would the world be without sausages?

The road taken in the evidence class has a "process" side, too, a potent lesson quickly taught about how to treat people. Student Brown not only suggested that truth has something to do with trials, but he also suggested that he cared about the point. The process question was: How do you treat people who tell you they care about something? This is a relevant question in the practice of trial law. It comes up when lawyers and clients decide on trial tactics; when they decide whether to settle a case or not; when they decide whether there is even to be a case or not. The lesson about that, quickly taught, says: What the other person cares about is just as irrelevant as truth is. Student Smith, when he takes over the dialogue from Brown, if Smith is as clever as most law students are, will answer with a concept. What he says will have nothing to do with his feelings about truth or about his aspirations for practicing law as a trial lawyer. He will have learned, at student Brown's expense, that his feelings have nothing to do with the law. He will have begun to learn that his client's feelings have nothing to do with the law. "Society demands certain attitudes, reactions, etc., from certain types of people—as a lawyer, businessman, or whatever," one of my students wrote in his diary. "I seem to have no choice. Perhaps it is just me reacting to my legal education, but my education accentuates a careless indifference to people.... Personal involvement and the law don't seem to mix. If you want to be good you must be indifferent. I have yet to find myself in a situation where emotion has done anything for me other than to scramble my sometimes good judgment." He had learned his lesson. He had even learned to defend it.

The process issue presented by Brown in the evidence class goes beyond the reflection of feelings. Brown also presented a discussable issue. The issue is whether emotions are obstacles in the practice of law. A respectable argument can be made on both sides of that question. Professions that are more directly wired into behavioral science (the ministry, counseling, psychology) argue that emotions are the raw materials for being helpful; a growing amount of lawyer material makes the same argument and even makes it in reference to the practice of trial law. Interesting stories from and about American trial lawyers, and an almost romantic attachment to the traditions of the British trial bar, might argue in the other direction.

What was turned aside in about five seconds in this evidence class, therefore, involves two interesting and relevant propositions and, more important than propositions, a lesson on how lawyers are to treat people. The diary of a "resuming woman" who came to law school drives these points home: "There seems to be a strong identification in the public's mind of a lawyer as being a loud mouth, double-talking kind of person. He is characterized as searching for loopholes in order to win something for his clients. I even sense many people feel this way about their own lawyers, distinguishing a certain one, whom they like, as not like most lawyers you know. One neighbor friend's comment to me, on learning that I was going to law school, was: 'Don't you think this neighborhood already has enough smart asses?' "

Method ... unexplored positions. Avoidance of the moral is almost a sacred tradition in the culture of American lawyers. But it is not inevitable. A law teacher can—and many do—pursue the distinction between process and content in an exchange such as the one in the evidence class. The teacher can say, in effect: "Well, let's see. There is an interesting proposition in what the student says, and the student is, in speaking out, laying himself on the line. Whatever is to be done with his proposition, I think I should show respect for the student's point of view and in that way demonstrate that I care about his feelings." The result of this pedagogical stance will be an important moral lesson on how to treat people. It may not be any lesson at all on the truth of the student's proposition. Here is an example from a family-law class. The class was discussing the custody-by-kidnapping phenomenon, in reference to a divorce client. The father of small children who seeks legal advice can be told to obtain legal custody of his children by taking them across the state line:

McGee: You don't have a lot of choice in the matter.... The problem is being able to say, "Gee, you know, I really don't want to take your case. Maybe you want to get somebody else...." It puts you in sort of a bind.

Professor: But you think you have to do it [i.e., advise on the advantage of kidnapping], huh? You could call another lawyer ... and say, "You handle this matter...."

McGee: No. This is one of the disadvantages of being a junior partner, or not even that. A lackey.

Professor: Anybody in the class who thinks he'd decline to take the case, in the way that it is presented?

Meyer: Well, we do have a pretty good idea of what the situation is.... I think you could certainly feel that you could in good conscience advise him.

Professor: All he's asking you to do ... is to read the papers and do some research, huh? And there would not be anything out of the way in your doing those two things?

Brown: Ideally, you may have some objections but—unless you have another job lined up—technically speaking, I would probably go ahead and do it.... It's nice to be an idealist, but right now I would rather eat.

Timmons: Well ... let's put it this way: You advise him of what are his minimal legal rights; you don't necessarily wax eloquent.... You don't necessarily tell him he could kidnap the kid and probably get away with it.

Reynolds (to Timmons): Who elected you judge and jury? I mean—if you don't want to handle the case, that's one thing. But to give the guy shoddy legal advice—

Professor: Well, I think we can disagree on that issue, but I do think it's worth raising....

From the perspective of content, the teacher here is a referee. (From the perspective of process, he is much more than that.) Student answers in this sort of discussion are of the form "I would/would not do that." Sometimes they are of the form "I *just* would/would not do that. I'm sorry about it, but it's the way I am, and I am the way I am because I was raised (in the South) (in parochial schools) (by a good Baptist mother)." This is training in the ethics of isolation (Chapter 2). The dialogue has valuable potential in its acceptance of student feelings, and in what it teaches about the way people are to be treated, but its ethical content, beyond an implied principle of civility, is flimsy at best and fatalistic at worst. From an intellectual point of view, the professor's classroom scorekeeping establishes that the moral life has *something* to do with the practice of law. But it also follows the tacit norm of our American legal culture, that moral life is a private matter. Except as provided in the *Code,* there is no more accounting for a lawyer's morals than there is for his taste in beer. And one must learn what is in the *Code,* not because the *Code* is a moral document (it is not), but because one may offend disciplinary authorities and courts if he does not understand the rules stated in the *Code.*

The unexplored-positions device in law classes has value in establishing that there must be time for moral discourse, even in law school. But it tends to imply to students that there is no discipline in moral discourse. One cannot hope to come out with understanding. He cannot hope to be able to say, of a moral position, "That is a good position," as he can of a rule of property law.

Our family-law teacher was reverent in the presence of dim signs of belief among his students; he should, I think, consider being less reverent and more analytical about their beliefs—a tactic that would suggest that morals are worth as much intellectual attention as, say, the rule against perpetuities. The criticism I mean to make here is that these moral assertions were not *explored*; they were not drawn out, elaborated, learned about.

Why were these positions not drawn out? A prelude to an answer lies in a curious paradox: Law teachers (and other lawyers too) prefer to reason logically and intuitively; they are interested in concepts and in what the mind dredges up, but they distrust empirical information that might assist them in their reasoning. Our family-law teacher permitted full statements of positions on the issue of whether the client should be advised that he could probably get away with kidnapping his children. Those positions asserted certain information about the way young lawyers practice law and the way students perceive how law is practiced; for example:

1. Young lawyers in firms are not given the power to refuse to serve one of the firm's clients.
2. Young lawyers in firms do, though, get away with imperfect service when they are working for a client of whom they disapprove.
3. One way moral conflicts in law practice are handled is to recruit a second lawyer to serve the client's immoral purposes.

And so forth. These are all empirical propositions. They assert bits of information. If the class were to examine them thoroughly, it would have to examine them empirically. The teacher would have to point out their obvious weaknesses in apparent sources of information before he could undertake to reason about the dilemmas they present and the perceptions they betray. It seems to me that this family-law teacher refused to cope with empirical information, with the result that the discussion, such as it was, was not based on the truth.

The class was an important improvement on the way law appears usually to be taught. It was humane, for example, where the evidence class was inhumane. It demonstrated to students an openness to people, where the evidence class demonstrated contempt. But the family-law class was unsatisfactory in content—and this in an institution dedicated to the life of the mind.

Methods . . . unexamined positions. It is one thing—and a good thing—to listen to the statement of a moral position. Lawyers are not trained to do that. The evidence class is an illustrative case. It is a second thing—and a better thing—to test a moral position and determine whether it is based on reliable information. Lawyers are not trained to do that either. The family-law class is an illustrative case. (For example, older lawyers in law firms deny that young lawyers are forced to serve firm clients when the young lawyers object to what the client is doing, and some legal cultures—the French, for example—have rules to protect young lawyers in such situations.) It is a third thing to examine a moral position. Given the dynamics of approval with which my outline is proceeding here, I guess it is clear that the third thing is better than the second, as the second is better than the first. It is better to explore (explicate) *and* examine (evaluate) a moral proposition than merely to explore it. It is better to explore a moral proposition—and that only—than it is to turn it aside as irrelevant.

The examination of a moral proposition might mean subjecting it to logical analysis, which is the traditional way lawyers and law students examine *legal* concepts. This is sometimes done—i.e., lawyers do it—with sarcastic wit. The late Dean William Prosser noticed the rule that the owner of a dog is not liable to people the dog bites, unless he knows of the dog's propensity to bite people, and said that the law permits one free bite. He examined cases where a man was held not liable for making a lewd proposition to a woman and said that the law is that there is no harm in asking. Justice Holmes stated it as his opinion that a state legislature should be deferred to in deciding to sterilize a fertile person who has a mental deficiency, noting that the legislature might well have decided that three generations of imbeciles are enough.

The examination of a *moral* proposition might be carried out in the same way. Or it might be examined by subjecting it to the tools of analysis used by students and teachers of ethics. These reach, with remarkable expertise, from Aristotle to Kant to Joseph Fletcher. Ethics is the science of thinking about morals; if a law teacher were to propose both to explore and to examine moral assertions—his own, his students', and those to be found in the literature of legal ethics—he would reasonably be expected to show familiarity with both approaches. It would not do (I assert this as my view) to deal with moral assertions only by subjecting them to legal logic, wit, and sarcasm. If one is to talk about ethics in a university, he can reasonably be expected to know something about Aristotle, Kant, Richard Niebuhr, and maybe even the Bible. Default on that reasonable expectation—I assert this as a hypothesis—might explain why one rarely hears of a law class examining moral assertions.

Another reason law classes do not examine moral assertions is that the assertions are heard as if they were principles and law students are learning a cultural disrespect for principles. At least they are learning disrespect for *legal* principles and may, therefore, either lack respect for moral principles or be afraid to develop respect for them. Scholars in the early part of this century began to make it clear to lawyers and judges, and those who study lawyers and judges, that the Anglo-American legal system changes constantly. Dean Joseph O'Meara told us first-year students, in the era of the sandbox cases, that he could demonstrate that there was scarcely a legal rule that had not changed from its opposite within half a century. And this was not the part of the law that is decreed by legislatures, or the part that is insinuated by administrative agencies. This was the *common law,* that ancient protector of stability that rests on the principle that judges must follow precedents. Even in following precedents, the law changes twice in each century. Change occurs because lawyers and judges are skillful at dealing with precedents and because *they are not awed by legal principles.* Lawyers' law is a complex art. We work with what courts *do* rather than with what they *say* – so that the judges of the future are bound by results based on facts rather than by explanations of results. One who is trained in that system – and much of what "thinking like a lawyer" means is bound up in that system – loses his respect for legal principles. Legal principles are explanations for results. They are not the stuff of the law, and one who proposes to deal with the stuff of the law has to go through principles to facts and results. A lawyer has to write new principles to fit the needs of his clients. For this reason, a lawyer can, with no guile, engage in a dialogue in which someone asks him, "What is the law in this situation?" and he answers, "That depends on what you want the law to be."

This common-law legal system (and, notice again, we lawyers are all trained in it – trained rigorously in it – whether or not we use our training) provides stability. Every new result has to be reconciled with past results, so that the law seems not to change as it changes. The end of the process, after all, is the confidence of citizens in that part of their government that resolves disputes. Any system that attracts and keeps that confidence has to be stable and at the same time able to change.

A lawyer knows that no legal principle will stand forever; there are few legal principles he or some clever colleague cannot argue away. There is no cynicism in this. It is necessary that the legal system change and be stable, and it is necessary that it explain itself in principles that are impersonal, equal, and certain. But the result, in a lawyer's way of looking at things, involves low respect for legal principles. This, as David Reisman noticed, can become troublesome when clients interpret it as cynicism: "The better schools have for a generation or more been training their students in the art of debunking legal rituals and debunking authority, especially the authority of upper-court judges. More generally, lawyers learn something about relevance, a concept that, to their constant frustration, seems nearly absent in most of the people they deal with. Above all, lawyers learn not to take the law (principles) too seriously.... But the layman is not quite sure how he feels about such a person, whose usefulness he may need and whose knowledge may fascinate him; the more he needs him, the more he may be apt to project on to him his own tendencies to cynicism about authority and procedure."

Law teachers, who are adept at manipulating principles in this fashion, may not be willing to apply their skills to manipulating moral principles. It seems less possible, in manipulating moral principles, to account for situation and for change. It is hard to think of moral principles as lawyers think of legal principles. Morals should not change every half-century. Moral principles are more important than that. One answer to the dilemma is that lawyers make a mistake when they show such heavy respect for moral principles. Maybe moral principles, like legal principles, are not the heart of the matter; they, too, may be merely engines of explanation for something that is more vital than principles.

A third explanation for lawyers' reluctance to discuss moral assertions is that in America it is not considered polite to argue about religion, and assertions of moral position in law school sound religious and often are. There is, surely, something to this explanation, but it would not cover situations where the context permits argument about religion and *still* the lawyer participants do not dissect moral positions as they do legal positions.

A final explanation for the fact that law teachers do not examine moral positions is that the examination of moral positions leads one to what Stanley Hauerwas calls tragic choices. The great ethical thinkers have always recognized that interesting moral choices are not those between good and evil, but those between good and good. The divorce-client discussion in the family-law class was such a dilemma. It is good to serve one's client well. It is also good to advise one's client to obey the law. The choice there was between those two good alternatives. The most interesting moral questions involve a choice between what appears to be a good alternative and adherence to a moral model a person tries to govern his life by. (For example, it is good to fight for one's country, but the life of Jesus is a testimony against violence.) Hauerwas even talks about a willingness to *die* and to *allow others to die* for one's morals: "To live morally ... means that we must necessarily be willing to risk our own and others' lives for those values we find necessary to maintain our life together. In certain crucial cases ... we must be willing to let ourselves and others die rather than to act against these goods." Lawyers may be peculiarly reluctant to explore moral reasoning to these tragic but consistent ends. Our peculiar self-delusion may be tied up in winning.

Stories and moral sensitivity in law school. We get into trouble with our lawyer culture when we begin to suppose that it is adequate. It becomes a devil when we allow it to become a god. The analytical distinction we make between law and morals is in the suburbs of Jerusalem—it is even mildly useful—until we begin to suppose that living amorally is what being a lawyer is about and that being a lawyer is what being a person is about. Some modern moral theologians describe moral life in terms of the story a person is living and the stories he considers important and, in one way or another, chooses and seeks to conform his life to. For example, the courage of Judge James Edwin Horton cannot be explained without considering both the story of his being a Southerner and a grander story that gave him a way to evaluate the story of being a Southerner. These "story theologians" say of moral principles what John Dewey said of legal principles—that the living of life is prior to principles; the living produces the principles. If you want to know what a person's morals are, you do better to watch him than to ask about his principles. The story of Jesus is more important to a serious Christian than the moral precepts of Jesus. It is the story of Jesus that is special. It is the story that is unusual. Schnackenberg demonstrated that few of the *precepts* Jesus taught were unusual. But his coming into the world, what he did here, his death and resurrection—these were unusual.

Other stories are important in moral life—the American story, for example; the mountain-western story for me, since I am a descendant of cowboys and frontier women; the story of those who cherish the life of the mind for those of us who succeed and fail in universities. And there are inadequate stories, corrupt stories that diminish moral life and make evil decisions possible. Inadequate stories, as Stanley Hauerwas develops his theory of stories, are those that are built on delusions. They are not truthful. The delusion of power, for example, leads to an inadequate story; Hauerwas and David Burrell analyze it in reference to Albert Speer. One can see the inadequacy of power stories in the contrast between Thomas More and Thomas Cromwell in Robert Bolt's play *A Man for All Seasons* (*see* Chapters 18 and 19).

My argument, in reference to the lawyer culture that makes a distinction between law and morals, and that makes other suburban distinctions as well, is that it does no harm until we allow it to become a story. *To be a lawyer* is not an adequate story, any more than "to be an architect" (even if it was Hitler's architect) was an adequate story for Albert Speer. Professional culture does not provide an adequate story for many reasons, one of which is that it ends us up in moral analyses that begin, "It is no part of a lawyer's job to..." It is a delusion to suppose that being a lawyer is adequate. Lawyers assist evil when they deceive themselves into supposing that the lawyer's professional ideal is enough. The result of that self-deception is, as Richard Wasserstrom has demonstrated, an immoral professional life in an immoral society. I often think that the only way to be both a Christian and lawyer is to ask, every day, "Is it possible to be both a Christian and a lawyer?" and to be open, every day, to the thought that it is *not* possible.

Being a lawyer is not an adequate story. But that is not to say that there are not morally helpful stories about lawyers, stories that bring more profit to first-year law students than the distinction between law and morals or the idea that morals are based on ethical considerations and disciplinary rules. My program for the study of ethics in law school would involve consideration of *lawyer stories,* rather than the story of ethical aspirations, and disciplinary rules that are formulated in reference to an abstraction—an abstraction one might call *the* lawyer story, and then, having called it that, label it inadequate. The difference here is between *lawyer stories* and *the* lawyer story. Mrs. Bowen's contrast of Edward Coke and Francis Bacon tells more about the morals of being in power and being a lawyer than consideration of the *role* of the government lawyer. Richard Kluger's book *Simple Justice* tells an equally compelling set of stories about powerlessness and being a lawyer. Consideration, by almost any lawyer, of the moral richness in the lives of other lawyers he admires, tells more about the moral aspirations of the admirer than the most elaborate recital of his principles.

The last point suggests another teaching device, the study of the professional conversion of the law student as he is being changed from a person who says "those lawyers" into a person who says "we lawyers." The device involves self-conscious study of the way a student feels about his teachers, his classmates, his courses, his school, and the lawyers he sees acting in the cases he studies. I have used, to good effect, student journals. I quote some of them in this chapter. Andrew S. Watson has suggested that law students be encouraged to talk in class about the way they feel about the parties and witnesses (and lawyers) in the cases they discuss. The idea is that the student see himself, and study himself—read his own story, as he is living it. One way or another, we lawyers need to learn how to test our stories against truthfulness and against our inevitable tendency to delusion, especially to the delusion that being a lawyer is in itself a moral way of life.

CHAPTER SEVENTEEN
Law Faculties and the World

The mission of a prophet is moral witness to (and usually within) an institution (Chapter 10). From a Jewish and Christian point of view this witness is through institutions to people. My argument in this chapter is that American law faculties are to the American legal profession what the Old Testament prophets were to Israel. I propose to make the argument with a New Testament story.

The last chapter of the Acts of the Apostles is the account of Paul's arrival in Rome. It is an account of three institutions, of their moral impact, and of a prophet within them. Here is the Pharisee, Saul of Tarsus, arriving a privileged prisoner of the Romans. His letter to Roman Christians has preceded him. And now he has come himself to be a religious leader for as long as the Roman bureaucracy can bear having Christians around. The Roman Christians come out of the city to meet him. The first meeting he has inside Rome is with the leaders of the Jewish community.

When it is convenient for the state to blame its failures on him and his followers, it will do so. Paul has two years of pastoral work ahead of him in Rome, five or six years of life altogether. After that he will go to his death at the behest of a mad dictator, as his Jewish brothers and sisters went to similar deaths, in similar circumstances, twenty centuries later.

I am interested in the three institutions Paul served—the Roman state, the nation of Israel, and the congregation of Christians in Rome. He had and used the advantages of membership in each of these institutions; he owed fealty to each of them and gave it. He was, in each of them, a prophet.

Law professors live, as Paul did, in a civil society, in a heritage of valued traditions, and in colleagueship with those who do as we do in pursuit of what might be described as a common belief. Belief is probably a metaphor here, but any law teacher who has grown to love his colleagues will see the point, even if it is only a metaphor. What we have in common is more a story than a set of dogmas; I am suggesting that our fealty to this story is what makes us a community and that one can talk about the fealty and the community with the metaphor of belief.

The State. Paul was a Roman citizen. He made claims upon and was a victim of the powers of this world. He was in Rome because of his privileged civil status; he had appealed to Caesar. And before his appeal he had demanded protection from the Roman army. But for his citizen status one or the other of the three factions which made up the Sanhedrin in Jerusalem would have disposed of him, as they had disposed of Jesus and of James and Stephen. Saul of Tarsus had been one of the persecutors of Stephen, on behalf of the religious authorities from which Paul, the convert, had appealed to Rome.

Paul lived in this Roman civil society as a stranger, as each of us law teachers lives in a society of strangers. Such common bonds of theology as we Americans might once have had are common no longer. For example, it would not have been unusual a hundred years ago for me to write for American lawyers from the Acts of the Apostles, but I suspect it is strange to do so now. There is literally no purely moral claim we Americans can make on one another. All we have in common is the law, and the law is a matter of procedures, as, for Paul, Roman law was a matter of procedures. It was procedure that had seen him committed to the lenient charge of a Roman officer, procedure that brought him to Rome. The substance of Roman law, which was the defense of the Roman state through fear, did Paul no good except to grant him the ironic benefit, finally, of martyrdom.

The substance of the Roman law, which was the maintenance of an empire through fear, had no interest in Paul and he had no interest in it. He had appealed to power and to power only, and power had protected him in Jerusalem and Caesarea as it would protect him and then kill him in Rome. Being a Roman had no *significance*; it didn't stand for anything except law. Paul would have understood what Aleksandr Solzhenitsyn said about a moral community built on law: "Whenever the issue of life is woven of legalistic relationships, this creates an atmosphere of spiritual mediocrity that paralyzes man's noblest impulses." Paul appealed to law for safety—as Solzhenitsyn did—and then only for a while. He did not appeal to law for meaning. And we had better not do that either.

That is our first institution and Paul's: the state. It is the most prominent institutional setting for moral witness by lawyers, but it is no help in deciding what the witness should be. It is important not to confuse justice with force. Force comes from the government, but justice does not come from the government. Justice is the gift we give one another as we go about living under the law, and as we go about making the law fit our lives. Our truthfulness in doing this is where justice comes from.

Israel. Paul was also a Jew. The first thing he did in Rome was to address the leaders of the Jewish community. He made a claim on the heritage he shared with those leaders. He got them arguing about his claim, and particularly about his further claim that the person of Jesus was the fulfillment of Jewish heritage. "They went on from dawn to dusk. Some were won over by his arguments; others remained sceptical" (Acts 28:24).

This claim was not a legal claim in the sense that Paul's claim on Rome was a legal claim. It was not legal at all, really; it was prophetic, in the Old Testament sense of that word. His moral claim on the Jews in Rome was a claim on their deepest beliefs and the consequences of those beliefs. "He spoke urgently of the kingdom of God and sought to convince them about Jesus by appealing to the law of Moses and the prophets" (Acts 28:23).

Paul's relation to the Jews in Rome suggests to me an analogy between the modern American law teacher and the legal profession. Our moral claim on the profession is like the claim Paul made on Israel. We are at our best, morally, when we speak to the profession prophetically but from within the tradition the profession claims. Our calling as part of this second institution, the profession, is to provide reminders of the consequences of its pretensions.

Law professors, when they speak from this common tradition, depend upon a shared lawyer culture but they (we) also speak from a narrower part of the tradition and the culture, a part I am trying to treat with the metaphor of belief but which others might call scholarly objectivity or (a bit too pretentiously) a commitment to truth. There is something from which we speak when we lead movements for law reform, something the broader profession shares, in the sense that it is common to our professional undertaking as lawyers, but also something to which the teaching branch of the profession is specially committed. The common source and the special commitment explain, I think, the peculiar (and what I would call prophetic) office of law teachers in bringing about such massive reforms as the Uniform Commercial Code, the Uniform Probate Code, major movements in the modern law of civil liberties, and the introduction into the modern American legal profession of women and members of minority groups.

The legal profession is tragic, as all institutions are. It tends to the acquisitive protection of its own. It tends to the exclusion from membership of those who are different. It tends, as all guilds do, to define social welfare in terms best suited to the profit of its own membership. Even at its best it will not admit the tragedy of its own prerogative. When law professors speak to the profession prophetically, as they (we) are specially able to do, we speak to it as Paul spoke to the meeting of Jews in Rome: "You may hear and hear, but you will never understand; you may look and look, but you will never see. For this people's mind has become gross; their ears are dulled, and their eyes are closed" (Acts 28:26–27, quoting Isaiah 6:9–10).

We law-school lawyers in America are somewhat less than three percent of the legal profession in our country. The prophetic claim we make on American lawyers is the claim of a small unrealistic minority. Listen, for example, to the recent attack on adversary ethics of one of the greatest of our prophets—Professor Harry Jones:

> If unbridled partisanship, single-minded and ... no-holds-barred, is unacceptable in the other affairs of life, is it acceptable in the context of the lawyer's professional functioning...? If the *Code of Professional Responsibility* is to retain the idea of partisanship as the measure of the counselor's obligation, it should be for some far better reason than that the all-out partisan model enables lawyers to participate as advisers in morally-dubious enterprises without being criticized for it and without feeling uneasy about it themselves.... Somehow it must be made plain that the lawyer's moral judgment is not for hire, that there are occasions when the lawyer as counselor is under a duty to act as a person of independent ethical concern with obligations not only to his client's interest but also to fairness and justice in the management of affairs.

What Jones is doing, it seems to me, is insisting that the profession step outside itself, criticize its own rules, and amend its traditions. The fact, though, that justifies my treating this sort of speech as prophetic and as a kind of belief, is that such talk, from such an unrealistic minority, is often effective. Law professors have the power, not in any way explained by their numbers, to call the profession to its senses.

The Congregation. Finally, Paul came to the church in Rome, and we come to our own most organic institution: the law school, our colleagues. This is the place where we are most likely to be deluded. The more insistent our moral witness in the society, the more likely are we to become smug about the corruption and tragedy of the academy.

My life among my own is an organic life. Here I learn the pain in being prophetic because I am always one of those who is addressed. My colleagues are partners in my prophecy as well as the objects of it. My relationships within the law faculty are based on faithfulness more than on rules. When Paul wrote ahead to the Christians in Rome, he delivered a polemic against rules. "Law intruded," he said, "to multiply lawbreaking" (Romans 5:20). And yet each of the little churches Paul tended in his ministry—Ephesus, Corinth, Philippi, Rome, Galatia, and the others—fell into contention and error as soon as he turned his back.

Each of the churches hit upon some way to certify its superiority over other people and to exclude the heathen. Each of them did what institutions always do—it drew lines, cast out deviants, and built pedestals. Each of them forgot its purpose. Paul railed against this tendency when he railed against the law—meaning the system of rules which the Jewish Christians inherited. When Karl Barth came to translate Paul's word "law," and to give it meaning for Christians in the twentieth century, he translated the word "law" as "church"!

The Christians were arguing, for example, over the issue of eating meat which had been sacrificed to idols. The vegetarians were well on their way to casting out the meat eaters. Paul said to them: "No one of us lives, and equally no one of us dies, for himself alone. If we live, we live for the Lord; and if we die, we die for the Lord. Whether therefore we live or die, we belong to the Lord.... Let us therefore cease judging one another, but rather make this simple judgment: that no obstacle or stumbling block be placed in a brother's way" (Romans 14:7-8, 13).

The idea and practice of tenure is a contemporary, agony-filled law-faculty example of the obstacle and the stumbling block. Tenure can be the occasion of moral growth within the academic fraternity—as abstinence from meat sacrificed to idols was in Rome—and a source of its corruption. It is either an opportunity to honor the collective aspiration of the Letter to the Hebrew Christians, "We ought to see how each of us may best arouse others to love and active goodness" (Hebrews 10:24), or a device for training young law teachers to hate one another. For the last four years, and particularly in university-affiliated law schools, the tenure system has come up against tight funding, an expected decline in enrollment, and a diabolical, recent invention called the tenure quota. A tenure quota is a limit on the number of members of a faculty who may have tenure. Because the American tenure system requires that a teacher either be given tenure or be fired within a stated period of time (typically six years), a quota comes to mean—not logically, but corruptly—that untenured members of the faculty have to be fired whether or not they are doing well. They must be fired because it is said that there are no places for them, and there are no places for them because the institution wants to save places for new or better teachers who have not yet come along.

The result is destructive competition among sisters and brothers, even in institutions which proclaim fealty to the ethics which demand that "no obstacle or stumbling block be placed in a brother's way." Young teachers who have professional interests, careers, and even neighborhoods in common can normally be expected to arouse one another to love and active goodness. However, when they are told that only half, or a third, or even fewer of them will be rehired after their probationary periods end, they tend to see advantages in cutthroat competition and even—some few of them—in less honorable paths to glory.*

The central problems in a brotherhood are that we sisters and brothers no longer see what we are doing; we forget how we come to be sisters and brothers in the first place. What we law teachers tend to do is to sanctify ideas of exclusive fraternity that are at worst wrong and at best tragic. And what we forget is that the way we treat one another has its effect on how each of us grows in active goodness and is, also, the principal moral model for our students on how lawyers should treat one another, as the way we treat our students is the principal moral model on how lawyers should treat their clients. We are, collectively, prophets—false prophets, sometimes.

Our ideas of rank, scholarship, academic freedom, tenure, effective teaching, community service, and faculty governance have tended to protect an insular white male oligarchy. They *tend* to do that—at worst they do it; at best they tend to do it. It is impossible to stand for anything without standing against something. It is impossible to recognize those who exemplify what we stand for without excluding those who exemplify something else. At best it is impossible to stand for anything without that sort of exclusivity, and that is what I mean when I say that at best our institution is tragic. The moral consequence is that we tell the truth about what we are doing and find out thereby if we want to do it—if we *should* do it. The great opportunities of our lives in this third institution are the opportunities of ministry in a community.

Here we can deal with one another in the ethics of fidelity, because we can see a possibility of being faithful. That possibility has been lost in the broader civil society: We live there, as Paul lived within Roman civil society, according to law. The ethics of fidelity are also unlikely in the broad professional society we have with other lawyers, because we who inhabit university law schools have chosen to separate ourselves into the academy. Teachers of medicine, by contrast, have not separated themselves into the academy, so that their moral witness has no prophetic character about it—they cannot be prophets. The result is that philosophers and theologians are hired to teach ethics in medical school. Morals are a specialty in medicine. If morals are a specialty in law, we professors are the specialists. We professors are prophets by our own choice—and false prophets sometimes.

---

*Law teachers moving into tenure have been compared to associates in law firms moving into partnership. But law partnerships have not been widely tempted to the adoption of quotas for advancement of associates; partners like to say, on the contrary, as senior law professors should also hope to say, that there is no obstacle but personal limitation between being an associate and being a partner. They like to say that there is benefit in associates helping one another.

Here we can still try to tell the truth to one another. Three truths that occur to me are that we are dependent on one another in our growth in active goodness; that we are professional models for our students—moral models; and that our fraternity, in its exclusivity, is at worst corrupt and at best tragic. But, even so, it is in these small organic, congregational institutions of ours that we are able to search for and revive the roots and consequences of a morality that has more to it than the suffocation of the law or the pretensions of professional ethics.

PART FOUR
Institutions

Introduction

Conscience deals with power in institutions. This part of the book explores that fact in reference to Thomas More's meeting power in sixteenth-century England, Franz Jagerstatter's meeting power in twentieth-century Austria, and my own meeting power in church institutions. Discussion of Tudors, Nazis, and Baptists may be too remote to be useful for lawyers in the 1980s, but I don't think so. I find a resonance that may connect themes here in Charles Morgan's experience in Alabama, both among those who are victims of America's institutions and among those who live the sedate life of a business-oriented law practice. Charles Morgan, in talking of this strange diversity, calls his professional life a matter of "law against order." Regarding conscience dealing with power in institutions, Powledge says of Morgan:

> The Birmingham law firm that Morgan had joined after finishing law school was one that specialized in municipal bonds, securities, corporate transactions, and taxes. He soon started handling cases for indigent defendants in his spare time. The state required at that time that a lawyer be appointed to defend anyone who, if found guilty, might be faced with the death penalty. "They didn't care, at first, what I was," Morgan has said. "At first, all they wanted to do was to put a body up there in front of the bench to defend the indigent. The body got one hundred dollars. I asked my law firm for permission to go out and handle criminal cases like this. I thought this would be something for a lawyer to do. As a matter of fact, I thought it was what lawyers were *supposed* to do."
>
> He defended a Negro man accused of murdering a Negro woman by first stabbing her and then beating her with the barrel of a shotgun. It was not the sort of case that a young attorney might hope to make much of a reputation with. The victim was a widow with four children, all living on welfare, and, what was more, she was paralyzed from head to foot on one side of her body. Also, the slaying had occurred at high

noon before a dozen witnesses. The defendant, whom Morgan has described as "one of life's losers," finally pleaded guilty, and in time died in jail of natural causes. But when in the preparation of a case that seemed utterly hopeless, Morgan conducted an exhaustive search for facts that could help his client in any way, or at least provide some explanation for his actions. "I was learning something about the ordered society I had grown up in.... After only a year of the practice of law in Birmingham, I had seen that for some there was no peace in our valley. There never really had been."

CHAPTER EIGHTEEN
Thomas More's Skill*

The seduction of power is as perennial as the threat of power spurned. Power is a medium for good and evil. Lawyers and politicians and their victims come and go, but the moral problems of how to use power, how to live with it and leave it behind, remain. I am interested, in this chapter, in adapting an attempt Hauerwas and I have made to suggest that the special way a lawyer uses power is through the virtue of skill and the skill of virtue.

The use of power is a moral problem. One inquiry about the problem is to ask how a virtuous person uses power in an institution, and lives there close to power, without losing the sense of self necessary to negotiate the temptations of power. We asked that question with respect to Thomas More (our effort was a present to him, on his five hundredth birthday), particularly with respect to the Thomas More of Robert Bolt's play *A Man for All Seasons*. We proposed to offer an account of the character necessary to maintain what Bolt's More called "that little area in which I must rule myself." We contend that consideration of More's character is a way to learn how to be honest about power and still to hope. We try to show how More's hope involved moral and intellectual skill—skill in the use of power, skill in serving power in such a way that he was not consumed by it, and skill in knowing when to spurn power and then to accept the consequences.

More was attractive to the dramatist because More's public life is a puzzle. There does not seem to be any satisfactory explanation for his decision to spurn power when he did—in the midst of a hard-won and successful public career, at a time when men of moral substance all around him adjusted themselves to the demands of the new English nation-state. The task of that generation of leaders was a titanic task. They learned how to live with a concentration of national power that, begun in More's childhood, has maintained itself for five centuries. They learned how to live with the central fact of modern history—

---
*Written in collaboration with Stanley Hauerwas.

nationalism—and More did not. More, who was a practical political man, a subtle schemer, a loyal servant of the principal actors in the policy of his time—Cardinal Wolsey, Henry VIII—declined the opportunity to be a titan. His spurning of the patronage of king and archbishop seems arbitrary if not perverse. The conventional way to account for it has been to explain it as martyrdom—that is, as an admirable stubbornness not quite accessible to practical reason.

A modern way to deal with the absurdity of More's "exit" from power is to regard it as eccentric—to view More as an existentialist hero defending, as Bolt's preface to the play said, an "adamantine sense of self." That explanation is as inaccessible to practical reason as martyrdom is; the difference, perhaps, is that the martyr hears the voice of God and the existentialist hero hears only his own voice. We contend that it is possible to suggest a deeper account for More's spurning of power. If one attends to the kind of hope that formed More's life, one can, we think, sketch a continuity between More's legal and political life and his turning away from power. Martyrdom, or the adamantine sense of self, is then a consequence of More's life rather than an explanation for it.

The crucial point to be made is that none of us can afford to be without the kind of hope that formed More's life. Few of us will be called to do what More did, but hope is important to any moral life and to all moral lives. Thomas More and those like him remain our masters in learning how to hope. We are not likely to learn enough about how to hope by reflecting abstractly on what hope is or on how hope relates to other virtues (such as faith and love). We can learn—we do learn—more when we look to those whose lives were hopeful; we learn not whether to hope, but how to hope. Our claim is this: Not only does hope employ and give the basis for certain skills, but it *is* a skill. It is a skill one learns. We do not learn to lay bricks without guidance from masters; neither do we learn how to hope without guidance from masters. The acquisition of a skill involves, usually, an initiation into a way of life. A master, who has gone before, usually presides over the initiation. Put in language Hauerwas has used elsewhere, we need a *narrative display* in order to understand how it is we should hope. From this perspective, the traditional theological virtues—faith, hope, love—are best understood as reminders of the narrative of the master, Jesus, a narrative that schools the self to serve God rightly. Such virtues become distorted if they are treated as independent norms for behavior. If the moral life is inseparable from the life of wisdom, then, in spite of a modern attempt to secure an independent status for "morality," our moral lives as lived continue to depend on the existence of masters. In this sense, we refer to hope as a skill and the use of skill as a way to hope.

There is a difference between *hope* and *optimism*. Optimism is not hope as we mean to talk about hope. Optimism differs from hope in that optimism can exist without truth. Because it can exist without truth it is defeated and perverted by power. Hope, when seen as optimism, is, in the poetic phrase, dashed.

An optimistic person whose "hopes are dashed" becomes a cynic. He becomes a cynic because he lacks a truthful way to locate and protect "that little area in which I must rule myself." Cynicism gives him a way to do that without requiring that he worry about the truth. Cynicism thus promises a check against power, against the persons, institutions, and roles that claim our lives. Both the hopeful person and the cynic have found a way to stand back from their engagements; but cynicism stills the imagination against the possible and therefore protects the cynic without requiring that he be truthful. The price of cynical protection is self-deception. The cynic abandons the human burden of deciding what is true and what is not; he does this by refusing to believe in anything. His optimism is fragile because he lacks the skill to turn optimism into hope; his refuge is a state in which he deludes himself into thinking that neither hope nor truth is necessary. He comes to believe that the moral life can be lived on negative premises. Cynicism leads to despair, because it is impossible to live a life based on negative premises. Despair is to hope what hypocrisy is to truth: Hypocrisy proves how much we need truth in our lives; despair proves how deeply we need hope.

In this way, despair could be seen as the result of optimism out of control, of overextension, of absolutizing the range of optimism, of having so much need for hope that one is willing to trick himself into being optimistic when, with skill, he might have learned how to be optimistic and truthful at the same time—to be, in a word, hopeful. This is, perhaps, what Aquinas meant when he numbered among the temptations to despair "the mere excess of good," which makes "the difficult good impossible to obtain."

Despair is the condition in which one no longer looks for alternatives. Cynicism leads to despair because cynicism does not look for alternatives truthfully. Optimism leads to cynicism because it does not pay attention to truth. Hope, as we are talking about it, as based on truth, forces the imagination to look for alternatives. If we are unable to look for alternatives we are forced to rely on power. *Hope is therefore an alternative to reliance on power.*

More's life illustrates how hope is an alternative to reliance on power. The point can be made in a preliminary way by comparing More's behavior in the play with the behavior of Cardinal Wolsey, Thomas Cromwell, and the Duke of Norfolk. All four men lived in circumstances in which power was available to them, but only one of them ultimately refused to rely on power. In all four cases, opulence, arrogance, "clout," and deference received tempted powerful men to a narrowed sense of what was possible. It was thus that power corrupted and, in the case of a fifth character, the king, absolute power corrupted absolutely. As Camus said, "[T]he truth is that every intelligent man ... dreams of being a gangster and of ruling society by force alone." Hope varies inversely with the extent to which power seems to be the answer—as it seemed to be the answer to Wolsey, Cromwell, the duke, the king, and Camus's gangster. This is not to say that hope varies inversely with the attainment and exercise of power; those who hold and wield power can be hopeful people, as More was. What we mean to say is that hope varies inversely with the absoluteness of one's *trust* in power. Hope declines as trust in power increases, and this seems to happen because hope declines as one's sense of alternatives narrows.

Our thesis is that More's response to power is an example of the hopeful life—the life lived truthfully and therefore with hope rather than with optimism; the life lived with a broad sense of alternatives to power and therefore without reliance on power. Bolt's play is the story of a hopeful life. More is particularly interesting for this book because he was both a Christian and a lawyer. The molding of a Christian lawyer's life is a power-centered task, and for this reason moral admonition addressed to the powerless—in, for example, Paul's letter to the Christians in Rome—at first seems useless. And such secular admonition addressed to lawyers as there is—in, for example, our *Code*—tends to a narrow sense of alternatives to power. Being a Christian and a lawyer seems to be a matter of learning about power and conscience, since lawyers wield power, even when they do not have it, and Christians wield conscience.

The lawyer's life is a problem when subjected, as a Christian life, to the New Testament. The New Testament is not about using power, but about how God provides the means to live hopefully rather than powerfully. Barth said of the New Testament, "What it impels the Church towards—and it is the Holy Spirit moving in it who does this—is agreement with the direction in which it looks itself. And the direction in which it looks is to the living Jesus Christ." But Jesus was not a lawyer (anything but), and almost none of the Christian lives traditionally given as examples to Christians were lawyers; almost all of these lives were lives of powerlessness. It is important that lawyers, and anyone who thinks about the way power is used in the United States (i.e., by lawyers), seek such examples as there are of the limits and possibilities of power in a Christian lawyer's life. More's life is a Christian lawyer's life. His martyrdom, in that respect, seems a paradox—and is—but our idea is that his martyrdom was a consequence both of his being a Christian and of his being a lawyer.

Thomas More was finally crushed by power, but we are attracted to him because his hope and his life, both of which he fought to save with every technique possible, were finally sustained by what Aquinas called the "arduous good" the world's possibilities cannot encompass. And thus More learned to hope, and the hope that guided his life gave him the freedom to see the world as it was and as it might be. This is demonstrated by his response to the Act of Supremacy:

> Roper: There's to be a new Act through Parliament, sir!
> More: ... Act?
> Roper: Yes, sir–about the marriage!
> More: Oh.
>
> * * *
>
> Margaret: (Puts a hand on his arm) Father, by this Act, they're going to administer an oath.
> More: ... An oath! ... On what compulsion?
> Roper: It's expected to be treason!
> More: (Very still) What is the oath?
> Roper: (Puzzled) It's about the marriage, sir.
> More: But what is the wording?
> Roper: We don't need to know the (contemptuously) wording–we know what it will mean!
> More: It will mean what the words say! An oath is *made* of words! It may be possible to take it.... Then let's get home and look at it.... God made the angels to show him splendor–as he made animals for innocence and plants for simplicity. But man he made to serve him wittily, in the tangle of his mind.... Our natural business lies in escaping–so let's get home and study this Bill.

More's hope allowed him to "escape" and thus to "act" more than most of us. But finally, it also helped him know when escape was impossible if he was to secure that area in which he had to rule himself. So long as truth is possible, hope is possible and, from the perspective of a lawyer like More, skill is possible; skill is hope and hope is skill.

Hope and skill. The ordinary hopeful way to deal with power is to apply to it the arts of the mind. Since More was a lawyer, this meant that More met power with *analysis* and with *knowledge.* This explains, and is illustrated by, More's confidence in his own ability to outwit his persecutors. He sees this ability as important, so important that he is willing to extend the protection of the law (that is, of analysis and knowledge) to the devil himself. He is willing, as a modern would say, to extend "due process of law" all the way to hell. One reason he is willing to do that is that he needs legal protection for himself or, to put that another way, if the legal protection is left intact for everybody, even the devil, More's persecutors will never be able to get More. That is a familiar argument for those who want citizens to support the rule of law.

However, Bolt sees More as doing more than simply trying to save himself:

> Margaret: Father, that man's bad.
> More: There is no law against that.
> Roper: There is! God's law!
> More: Then God can arrest him.
> Roper: Sophistication upon sophistication!
> More: No, sheer simplicity. The law, Roper, the law. I know what's legal not what's right.... The currents and eddies of right and wrong, which you find such plain sailing, I can't navigate. I'm no voyager. But in the thickets of the law, oh, there, I'm a forester. I doubt if there's a man alive who could follow me there, thank God.

This is more than survival. This attitude of More's is a kind of witness. More had hope not only for himself but for his time and for his society. It was a lawyer's hope. One could sum it up by saying that he, like almost any lawyer at almost any time, hoped that his society would preserve law – that is, government under law. Government under law was, and is, a radical idea. In England it finally led to the spectacle of the king himself being torn from the seat of power, deposed, and killed, because the king himself (Charles I) was seen as lawless. When More says, in the play, that "the law is a causeway upon which, so long as he keeps to it, a citizen may walk safely," he aspires more than describes, but he does aspire; he does have hope for his country.

The fact that More had this hope, that it was more than a hope for his own survival, and that it was a lawyer's hope is enough to make him a hero. (His use of cleverness to save himself, even to save his truth to himself, would perhaps not be enough to make him a hero.) But there is a further sense in which More's witness was both lawyer-like and heroic. More was bearing witness to the truth about the nature of power in the world. His witness went beyond the procedural idea that every person should have the full benefit of due process of law. His witness was to the truth that human governments are limited, that however much power they have – King Henry VIII had – they have less power than they think. "The King in Parliament cannot bestow the Supremacy of the Church because it is a Spiritual Supremacy!" After he finally says that much, and only after he makes that principal point, does More add that the Act of Supremacy also violated English law.

In any event, so long as the state followed the law, More was confident that he could cope with its power – to save himself, to save a fundamental legal principle, and to save the idea that governments, too, should be truthful about themselves. He was confident because he had hope *as skill*. Skill does not confront power; it calls power to rationality. It does not appropriate power, either. It is the special business of lawyers—this skill in the face of power—and lawyers rarely *have* power. Lawyers *use* power; they manipulate power. They do not possess it. One reason Bolt's play is so popular among lawyers, particularly among American lawyers, is that it exalts this use of lawyer skill.

Skill, character, and knowledge. This lawyer skill is not a matter of principles. Lawyers use legal principles, but they use them more to garnish their work than to carry it out. Lawyers, when being candid, admit scant regard for legal principles. Nonlawyers may think that lawyers disdain principles, or that we disdain the idea of government under law. But the lawyer thinks of legal principles as something to be taken apart and made to fit the client's needs. The lawyer thinks this work *is* government under law. Principles and facts are the lawyer's raw materials. What is sacred in the law is not legal principles. The sacred thing in the law, to a lawyer, is the fact that those who have power are bound to respect skill and knowledge in the wielding of power—skill and knowledge even among those who merely wield power, who do not have it. This is, at last, we think, the political side of a respect for *character*. With regard to what is *legal,* principles come last. Thomas More understood that. He lived it. It was important to him. Bolt understands that; it is part of the reason he thinks that More's life might stand up as an illustration of the courage to preserve one's soul—one's unbudgeable self—in the modern world.

Skill seen as hope is both larger than itself and smaller than itself. Larger, because skill seems here to be exalted into virtue, and, beyond any particular virtue, into character. The idea of skill, which might suggest facility at making omelettes as well as facility at making arguments, seems unable to bear this much moral weight. But skill can be made to bear moral weight when it is seen in the life of a person who is both skillful in hope and hopeful about his skill. More's was such a life, as were the lives, say, of Daniel Webster who, in story, could draw goodness from the depths of hell (Benét's play), or of Abraham Lincoln, whose aspiration for government *for* the people is precisely this idea of skill as hope at the service of an entire culture (a *people,* in the biblical sense).

Skill is also smaller than itself. It is a matter of craftsmanship, about which the craftsman will have aesthetic standards—matters of taste. It is important, particularly when one thinks of lawyers, to see skill, lived with hope, as character. And it is useful, again when talking about lawyers, to narrow the focus and analyze skill as a matter of craftsmanship and taste. Much of Bolt's genius (as the teller of More's story) consists in his way of describing More as a person who dealt with power, habitually, as a craftsman. And craftsmanship is important. A lawyer's craftsmanship calls for some of the best that is in him and some of the best that the grace of God adds to what is in him. Bolt's More had a respect for craftsmanship as a matter of taste; he disdained its absence as a kind of stupidity. He also had a respect for craftsmanship as a matter of hope—of the virtue of hope. He disdained its absence as a kind of despair. Both points are illustrated, in the play, when More tells Wolsey that Wolsey's Machiavellian diplomacy is not necessary:

> More: (Crisply) [after reading, at Wolsey's request, a letter from Wolsey to the Vatican] It's addressed to Cardinal Campeggio.
> Wolsey: Yes?
> More: Not to our ambassador [which would have been proper, as ignoring the ambassador is improper].
> Wolsey: Our ambassador's a ninny.
> More: (A smile) Your Grace appointed him.
> Wolsey: (Treats it as the level of humor, mock exasperation) Yes, I need a ninny in Rome! So that I can write to Cardinal Campeggio!
> More: (Won't respond; with aesthetic distaste—not moral disapproval) It's devious.
> Wolsey: It's a devious situation!
> More: There must be something simple in the middle of it. (Again this is not a moral dictum; it is said rather wistfully, as of something he is beginning to doubt)

More regrets the absence of craftsmanship because Wolsey's use of deviousness seems distasteful and also because Wolsey's behavior evidences a lack of skill, *that is, despair.* But Bolt directs the actor to suggest a deeper regret, too. There is more here than craftsmanship and good taste. The theme of the play is in this scene. More is beginning to doubt the success of lawyer skill in the matter he and Wolsey are discussing: the king's marriage. More's hope is that the use of skill will save something. He thinks of saving his own life and of saving a way of life.

Another art of the mind that can cope with power is knowledge—knowledge in the sense of an intellectual command which liberates, makes one less afraid and therefore better able to look power in the eye. English law in More's day was a recondite and complex body of knowledge—as, perhaps, law always is, since its office is to analyze principles and principles do not yield easily; they offer too much security for that.

More knew that knowledge can often confound power, even when knowledge has no power of its own. An anecdote illustrates this. When he was a law student at Bruges, one of the professors there invited any comer to debate him. He would, he said, dispute any question in science. More asked him whether beasts of the plow, taken in withernam, were capable of being replevied. The professor could not deal with that; Erasmus, who was present, said the professor retired "with his withers wrung and More's withernams unwrung." Knowledge, in situations like that, is not power; it is a way to deal with power. More, who had that sort of knowledge and knew he had it, could find what he had more useful than his belief in principles of right and wrong: "The currents and eddies of right and wrong, which you [Roper] find such plain sailing, I can't navigate. I'm no voyager. But in the thickets of the law, oh, there, I'm a forester."

So long as law is able to hold power at bay, More is dead certain that he and his way of life will be all right; he has humility about himself as a lawyer—humility which, in this case, means that he sees himself, without illusion, as a superb lawyer. He also has humility about law itself. He knows that the time may come when the law itself will not protect him. Late in the play, power is brought to bear on him lawlessly, i.e., through perjury, planned and executed by the state itself. Early in the play More knew that that time might come. That is possibly the meaning of his hint to Wolsey that he is beginning to doubt whether the simplicity of skill and knowledge is dependable. More senses a swelling of power his skill will not be able to contain. In that swelling, of which Wolsey and Cromwell will be victims as much as More, power will destroy unless it is appropriated. This new power will not yield to law; it will be popular and irrational. (It will be—and is already—the power of nationalism.) Bolt illustrates this point, in the play, in the character of the Common Man. When Roper says to More that all of England is buzzing over the matter of the king's divorce, More replies, "The Inns of Court may be buzzing. England doesn't buzz so easily." When England buzzes, More's humility tells him, discussions of the writ of replevin will not hold power back.

The point is that analysis and knowledge will go a long way toward containing power. That is the most elementary hope that law has—law as something to live, as lawyers live it.

The despair of character and characters of despair. Despair decides that the mind and the arts of the mind will not be enough when, with hope, they might be enough. (An American example is Thurgood Marshall and the small group of lawyers who, in the early 1950s, assembled the precedents and set out to demonstrate that *the law* required an end to school segregation.) This despair shows up in other characters in Bolt's play; he uses them to give background to More's hope and to make Thomas More, *as a lawyer,* interesting. As examples:

Bolt's *Wolsey,* naked to his enemies, no longer has power. He struggles to save himself with old arts of deviousness that are not only unattractive and unnecessary but also futile. Deviousness is despair; it is untruthful (because unnecessary and futile); it is contrasted in the play with More's character. More's character is fashioned with habits of skill as hope and of hope as skill.

Bolt's *Roper*—who was, as a matter of history, clever enough to save some of More's property from the relentless Cromwell—yields to the despair of violence. In Bolt's drama he holds the place of the Zealots in the gospel. More's (and Jesus') lives are lives of hope and therefore of peace. This life of peace is not so much a matter of convictions and certainties as it is a matter of *character*. More says to Roper, "Will, I'd trust *you* with my life. But not your principles. You see, we speak of being anchored to our principles. But if the weather turns nasty you up with anchor and let it down where there's less wind, and the fishing's better. And 'Look,' we say, 'look, I'm anchored . . . to my principles!' "

Thomas *Cromwell* was an abler man than Bolt portrays him to be. He followed More to the block, but his family held high power in England through the reigns of the next half-dozen kings and queens. The curator at the Frick Museum probably had it better than Bolt does, historically, when he put Hans Holbein's More on the left side of the fireplace, Hans Holbein's Cromwell on the right, and El Greco's Saint Jerome above them in the center. (More would have enjoyed that arrangement.) But, for Bolt, Cromwell is a study in the despair of corruption. Cromwell destroys people—destroys character in people—and that is about as despairing as a person can be. Cromwell's is the delusion Karl Barth calls "the syndrome of the two kingdoms"; Cromwell seems to suppose he can lead a decent private life which, in public, follows "chance or laws of its own." Bolt's Cromwell speaks of "the constant factor" of giving the powerful what they want; government is more accommodation, he says, than corruption. "Our job as administrators is to make it as convenient as we can." Bolt is an old-fashioned (and, we think, accurate) moralist when he poses that delusion as the essence of evil.

The *Common Man,* not a historical figure—or, rather, the most historical of them all—despairs of virtue and lives as if the only value were survival. It is he who keeps the world going, who says, at the end, "if you must make trouble, make the sort of trouble that's expected." He proves that evil is banal.

In each of these cases, the absence of hope is despair about skill and knowledge. In a narrow, dramatist's sense, Bolt makes More's story interesting and finds it meaningful by touching on More's lawyer qualities and making them resound far beyond themselves, so that they approach what Paul meant when he told the Christians in Ephesus that his prayer for them was that they realize the hope to which they were called and the power that was theirs by virtue of hope. "This power in us is the same as the mighty strength which he used when he raised Christ from death, and seated him at his right side in the heavenly world" (Ephesians 1:20).

CHAPTER NINETEEN
Thomas More's Hope*

> *Rarely are we able to be the intelligent spectators of an historical event, more rarely still its actors. At such times the darkness lightens and the space contracts until we apprehend the rhythm of our daily actions as the rhythm of a larger welcome which has included us within its composition.*
>
> Iris Murdoch

Bolt's More had three critical moments in his hopeful dealing with power. The first occurred when he was faced with the king's and bishops' decision, as he put it, "to declare war on the Pope." The second occurred when the power of the state began to be applied to force him to take the oath. The third occurred when the state, sunk in the despair of corruption and of the delusion of the two kingdoms, concocted perjured evidence—gave up the game, so to speak—and confirmed More's martyrdom.

More reacted differently to each of these events. When the state took to force (the second crisis), he used the skills and the hope we talked about in the last chapter, in terms of analysis and knowledge. His reaction to this pressure is the main focus of Bolt's play and it is what makes the play, and More himself, interesting to modern American lawyers. When the state corrupted its use of force with perjury (the third crisis), More reacted (in fact and in the play) as Jewish and Christian martyrs always have. He knew how to act, because his hope was faithful. In a sense, his reaction then was based on faith more than hope—faith, in Barth's phrase, as "hope against hope." More saw God—"love right through"—reaching to draw down the curtain. He proclaimed the Kingdom, as his Lord had, and he accepted his happy sentence with relief. The climax of the drama, and of his life, was the realization of

---
*Written in collaboration with Stanley Hauerwas.

the glory he had avoided: "If he suffers us to fall to such a case that there is no escaping then we may stand to our tackle as best we can, and yes, Will, then we may clamor like champions ... if we have the spittle for it. And no doubt it delights God to see splendor where he only looked for complexity. But it's God's part, not our own, to bring ourselves to that extremity! Our natural business lies in escaping." When the time came, More spoke his mind about the King and the Act of Supremacy, and Cromwell (and the world, as it always does) said: "Now we plainly see that you *are* malicious!" And power killed him. More's sentence of death is not the climax of the play, though, because his death is—even in Bolt's view—a settled matter of Cross and Resurrection. Rather, the climax of the play is the clash between hope and despair.

The first of the three crises, the resignation, is the one that interests us as we consider a different way in which hope deals with power—the way of *confrontation*. More resigned as chancellor rather than get involved in the case of the marriage. In our reading of the play (and of More's life), that was a matter of his refusing to "work within the system." There seems to have been no need for him, as a matter of conscience, to step out of his position so early in the game. He did so against the king's urging. It was possible, at that point, that the case might still have been resolved—as so many royal marriages had been with Rome—without the Act of Supremacy and the creation of a separate English church. It was nothing new for a king to declare war on the pope, and few Christians felt it necessary, as Christians, to take sides in such wars. There was in the marriage case room for the application of the hopeful skills of analysis and knowledge, both as to the king's attitude (what lawyers call counseling) and on behalf of the king (what lawyers call advocacy). Why, then, did More resign with such imprudent finality?

The reason seems to be that More knew that hope required his retreat from that situation. Optimism was possible, for all the reasons mentioned in the last paragraph. But those reasons could not survive the *real* test of hope in the face of power, the test that says hope must be truthful. Hope must keep a sense of the alternatives to power. Optimism—hope without truth—is not sufficient for dealing with the pretentious powers that determine a person's existence in the world. The use of power can be a hopeful art, but only so long as the use of power is not an end in itself. Hope—that is, the person who lives a hopeful life and lives it well—knows the limitations of power. It knows that optimism needs the truth. The hopeful life must bend to the demands of truth or it will (by a paradox as certain as the fact that power corrupts) lose its hope, become mere optimism, then lead to cynicism and finally to a despairing life.

We have been talking about power as if it were often a clear menace, and at best a circumstance. Power may also be an incentive to delusion, a subtle temptation. Power as delusion is a peculiar risk for lawyers, and especially modern American lawyers, because power seems to offer a way to improve society. Lawyers are always being asked to bend a little so that power can work and things can be made better; lawyers are always being told—always telling one another—that the essence of their profession (what we have been calling the hopeful skill in it) lies in working within the system. We are always being told that someone has to do the job, that if we don't do the job someone worse will do the job. Things have to be done in office that cannot be done with moral comfort in private life, but that is the way office (including the license to practice law) is. The words for *that* play are, "Somebody has to do it," or, "What else are you going to do?" This is a play about the syndrome of the two kingdoms. It is interesting to us that Thomas More declined the temptation even when he knew—or maybe *because* he knew—that he would be good at acting in that play.

Truthfulness and compromise. We are talking about a compromise with truthfulness, a compromise demanded of public persons, that comes about because the person who makes the compromise is optimistic. It is important to notice what we mean by compromise. It is not compromise, in this sense, for the public person to adjust his views to the views of others when there seems to be no clear right or best thing to do—when, in other words, he needs their views as much as they need his, when all of those most immediately involved are seeking truth. It is not compromise, as we mean it, to commit oneself to the discovery of the truth through a willingness to share the variety of ways people discover when they set out to lead good lives. What we mean by compromise is an agreement to bracket one's basic convictions in order to achieve certain limited ends. Compromise, as we mean it here, assumes that *the good society is based on power.* Compromise is what we talked about in the last chapter as the despair of Thomas Cromwell. It needs to be distinguished from respect and civility and the concessions people make when they work together on the assumption that *the good society is based on truth.* As Bolt states in his preface and illustrates in his play, compromise asks the loss of self; we think that it also destroys the possibility of good societies.

Compromise is destructive because it becomes institutionalized and accepted as a proper way of life. When that happens, the distinctions between the public and the private, between the kingdom of the world and the kingdom of God, become a sign of despair. The distinctions come to say that the social world cannot be held together by truth. A society afflicted by the syndrome of the two kingdoms raises up leaders who have trained themselves to believe that their public roles *are* their selves, who define themselves by roles (e.g., the role "lawyer"). They are compromised before they enter the fray. When this happens, as it may well already have happened to us Americans, it is no longer honest to distinguish between the public and the private person. Privacy has already been voluntarily offered to feed the public role. There is no private person left. Power, as requiring the surrender of the private person, is what Bolt saw More struggling with. Power threatened the private, adamantine sense of self More sought to save. "There's a little ... little, area ... where I must rule myself."

Here, virtue is a tangled trail through a dark forest. The practical man or woman of affairs tends to believe that it is egocentric not to make the compromise. Refusal seems to betray hope (optimism). To be unwilling to compromise is to cease to be effective, and it is important to be effective. The way power corrupts is by gradually convincing those who have power that the most important thing is to be effective. Thus, for most of More's contemporaries in the English establishment—including even Alice More, his wife, and Margaret Roper, his daughter—More's refusal to remain in office seemed to be a betrayal of hope; he seemed hopelessly to abandon his public role, the possibility of reform in the government, and the possibility of saving England from schism over the marriage.

More's choice to resign seems to us, though, to witness that a choice against compromise is a hopeful choice. Hope, unlike optimism, retains a sense that there are alternatives to power. Hope, unlike optimism, is truthful. Hope, like love, rejoices in the truth. Compromise would have required delusion. Beyond that, More's choice seems to say that living hopefully—that is, truthfully—has social consequences *beyond* his sense of self, because social consequences are dependent upon the maintenance of the self—on, that is, a decision to live truthfully.

Our conclusion from this is that More's was a hope that knew that effectiveness cannot justify power. Only goodness can justify power. Faith and love can join hope because *the truth is* that God is "love right through." Because this is the truth, Paul sees the Roman Christian, in a sweeping paradox, as "rejoicing in hope" (Romans 12:12). "The great hope God sets before men compels them to demonstrate against the course of the world," Barth said. "But is there any one who does not hope? What is it that makes of our hope an ethical action? Surely, it is our rejoicing!"

More's quiet confrontation, when he resigned as chancellor, was not quiet at all. All that followed was implied in the resignation—so that the resignation itself, and More's willingness at that point to speak his mind to the king (that is, to speak the truth about the marriage), *was* a confrontation with power, rather than a choice to exercise skill in wielding power. That would then seem to have involved More's own realization that his hope, because it was truthful, could not avoid confrontation with the power of the world. Bolt seems to understand the point. He wants More to have that realization early in the drama. He hints at More's limited expectations for craftsmanship when More talks to Wolsey about the letter to Rome and when More intimates to Roper that lawyers' gossip is not serious but that gossip that "sets England buzzing" will be serious and will be a force that cannot be contained by skill or by knowledge.

The point is that the powers of the world fear the truth and fear those who trust in truth to guide their way. Power sustains itself by resort to violence (as in the play), which means that it always fails to sustain itself. Power cannot face its own powerlessness, and truth's (hope's) demand is that power face its own powerlessness. The incongruity between truth's demand and power's need is the reason people such as Thomas More become martyrs; they are, as Cromwell would have put it, an administrative inconvenience. They too vividly remind those in power that their pretensions to rule the world really are pretensions. The gospel seems to pose an alternative: Those who wield power must either comprehend that God is the Lord of our lives or resort to violence as a means for denying that God is the Lord of our lives. The truth is that the Kingdom is here, whether the world says so or not.

Speaking of hope as a virtue that depends on truth, and of confrontation with power as a necessity to be expected in the lives of those who wield power but who try to live truthfully, may suggest that the hopeful person is one who forces the world to violence. That issue has to be dealt with. If More was one who forced the world to violence, then he was deluded when he said, "I am the King's true subject, and pray for him and all the realm.... I do none harm, I say none harm, I think none harm. And if this be not enough to keep a man alive, in good faith I long not to live.... And therefore, my poor body is at the King's pleasure. Would God my death might do him some good."

It is not the *intention* of the hopeful person to force those who would rule to resort to violence. To live so as to force violence would be itself to fall into despair. It would be self-righteous and anarchic. That view of the hopeful person would deprive us of needed heroes, from Socrates to Martin Luther King, Jr., and Cesar Chavez. But, at least for Christians, hope does not provoke violence because our hope is grounded on the conviction that in the life and death of Jesus Christ God has shown once and for all that his love is deeper and more profound than the evil we find in the world. We trust that this is the case. Not to trust that it is would abandon the world to sin and thus deny that *God's work* has been effective.

Thomas More, as we see him with respect to this issue, was committed to hope as skill—that is, to working within the limits of power as far as he could. And this was a long way. So long as the state (Cromwell) was minimally honest, More's skill kept him (More) from the scaffold. And, in More's case at least, it kept the state from violence. However worldly-wise he may have been, More was convinced that the power of truth ruled over the power of sin and fear. He was thus committed to public life, and to the idea that his business lay in a lawyer's skill, because he was convinced that it is in and through our everyday commerce with one another that God's love is known.

Viewed this way, More can be understood as knowing that a refusal to "work within the system" was not only a matter of conscience (which is always admirable but sometimes seems to suffer from a tinge of solipsism), but a *social* responsibility. More's act of conscience was not something discontinuous with his work as a lawyer or as a chancellor. He saw the act of conscience as required by and consistent with the character of his public commitment. More trusted the law because he insisted that he must be able to live in a society that could be trusted, and he had an obligation to stand by what he knew as the truth because the truth is finally the only safeguard a society can have. Societies need a trust that is grounded on truth. Without it, violence comes all the sooner.

Society's dependence on truth. Thomas More could equivocate on much of the conceptual content in the issues he faced—or, at least, he played a diplomatic game of disguising truth in ambiguity. But he refused to take the oath. Equivocation stopped there. That was because for him oaths reach to the heart of what society is, to truthfulness itself. "When a man takes an oath he's holding his own self in his own hands." A society that does not demand truthfulness is a society that cannot be trusted. In our view, More's understanding of the necessity to maintain a sense of selfhood—"that little area in which I must rule myself"—was not so much the unique act of the existentialist, authentic man, as it was the normal obligation of all people—*all lawyers*—who seek to live in a truthful society. An untruthful society is not only dangerous but corrupting. It encourages those who live in it to distrust one another.

And the reason More, the statesman who resigns, cannot forsake his own conscience for the sake of public duties is not only because he wishes to maintain personal integrity but because personal integrity *is* a public duty. A leader who does not insist that we be truthful leads us to moral chaos. He may trade in optimism but he does not trade in hope. His leadership may take the appearance of stability, but that is only because it trains people for roles in which they are not capable of being truthful, roles in which they dare not hope.

More's hope was built on the conviction that truth finally transcends power. His hope insisted that our existence, and in particular our social existence, is held by a power beyond that of the state. Because of that conviction he was schooled in hope and his hope was not diluted by those who were optimistic. The time for him to begin refusing to attempt to use power was the moment he began to have to be untruthful, to sacrifice the truth that was the ground of his hope. Two generations later, English lawyers would remind the king of Bracton's thirteenth-century principle, *non sub homine, sed sub Deo et lege*,* but it may have taken the blood of More, and other lawyers, for England to get that far.

More's claim that God is "love right through" was not only a "religious claim" but a political statement. Such love, which is beyond skill and knowledge, is the necessary condition for society because it provides the self with the depth that is necessary for the social order. It is important that we understand this point, because this is the answer to the common misinterpretation of More's refusal to condemn anyone who did take the oath. It is at best anachronistic to make the liberal assumption that More thought that a good social order should allow freedom of conscience in the sense that each conscience is private. (And Bolt is not so naive as to suppose otherwise.) The reason that the first duty of every loyal subject is to be loyal to his conscience is not that conscience is an end in itself, but that the subject's failure to be true to himself is a failure to be true to the love that provides us a basis for being able to trust and share ourselves and to accept the trust of others.

More would say that the reason one must stand on one's conscience is not that the state is just, but that it is not just. Thus, in response to Margaret's argument that he is trying to make himself a hero unnecessarily, he says, "That's very neat. But look now ... if we lived in a state where virtue was profitable, common sense would make us good, and greed would make us saintly. And we'd live like animals or angels in the happy land that needs no heroes. But since in fact we see that avarice, anger, envy, pride, sloth, lust, and stupidity commonly profit far beyond humility, chastity, fortitude, justice, and thought, and have to choose, to be human at all ... why then perhaps we *must* stand fast a little—even at the risk of being heroes."

Margaret answers, "But in reason? Haven't you done as much as God can reasonably *want?*" And More says, "Well ... finally ... it isn't a matter of reason. Finally it's a matter of love."

Thomas More's confrontation with power came about because he was truthful and because he insisted on hoping that truth is deeper than the optimism of those who too quickly resolve differences

---

*"Not under man, but under God and the law."

through the use of power. More was not seeking martyrdom. He was not even seeking an argument—the issues, as he saw them, were too serious for that. He was seeking, and insisting on, the existence of the truth. The fact that the truth led to his death is not an indication that More's convictions were mistaken. It is an indication of how deeply our institutions are built on fear.

CHAPTER TWENTY

Franz Jagerstatter's Hope

> *The complicity of Christians with Auschwitz did not begin with their failure to object to the first slightly antisemitic* [sic] *laws and actions. It rather began when Christians assumed that they could be the heirs and carriers of the symbols of the faith without sacrifice and suffering. It began when the very language of revelation became an expression of status rather than an instrument for bringing our lives gradually under the sway of "the love that moves the sun and the other stars." Persons had come to call themselves Christians and yet live as though they could avoid suffering and death. So Christians allowed their language to idle without turning the engines of the soul . . . their lives were seized by powers that they no longer had the ability to know, much less to combat.*
>
> David Burrell and Stanley Hauerwas

Franz Jagerstatter was a farmer and parish sexton in the village of Saint Radegund, a part of the district in Austria that produced Adolf Hitler (Braunau-am-Inn) and Adolf Eichmann (Linz). Jagerstatter was exceptional, if at all, only for a somewhat more pronounced piety than the villagers ordinarily thought necessary for agriculture and for relatively strong misgivings about the *anschluss* of 1938 and the growth of national socialism, in the fragments in which Nazi politics was manifested in rural Austria. He was married, the father of three children, and the support of his mother.

Jagerstatter was summoned for compulsory military training in 1942; he reported and served an obedient novitiate in the German army. In 1943 he was ordered to the seat of his diocese, Linz, for induction into active duty. When he arrived at the induction center he refused to accept service or to take the oath required of noncombatant soldiers. His stated reason for refusing service was that Hitler's war was unjust and that a Christian could not fight in it. He was arrested, imprisoned, tried by a military tribunal for the statutory crime of resisting the war effort, and sentenced to death. On August 9, 1943, in Berlin, Jagerstatter was beheaded.

Jagerstatter acted against moral advice. As nearly as one can tell from the documents and interviews on which his biography is based, no one who claimed special learning in ethics—no pastor—encouraged him in his conscientious objection. All of the official representatives of Jesus Christ from whom Jagerstatter sought help in his agony told him the right thing to do was to fight for Hitler. It is remarkable that he retained his conscientious objection, that he refused to fight for Hitler, that he went to his death instead and left five dependents without support—all the more remarkable when you consider that he was poor and rural, worked with his hands, was not well educated—a simple Catholic in a Catholic country. The world supposes that such people are dependent on the clergy for religious decisions.

Interviews about Jagerstatter, statements from those who knew him, taken after the war, fall into two general categories in terms of explanations offered for his choice. Most of the priests from whom he sought advice said that Jagerstatter was not a fanatic; the first priest he talked to, a temporary curate in the church at Saint Radegund, said that he thought Franz to have been "thoroughly sound in his approach to religious matters." That was also the judgment of other priests who helped him, including the prison chaplain, and was true as well of Jagerstatter's lawyer. Laymen, on the other hand—Franz's neighbors—said they found him too pious. They admired his fealty to conscience, but they thought he was odd.

Saint Radegund has its curious symbols of these attitudes toward the village martyr. Jagerstatter's name is on the war memorial there; his ashes are buried in a place of honor in the churchyard, with the remains of the fifty-three sons of the village who died fighting for the Third Reich. The clergy seem to be saying that Franz has to be placed safely within their tradition, and the village seems to be saying that he has to be placed safely within the war. It seems to have been important, both to those who saw him as sound and to those who saw him as odd, to make him a part of their history—possibly because they cannot bear a memory of him which says that the church, the village, and those who died in Hitler's army should *not* have been a part of that history. Saint Radegund's Christians know they should not have been in—have been—a church that tolerated Hitler; they should not have been loyal soldiers in Hitler's war. Therefore Jagerstatter can be a hero only if he is made into an eccentric or a collaborator.

The truth is that Franz Jagerstatter was not a fanatic and that he was a witness not for the church but against it. His reasons for refusing military service are calm and clear; they don't appear to be eccentric. He said, for instance, on several occasions that he could not support a regime that was persecuting the church. His belief that Hitler was persecuting the church must have embarrassed clerics who had, at the beginning, opposed national socialism, and even had denied the sacraments to its adherents, but who had found it possible to advise loyalty after the party began winning elections. The same argument had been made, much of it in Germany, after 1933 by Karl Barth, who said that the evil in national socialism was that it could not exist with the church; it had to replace the church. Nazism was, he said, "the deification of Caesar." I say this to illustrate that Jagerstatter's argument was not the argument of a fanatic, and not because I suppose that Jagerstatter, whose reading was sentimental biographies of saints, had read Barth on the point. (Catholics were as a matter of morals forbidden, then, to read Protestant theology; their church could countenance union with Hitler but not the theology of Calvinists.)

Franz also told more than one person that he refused to enter the army because it involved too many temptations to an unvirtuous life. These remarks seem hardly consistent with his acceptance of military training, or, for that matter, with his acceptance of prison. They might be understood as conversational arguments, but I think they are marks of a searching conscience, a conscience struggling for answers, especially struggling for answers *from the church*. Jagerstatter had begun to understand where he was being led—as Thomas More had begun to understand even before his resignation from the woolsack, and as Judge Horton had as early as when the young doctor talked to him personally. They had begun to see that they were being led, but they had not yet found a way to explain where they were going. Jagerstatter was confused. He is not a hero from hagiography; he is a real hero.

Another explanation for Jagerstatter's choice is that he was a pacifist. He had contact with members of the Jehovah's Witnesses; his cousin was proselytizer for them, and no fewer than twenty members of this curious group of objecting Christians had been killed for refusing to accept military service. Their theology on the point is a theology of pacifist noncooperation. Jagerstatter's bishop, writing after the war, argued that Jagerstatter's position was similar, and then concluded, on the apparent assumption that Jagerstatter had adopted Jehovah's Witnesses theology on the war, that, although "all respect is due the innocently erroneous conscience ... for the instruction of men, the better models are to be found in the example set by the heroes who conducted themselves 'consistently' in the light of a clear and correct conscience." Jagerstatter's biographer meditates for a while on this male playground identification of morality with virility; he even compares it with an argument, opposite in effect but similar in method, from Thoreau: "Must the citizen even for a moment, or in the least degree, resign his conscience to the legislator? Why has every man a conscience then? I think we should be men first and subject afterward."* It is better, I think, to identify the false assumption in the bishop's reasoning than to argue with him about what "being a man" means; the bishop assumed that Jagerstatter was a pacifist, when the evidence is that Jagerstatter was an old-fashioned Roman Catholic following traditional Roman Catholic theology.

Jagerstatter's biographer, Gordon Zahn, is convinced, principally from the village interviews, that Jagerstatter would have taken up arms against Germany had the *anschluss* been decided the other way. Jagerstatter was the only citizen in Saint Radegund to vote "nein" in the referendum on *anschluss;* he thought union with Hitler was wrong. His view of the morality of military service depended on his faithful understanding of traditional Catholic teaching on the just war. He was, as we came to call them in the Vietnam War, a "selective objector." The fact that there were few selective objectors in Catholic Austria in those days—Jagerstatter, before he died, only learned about one other—is evidence that clergymen such as his bishop were more interested in election returns than they were in their moral tradition. The traditional explanation for Jagerstatter's martyrdom would be that he believed the German army was waging an unjust war and—more important—that the individual Christian, once he had reached that conclusion, was obliged to resist his own country's war effort. Jagerstatter's dying words were, "I cannot and may not take an oath in favor of a government that is fighting an unjust war." "Naturally," he had written a year or so earlier, "the words sound sweet to our ears when we are told that others bear the responsibility for the results."

Because Jagerstatter had been convinced that the Nazi regime was unjust before it even became a regime, his conclusion that its wars of conquest were unjust was hardly surprising. His immediate problem was not this intellectual judgment, but the question of what he should do about induction. His experience, his reading, and his introspection all argued for resistance, but, like Thomas More, he was unwilling to resist if there was a moral alternative. More's careful position on the oath demanded of him by Henry VIII was that he refused the oath but refused also to risk greater royal displeasure by explaining why: "I feared lest the King's Highness would as they said take displeasure enough toward me for the only refusal of the oath. And that if I should open and disclose the cause why, I should therewith but further

---

*More's aphorism was better—"The king's good servant, but God's first."

exasperate his Highness, which I would in no wise do, but rather would I abide all the danger and harm that might come toward me, than give his Highness any occasion of further displeasure than the offering of the oath unto me of pure necessity constrained me."

Almost everything Zahn's considerable research unearthed argues against Bishop Fleisser's flippant postwar conclusion that Jagerstatter "thirsted for martyrdom and for the expiation of sin." The more persuasive conclusion is that Jagerstatter thirsted for pastoral advice against martyrdom but that he was honest enough to know complicity when he saw it, even—or especially—complicity by the church. "[T]here is no longer any likelihood that there will be a bloody persecution of Christians here, for virtually anything the Nazis want or demand Christians will yield," he said. "Almost all of us are quite willing to glut ourselves on the spoils of thievery, but we want to saddle the responsibility for the whole dirty business on one person alone!" His essays and letters are filled with a desperate cry for courageous guidance:

> I cannot turn the responsibility for my action over to the Führer.
> No one wants to accept responsibility for anything.
> One really has no cause to be astonished that there are those who can no longer find their way in the great confusion of our day. People we think we can trust, who ought to be leading the way and setting a good example, are running along with the crowd. No one gives enlightenment, whether in word or in writing.
> If road signs were ever stuck so loosely in the earth that every wind could break them off or blow them about, would anyone who did not know the road be able to find his way? And how much worse is it if those to whom one turns for information refuse to give him an answer or, at most, give him the wrong direction just to be rid of him as quickly as possible!
> If people took as much trouble to warn men against the serious sins which bring eternal death, and thus keep them from such sins, as they are taking to warn me against a dishonorable death, I think Satan could count on no more than a meager harvest in the last days.

One is reminded of Lewis's remark about Gethsemane as the model for martyrs—lonely, inadvisable, a death without honor, and no place for a gentleman.

None of the professionals wanted to see Jagerstatter die. None counseled him that his accepting death rather than military service was subjectively sinful—although many, including his bishop, continued to say, even after the war, that Jagerstatter was in error. The argument made to him—by village curate, prison chaplains, bishop, defense counsel, and military judges—was that he should think first of his farm and his family. And Jagerstatter answered: "[I]f I had ten children, the greatest demand upon me is still the one I must make of myself."

They even argued that there was a distinction between defense of the Fatherland and support—incidental support, perhaps—of a regime that could be overthrown after the war was won. But Jagerstatter found it impossible to support the regime without bearing guilt for what it did. "Many people believe quite simply that things have to be the way they are," he said. "If this should happen to mean that they are obliged to commit injustice, then they believe that others are responsible." Across Europe, Jean-Paul Sartre thought similar thoughts, which might have been, in a way, harder, because Sartre did not look, as Jagerstatter did, to an assurance of victory beyond the grave. Sartre said: "What is not possible is not to choose. I can always choose, but I ought to know that if I do not choose, I am still choosing.... I am responsible for myself and for everyone else. I am creating a certain image of man of my choosing."

Jagerstatter's choice, although he made it in faith, was, like Horton's or More's, an utterly lonely one. In all of the months he faced death, while at every moment he could have escaped death with the moral rationalization urged upon him by his confessors and his bishop, he found only one moment of objective encouragement—the news that Franz Reinisch had been executed for the same crime. The evidence, mainly the observations of persons near Jagerstatter when he received this news, is that it had an enormous influence upon him. The effect that a word or two of encouragement meant to a resister in those dark days is described by Sartre: "Because the Nazi venom seeped into our thoughts, every accurate thought was a conquest. Because an all-powerful police tried to force us to hold our tongues, every word took on the value of a declaration of principles. Because we were hunted down every one of our gestures had the weight of a solemn commitment."

But no other word of encouragement came to Jagerstatter. The Roman Catholic church had long since capitulated; Jagerstatter said, "For us Austrians, our Maundy Thursday was that infamous April 10, 1938, the day the Austrian Church let herself be taken prisoner, and ever since, she has lain in chains. And not before this *Ja* (which even then was given very hesitantly and anxiously by many Catholics) is balanced by resounding *Nein* will there be for us, too, a Good Friday. We are already being called upon to die, but not for Christ."

The important things to notice about Jagerstatter's witness, in this book about being a Christian and, of all things, a lawyer, are that his act was a political act; that his act was a witness against the church; and that his courage and character, formed as they were without professional help, without the professional ethics More and Horton had, have something important to tell lawyers about the sources of our information for making moral judgments about power.

Political act. The people of Saint Radegund made Jagerstatter a war hero. The churchmen of Saint Radegund made him a saint. And both argued that the reasons behind their purposes was that he was loyal to his conscience. Both parties made the error a modern liberal makes in respecting the consciences of others. It is easy to treat a martyr as a conscientious objector. It is more than just easy—it is too tempting, because it is a way to avoid treating the martyr as a bearer of truth. Neither people nor priests in Saint Radegund wanted to look upon what Jagerstatter said and did as a statement of the truth. If what Jagerstatter said was the truth, then the sons of Saint Radegund who died for the Third Reich died in support of evil; it would be they, and not Jagerstatter, who would have to be explained in terms of obedience to erroneous conscience. If what Jagerstatter said was the truth, the church had failed to be a witness to God's lordship; it had, in fact, witnessed to the opposite view of power. It was particularly important for the church to discount Jagerstatter's truth because the *sin of the Catholic church* cannot comfortably be explained by talking about loyalty to erroneous conscience. So it is better, from the church's point of view, that Jagerstatter be seen only as a saint, an exceptional person, like Joan of Arc. It is understandable that the leaders of the church might not comprehend the admonitions of a Joan of Arc, but not so understandable if they fail to hear the truth when it is spoken to them by a farmer.

The important thing about Jagerstatter's truth was that it was political. John Calvin's explanation of his preference for democracy—in the political order, at least—was that "the vice or imperfection of men ... renders it safer and more tolerable for the government to be in the hands of many ... that if anyone arrogate to himself more than is right, the many may act as censors and masters to restrain his ambition." The state exists, in the first place, to restrain mankind's tendency to sacralize itself; democracy exists to restrain each ruler's tendency to sacralize himself, the aspiration being that those who participate in government—and, I think, in Calvin's view, it was impossible for a citizen *not* to participate in government—tell the truth and be able to hear when others tell the truth. Jagerstatter's witness was then as much a political act as Horton's rejection of a racist verdict or More's rejection of the idea that Henry VIII could become absolute even over the church. Attempts to put Jagerstatter among the saints are as deluded as attempts to put him among the eccentric. Both are ways not to listen to the truth.

Witness against the church. The remarkable thing about Jagerstatter is not his martyrdom. That is remarkable only in context—the context being that the Christian church produced so few martyrs in twentieth-century Germany when it produced so many in first-century Rome.

The remarkable thing is that a person who was supposed to be docile in the face of clerical advice, and who believed in the teaching authority of the church, and whose reading was confined to biographies of the saints, could decide and then say that the church was wrong.

It is not remarkable either that the "simple people" of Germany and Austria were taken in by Nazi propaganda. The sources of information they had—particularly by 1942 and 1943—were efficiently dedicated to the accurate principle that "in the long run, people believe what they hear—if they hear nothing else." The most effective propaganda in those days did not even need to be false; news reports from the Russian front did the job. The remarkable thing, the pathos sounding through the understandable popular sentiment of Jagerstatter's time, was that the church *did not need to be silenced*; it had silenced itself. It retreated to its corner and contented itself with applauding those who fought for Hitler as "the example set by the heroes who conducted themselves consistently, in the light of a clear and correct conscience."

Jagerstatter's behavior in this climate is the point that interested Gordon Zahn, who compiled information on Jaggerstatter as, in part, a sociological enterprise. (Zahn is a sociologist.) Jagerstatter's was a "social background one would not ordinarily associate with such an overtly rebellious act," Zahn says. In his analysis of rebellion against authority, and of Jagerstatter as a curious kind of rebel, Zahn makes two distinctions—between on the one hand (1) a rebel who cannot identify himself with any institutional or historical position and (2) a rebel who looks for support to an institution to which he can remain loyal even while he defies his society; and, on the other hand, between (1) the church as an almost governmental institution, as part of "the power and dominion," as an institution which, like all institutions, finds it awkward to resist what civil authority does, and (2) the church as a community of believers that looks to its historical tradition for its sanctions rather than to the values of the society surrounding it.

Zahn decided that Jagerstatter was a rebel who sought his sanction in the life of Jesus and the stories of saints, rather than a rebel who had no historical identification at all. The institution (church) failed to encourage a similar communal reaction in others because it ignored its history. It takes no great sophistication in behavioral science to understand that; at any rate, Franz Jagerstatter appears to have understood it. "[M]ost institutions," as William James put it, "by the purely technical and professional manner in which they come to be administered, end by becoming obstacles to the very purposes which their founders had in view." But, to the devout Catholic, that sort of judgment about the church *as a community of believers* would be difficult. It is hard to see Franz Jagerstatter as rebelling against the church, but he clearly did rebel against something ecclesiastical. Zahn resolves the problem in terms of his second distinction—a distinction between the church as part of "the power and dominion" and the church as the people of God. "The Church with which he linked his refusal to serve was the Church of prophets and martyrs that had been abandoned and rejected by those who constituted the acting Church in Nazi Germany and Austria."

And so, Zahn says, Jagerstatter's action is explained as an act of loyalty to the church and an act of rebellion, out of loyalty, against two corrupt institutions—the Third Reich and the Roman Catholic Church in Austria. Zahn explains this by noting that Jagerstatter understood correctly the teaching of his Catholic moral tradition, that the Christian has an obligation to decide, for himself, whether the wars in which he is summoned to fight are just wars. "If the Nazi war effort did not meet the traditional requisite conditions of the just war, and I have seen no serious theological effort to prove the contrary, it would seem that ... the Bishop, not the peasant, and all of the Catholics he regarded as greater heroes were acting in erroneous conscience, that only Jagerstatter acted in accordance with the *objective* fact that Hitler's wars were not the just wars in which the Christian is permitted to bear arms."

Zahn used his analysis to make a point about the difficulties of the traditional just-war theory of military service. (It is probably a valid point; I think Zahn used it not only to explain Jagerstatter but also to explain his own conscientious objection to the Vietnam War.) The peculiar travail of the selective objector—who is not accommodated by American selective-service law any more than Jagerstatter was accommodated by the Nazis—is personal decision. Pacifism always requires courage and usually turns on faith; but selective objection seems in addition to require a victory over self-deception. A citizen who takes general moral comfort in the decision of his governors can go to war without guilt, while a pacifist, whose doctrine is that no war is acceptable, can go without guilt to prison or even to his death. In each case, the principle is settled. That is not true of the Jagerstatters of the world, who must find their principles in the facts and in their own hearts.

Sources of information. Zahn's distinction between the church as a tradition and the church as an institution, a distinction that allows him to explain Jagerstatter in terms of just-war moral theology, has something to be said for it, but it also diminishes the significance of Jagerstatter's lonely witness. Zahn argues for the distinction because he is intent to preserve the Catholic notion of what the church is. He is less reluctant than I am to see the church as sinful or as tragic. Treating selective objection as a matter of traditional moral theology is part of his difficulty, because that analysis suggests that the institutional church ought to support selective objectors when the fact is that it almost never has. The church of selective objectors is not like the church of pacifists because, when it comes to "the power and dominion," the church of pacifists is part of the solution and the church of selective objectors is part of the problem.

The church of pacifists supports its adherents out of church doctrine. You really shouldn't be in a "peace church" unless you're a pacifist. Since the pacifist doctrine is settled, it is part of what the church stands for; it is not vulnerable to hawkish patriotic delusion, because no war will do. Patriotism always supports war, as pacifism always refuses. However, this refusal is not characteristic of the mainstream (non-pacifist) church, which usually it lines up with the patriots and begins to talk about the honest but erroneous consciences of objectors. Lawyers who advised selective objectors in the Vietnam War saw this when our clients went before draft boards to seek conscientious-objector classification: Presbyterians, Catholics, Methodists, and Episcopalians were *not supposed to be* conscientious objectors; it was not as if they were Quakers or Mennonites.

Another way to look at this difficulty is that pacifists, since they can never be allowed to be more than a small minority of any healthy nation, do not have to be taken as speaking the truth. They can be—have to be—tolerated (or not) and dismissed. They have to be relegated to the class of deviants labelled as eccentric and religious, as if they were objecting to blood transfusions or insisted on wearing hats in the house. A selective objector is much harder to deal with because, except for his peculiar opinions about the war at hand, he comes from the mainstream. The draft boards seem to say that if Catholics, Methodists, Presbyterians, and Episcopalians did not, generally, and as a matter of theology, *approve* of the war, we wouldn't have one. An adherent of the mainstream Christian religion who objects to the war tends to challenge that certainty; he has to be classified as misguided or, after he is safely dead, as a saint.

I think, then, that it misses too much of the point for Zahn to put Franz Jagerstatter back into the mainstream church tradition. He belongs in that tradition only if he is seen as the rare Christian who pays attention to the implications of the tradition. It is better, I think, to see Jagerstatter's witness as a witness *against* the church, to see him as saying that the church's theology was right but that the church was wrong in trying to be the church and at the same time to be successful in the world. The Jagerstatters of our battered faith say, always, that the choice is between complicity with evil and the tragedy of bearing witness against the world and going on up to Calvary.

CHAPTER TWENTY-ONE
Tragic Communities

The word "attorney" means "someone who goes to town for you"—which in context means "someone who goes to *law with you,*" because the town where lawyers work is where the law is and, although your attorney goes to town for you, you can't send him alone. You have to go together. And so, even in the words we use to name ourselves, we lawyers are bustling back and forth between the powers that be and the beings who, because of the powers, have had to seek the companionship of a lawyer. The sense in which I would like to talk about our going to town, in this last chapter, is the sense in which the lawyer is an expert on communities, and an expert particularly in his coming to understand the fact that the community is sinful and tragic. I would like, here, to think about a lawyer as the representative of those who bear the burden of the community's sin and tragedy.

The scriptural image for this is the leper. It is clear, in scripture, whenever lepers are mentioned, that the community is either sinful or tragic and is probably both. The Mosaic law, which God gave when he made his covenant with Israel, established a community and then decreed that certain people be driven from it. The leper is a prototype. It is decreed that he "wear his clothes torn, leave his hair dishevelled, conceal his upper lip, and cry, 'unclean, unclean.' So long as his sore persists, he shall be considered virtually unclean...* He shall live apart and must stay outside" (Leviticus 13:45-46). Jesus touched such a person. He "stretched out his hand, touched him, and said '... be clean again.' " As a result, and as the law provided, Jesus became unclean and, as the law also provided, was unable to enter the towns openly. He—so to speak—lost his license to practice and then had to practice only on his license from the Father (Mark 1:42).

---

*That is, although he is not unclean, he is to be treated as if he were, so that the leper represents both the innocent and the guilty and shows—which is something like the thesis of this book—that there is no difference.

217

Communities are exclusive and cruel. A benign community—"community of believers," say, or "Christian community"—is a contradiction; it is, in the most radical sense, impossible. If it is to become possible, it will be because a miracle allows it to be in the first place and then allows it to continue. Jews and Christians call this miracle the covenant; Christians also call it Pentecost. This kind of community, which exists in the first place because of a miracle and which continues because of a miracle, will, despite the miracle and like all communities, be sinful and tragic. The difference is that the community that exists because of a miracle has a right to hope. I propose to talk about the community of the church here, but I think that what I have to say relates to more immediate lawyer communities in two ways. First, the church is a metaphor for communities such as law firms, civil communities controlled (as most of them are) by lawyers, and even voluntary associations in which lawyers work, as they think, for the public good. And, second, in a more specifically scriptural sense, when two or three are acting together, as Jesus said, "in my name," they are the church; this applies even to lawyers. They are sinful or tragic or both, but they are entitled to hope.

Sinful community. I grew up in the First Baptist Church, Fruita, Colorado (population—town, not church—1400). A Baptist congregation is an example of a sinful community, but one not surprised to be so. When President Carter was only a candidate and had been candid about his Southern Baptist faith, a newspaper reporter asked one of the Baptists in Plains, Georgia, about the theology of the Baptist church. "God knows men are a bunch of bastards," the Georgian Baptist said, "but he loves them anyway." This is not to say that the church in Plains or my boyhood church were unusually bad. In fact, my church was a good church and I was regular in doing what a boy in the church did. I went to Sunday school, studied the Bible, went to vacation school, put pennies in the little bank on my birthday, sang "Jesus Loves Me"—and believed it—and went to meetings of the Baptist Youth Fellowship. When the time came, I made my decision for Jesus, proclaimed to the congregation that he was my Savior, and was baptized in the tank behind the pulpit. That was a regular way to grow up in a community that thought it had a right to hope and hoped that it was right.

But my church also knew that it was sinful. The Baptist church failed to aspire and failed in its aspirations. Its principal aspiration was and is evangelism—to bring Christ to the nations. My church was smug and comfortable and did not work very hard at winning souls for Jesus (*or* at tending the lepers). We worked harder than most other churches did, but still not very hard. We deserved the tirade of Billy Sunday about churches and—this is the point—we *knew* we deserved it:

There we were, trying to bring that God-forsaken, whiskey-soaked, gambling-cursed, harlot-blighted town to her knees, and the church calmly looked on. I sometimes doubt that the church needs new members one-half so much as she needs the old bunch made over.... If I had a hundred tongues, and every tongue speaking a different language in a different key at the same time, I could not do justice to the splendid chaos that the world-loving, dancing, card-playing, whiskey-guzzling, gin-fizzling, wine-sizzling, novel-reading crowd in the church brings to the cause of Christ. There is but one voice from the faithful preacher and worker about the church, and that is, "she is sick"; but we say it in such painless, delicate terms that she seems to enjoy her being invalid. About four out of five who have their names on our church records are doing nothing to bring the world to Christ, and the church is not one whit better for their presence.... One of the great dangers, as I see it, is assimilation in the world, the neglect of the poor, substitution of forms for the facts of godliness, a hireling ministry, all of which summed up means a fashionable church with religion left out.

Much of this is quaint, and much needs metaphor before it is applied to the sinful communities of and under lawyers that I am talking about. But one point can be taken through almost directly, an old and fundamental point about revival preaching in America: The revival preacher was out, not to win adherents to the church but to win adherents *despite* the church. The metaphor is that lawyers do their best work despite the profession.

The failure of us Baptists at evangelism was sinful, and we knew that, and we knew we were forgiven. There were other sins the Baptist church did not repent of, which were therefore worse. For one thing, we were bigoted. Those the church did recruit it condemned. I can remember when my dad bought me a little burro—a Rocky Mountain canary—and pointed out the cross on the animal's back. That, he said, was there because Jesus rode on a donkey. I told my pastor's wife, and she said, "Who told you that? Some Catholic?" Her husband passed out anti-Mormon leaflets at the town park and said the Catholic church originated when Constantine forced baptism on the Roman army. Disgust at that sort of thing—disgust traceable more to adolescent rebellion than to moral indignation—caused me to answer a Knights of Columbus ad, and take instructions, and, at the age of seventeen, enter the Roman Catholic church. And it is in the Catholic church, still, despite everything, that I muddle along trying to ply my mere Christianity.

Conversion was a peak experience—maybe the first thing I had done all by myself—but it did not bring me into a purer community. I had exchanged one bigotry for another. I was required to recite a formula written in the sixteenth century, a formula that denounced

Protestantism, and I was required to be baptized all over again. The rebaptism is funny; if there is one thing they did well in my boyhood church it was to baptize people. Catholic ritual is, in that respect, a pale imitation of Baptist thoroughness. I cooperated in Catholic bigotry with enthusiasm, learned quickly to despise all the Protestants from Luther on, and revelled in the sound administration, ethical soundness, and correct teaching of the Catholic church. The earnest young priest who rebaptized me told me that God makes allowances for the invincible ignorance of Protestants but that he would not make allowances for me, if I should slide back to the Baptists, because now I knew the truth.

My new church also failed to aspire and failed in its aspirations. When it comes to neglecting evangelism, Catholics are much worse than Baptists. The New Testament is clear about the duty of Christians to bear witness, to speak of the Lord, as Paul says, "with our lips." Jesus did, and still does, want me for a sunbeam, as the song said in Sunday school. We Catholics listened at mass to the English translation (from the Latin, which was read first, officially) of the parable about the seed fallen on fallow ground, the light put under a bushel. We heard the mandate to preach the gospel to all people. But, looking around a Catholic parish in 1951, or now for that matter, you have to conclude that Catholics leave that sort of thing to priests and nuns, and priests and nuns leave it to missionaries (most of whom, in 1951, seemed to have come from Ireland). You hardly ever heard of a Catholic street preacher; there have been some, but the only one I knew about was Father John A. O'Brien, a stubborn apostle, evangelistic and ecumenical before his time, who made a spectacle of himself on the streets of Urbana, Illinois, in the 1950s.

For another thing, there is a pharisaism that is almost unique to Catholic parishes. (Christians always have to worry about pharisaism, I think—if they take Jesus seriously—because the Pharisees tried so hard and were such careful, pious people, and Jesus was so hard on them.) I found that the Catholic parish was turned in on itself. It disdained evangelism, which should have meant that Catholics were free to minister to one another instead of to the heathen, but Catholics didn't do that either. The local church was a filling station; people dropped in to get their holy fix, in Latin, and that was that. The oldest charge of the Reformation was that Catholic piety duped people into believing that they could make it to heaven through what they did, when the New Testament is clear: Christians make it into heaven because of what *Jesus* did. There isn't any way, ever, you can do that for yourself. If you think you can, you're a pharisee.

The metaphor is that groups of us lawyer Christians go along without mutual, self-conscious awareness of our being the church. We fail to speak with our lips to other lawyers or to clients, the simple economics of which neglect should leave us free to minister to one another; but we fail to do that too. We get our fixes at the altars of the world and pretend that our customary, cultural religious life is something that takes care of itself and is entirely private. "Fashionable," Billy Sunday would call it, "with religion left out."

The Reformation charge against the Catholic church was that it believed—or at least acted as if it believed—in a theology of works. Catholics thought that if they followed all the rules they would be all right. There is evidence for the charge in the little prayer books which were extant when I came into the Catholic church: The theology of works did seem, then, to be the operative theory. The irony was that the church managed to keep guilty all of those who were serious about the faith—to keep them guilty until, finally, they were told that it was a serious sin to be so scrupulous! And the Baptists, who knew that there was no way you were ever going to make it unless God, for Jesus' sake, looked the other way, were relatively relaxed. The Baptists, who were supposed to be especially evangelistic and outward looking, neglected evangelism and took better care of one another than the Catholics did. A Baptist church is a friendly place to visit. You are met at the door; you often even get a flower for your buttonhole. The minister will introduce you to the congregation—publicly if you give him a chance. You are met again as you leave and, in between, you are asked to come to the Lord. This, in an outer-directed church, contrasts in my life with the coldness of Catholics when they worship together in an inner-directed church. The life of the children of God is a thing of ironies, especially when they act together.

I say all of this to show that the church is sinful, and, in metaphor, that any community of earnest people, working together, is sinful. Irony is not the point here, except that irony gives us a way to look at all of this failure and to forgive ourselves and get along. The main point is that communities are sinful. There is nothing here that argues for or against the right of the church to exist. When Karl Barth spoke to the Augsburg Synod in 1935, when national socialism was strutting all around (and in) the German church, he said, "Christianity which wants the world to give it a reason, and indeed a justification for its existence, has come to an end." The issue of pharisaism no longer separates Christians as much as it did in 1951. We Catholics now know what Protestants knew when I was a boy—the terrible burden of freedom of conscience. We know, too, that Jesus is Lord. If you have him, you have it all. And if you don't have him, you don't have anything. We know that he comes to each of us, all alone; nobody can bring him to us, and nobody can keep him away. He died for me, and he loves me, as the Billy Graham hymn has it, "just as I am." There is nothing

I can do to make him love me, and nothing I can do to keep him from loving me. Everything else is politics, a politics which is sinful and tragic with a right to hope.

Tragic. Neither church made much of an issue about the poor or lepers. Both worried more about buildings than about the sick or those in prison. "We wonder why this old sin-blighted world is not on her knees," Billy Sunday said. "I am amazed that God is doing as well as he is, with the crowd he has to work with." But, when you talk about lepers, something else is at issue, something that is not to be called sin, but which I would call tragic. There is something in the issue about lepers that says that communities have to operate tragically, that they can't possibly avoid tragedy.

There were sound reasons to require the leper to live outside the settlement, and even sound reasons to require him to call out and to keep people away—so that they could not touch him and contract his disease. There were sound reasons, in Jesus' day, for Jews to avoid Roman soldiers and exclude tax collectors, who were Jewish lackeys for the Roman army of occupation. It is hard to see how the Jewish community could have taken in those jailers and collaborators and have remained a Jewish community; the scriptural history and tradition of that community was a history of having to exclude the heathen; and lepers, soldiers, and tax collectors were aggressive and therefore even more dangerous than heathen. You get a hint of how hard that issue was in the Acts of the Apostles, when God tells Peter to admit a Roman officer to the community. God literally wrestled with Peter over that—and Peter was the rock! He had seen the Resurrection!

Two examples here are the leper Jesus touched—on pain of himself becoming a leper—and the woman taken in adultery. Jesus did not tell the law professors who brought the woman to him that they were wrong to apprehend and accuse her. He did not even tell them that capital punishment according to the law of Moses is too harsh. He just took her by the hand and saved her. He became her lawyer and won the case, cleverly, even though she was guilty. The community had *rightly* condemned her; it could not have done otherwise and still have been what it was; but love lifted her, as the Sunday school song puts it. The point here is not a sentimental point; it is, in fact, a lesson in tragedy. Jesus seemed to concede that the rules of the community were inevitable and, if not inevitable, that they were proper. His action was consistent with the advice he gave to his more immediate Christian community on what to do with the sinner who would not repent after the whole congregation argued with him. "You must then treat him as you would a pagan or a tax-gatherer" (Matthew 18:17). In one case he set down a rule for the Christian community; in the other case, he acted despite the rule of the Jewish community but without challenge to the rule.

When Jesus announced the rule for Christians, he sounded tough in his concern for the community that is challenged by the stubborn delinquent: "Treat him as you would a pagan or a tax-gatherer." But it pays to notice how Jesus treated pagans and tax gatherers. The centurion whose servant he healed was a pagan, as was the officer Peter admitted to the Christian community. Matthew was a tax gatherer, as, apparently, were several others of Jesus' friends. Jesus' action toward pagans and tax gatherers is like his action toward the leper and the woman taken in adultery; he is, assuming the rules of the community, doing something spectacular about those whom the rules must condemn and exclude. He became a leper because he touched a leper. He became a criminal and took a criminal with him to paradise. He became the advocate for a guilty woman and won her case for her.

These New Testament stories illustrate what is inevitable about communities: They kick people out. The stories also illustrate two facts about Jesus Christ: (1) He saves those who are kicked out, even while (2) he does not change the community's rules. This is what I mean by tragic; I am using the word as Stanley Hauerwas uses it (in *Truthfulness and Tragedy*). Tragedy is the triumph of meaning over power. Jesus did not, in these leper stories, confront the community. He triumphed over the community by healing, not the community, but the outcast. What he does has meaning; the stories have meaning; and the meaning is that meaning triumphs over power.

In this sense the Christian community, the church—and, by metaphor, the benign communities we lawyers have and sustain—are contradictions. They have rules and traditions and try to stand for something. And they propose, in some collective way, to reach out and rescue the necessary, tragic victims of community. The issue, once the tragedy in these operations is clear, is how we are going to be a community and at the same time practice rescue operations that undermine the community's ability to stand for something. Any answer to the issue is bound to be a contradiction.

The Roman Catholic church has seen this contradiction played out again and again in the thirty years I have been a member of it. When Nancy and I were married, couples who practiced artificial birth control were out; you could not do that and be a Catholic. Now it is not clear how you can continue in the Roman Catholic church after you have committed the super sin of divorce and remarriage. The status of self-professed, practicing homosexuals is a similar question, for my church and for many others. Is it possible to reach out and include such people without giving up the doctrine that caused the problem in the first place? Is it possible for communities of lawyers to show special concern for deviants whom the law properly—or at least invariably—condemns? Probably not, although with God all things are possible. But, if it is not possible for a community to proclaim its values and at the same time to minister to those whose rejection is the language the community uses to proclaim the values, then the community has come upon its tragedy. (Not its sin; I don't claim that sin is inevitably the result of action in the world.)

Hope. Communities also need the apparatus we lawyers invent for them, and administer for them; but policies and structures, sound administration, correct teaching, and ethical thoroughness won't relieve the tragedy of communities. This is true prototypically of the Christian church and metaphorically of other communities, especially professional communities. Structures don't solve the tragedy of exclusion; they make it worse. Christians don't solve their collective problems with structures, even if the structures are necessary. Baptists understand that better than Catholics do. Karl Barth—not a Baptist, but more a Baptist than a Catholic—said of the church: "It need not die, if only it would not so grimly struggle to live." Even Catholics understand that now, better than we did in 1951.

Neither is planning the idea. Drafting new codes of ethics, for example, is not the idea. Hope is the idea. Hope is a combination of optimism and truth; optimism by itself is a lie; truth by itself is despair. Our optimism, in Christian communities of all kinds, is the promise of Jesus that he is with every two or three of us. Our truth is our understanding that the church, defined in this whenever-two-or-three-gather way, and so even the church including groups of lawyers, has to accept the fact that it is not possible to stand for something without causing pain. Optimism and truth come together in our hope to find a meaning for the pain and our hope that this meaning—the meaning of the stories of the lepers in our community life—will triumph over power.

There are a number of signs—in the Bible, most of them—of what the hopeful life in a benign community ought to look like. The benign community should stand against the world, for one thing. It is hard to explain a theory for standing against the world, since the community *is* the world; I find some guidance in the scattered political theology of Karl Barth, who said, first and foremost, that the Christian community (and, I think, the Jewish community) witnesses to the fact that real power is *not* in the world. "The Kingdom of God does not first begin with our movements of protest. It is the revolution which is *before* all revolutions, as it is *before* the whole prevailing order of things." He said that in 1919, when he was active as a Christian socialist. Thirty years later, when he was trying to make sense of what had happened in World War II, he said, "God has not abdicated his lordship over us. . . . All that is required of us is that in the midst of the political and social disorder of the world we should be his witnesses. We shall have our hands full simply in being that."

Being a witness in this sense is a matter of reminding the world of its relative powerlessness. Barth taught that this witness is not an ecclesiastical act but a political one. In 1932, as Hitler was coming to power, and Barth–a state-appointed German professor–was beginning to realize that Hitler represented something entirely unacceptable, Barth said that "the proclamation of the church is by nature political in so far as it has to ask the pagan *polis* to remedy its state of disorder and make justice a reality. This proclamation is good when it presents the specific commandment of God and not good when it puts forth the abstract truth of a political ideology." There are not two kingdoms in which people act, but only one. The witness of Christians (and Jews too, I think) is the witness that says that the power of the world (in state, in church, and in communities of all kinds) is limited. When Barth came, in 1935, to oppose Hitler openly and lost his appointment and was banished from Germany, it was because he condemned–violently condemned–"a totalitarian state which as such cannot recognize any task, proclamation, or order other than its own, nor acknowledge any other God than itself."

The primary witness a believer has to give in the world of power is a witness of limitation; I think this was the witness of Thomas More against the Tudor monarchy, the witness James Edwin Horton made against the popular sentiment that raged around the Scottsboro cases, and the witness Franz Jagerstatter made against the church. Christians (and Jews too, I think) can never be quite comfortable with the government, or the military-industrial complex, or the welfare complex, or the academic community, or the culture of lawyers. The drift toward comfort in the Protestant churches in the nineteenth century destroyed Christian polity in America. Theirs was not an issue about church and state; it was an issue about Christian witness in the communities of both church and state. Catholics did the same thing with different methods in Spain and Latin America. Jesus the Prophet is forgotten when Christian communities are comfortable; he slips out of town and lives with the lepers.

For another thing, a biblical community should be concerned about prayer. "We know," Barth said, "that the meeting place of God and man is not an arena where men crown each other with laurels or refuse to confer that distinction, but a point where God and man meet in order to separate and separate in order to meet. In other words, we know that we–all of us–can only fear and love and worship God." This is what we stand *for* as we stand *against* worldly power, as we witness its limitation. We witness real power as we witness the limitations of the power that, however powerful, is not real.

It seems, finally, that a biblical community will be among the poor. I don't know why Jesus harped so much about the poor; it was not that there was a lack of suffering elsewhere—the Pharisees were suffering; the temple priests were suffering; the Romans were suffering—but he did harp about the poor, and I suspect, but do not understand, that it had to do with his being Jewish. Jews—modern Jews, in America—are always, in significant numbers, among the poor. Jews in America, in significant numbers, are always buried in dams in Mississippi, in prison out of a protesting social witness, and among those who tell us that we cannot accept poverty in the midst of such wealth.

Afterword

This book has been five years in the writing and has been revised more than I want to admit. It has been difficult. I don't know what I would have done without the encouragement of my faithful friends Robert E. Rodes, Jr., and Stanley Hauerwas. I don't know, either, what I would have done without the forgiveness of sins—this in a personal sense and in theory. A writer about ethics meets a special challenge; the trick is to speak as a fool but to speak anyway. I also find, intellectually, as Barth said, that "the forgiveness of sins is the fundamental answer to the ethical question." Only because of this can I speak of law for the innocent.

I began this enterprise, and continue it, as a law teacher—nothing more than that, but nothing less. Not a word is written ex cathedra. How could it be? But every word is written because my students raise personal, confusing questions about being lawyers and Christians and Jews. My confusion was blessed, early on, by a group of law students at the University of Virginia, in 1975 and 1976. They were members of the Christian Law-Student Fellowship there and were enrolled in a group-study venture, in which I taught and learned, that was called law and religion. All of them are now about their professional apostolates; I think of them often as a special audience for what I write. They are Steven Agee, Richard Bersin, James Blane, Robert Cochran, Anthony Fussa, Jon Glenn, Croxton Gordon, Donald Lemons, Raymond Martin, Frank Rawls, George Reed, Dean Shahinian, Debi Standiford, Steven Whiting, and James Wootton.

My colleagues at Notre Dame and at Washington and Lee have inspired, admonished, corrected, and informed my work. I thank especially Joseph Bauer, Frank Booker, Fernand Dutile, Edward Gaffney, Peter Glenn, Roger Groot, Louis Hodges, Frederic Kirgis, Lewis LaRue, Andrew McThenia, David Owen, Daniel Snow, and John Yoder. Thanks, too, to Larry Churchill (University of North Carolina), James Childress (University of Virginia), Donald Klinefelter

(University of Tennessee), Richard Wasserstrom (UCLA); Nancy Shaffer, Thomas M. Shaffer, and Joseph Shaffer, at home; and Nancy Wesolowski and Margaret Williams.

This book was completed on a leave from Notre Dame supported by two generous grants, one from the Lilly Endowment and the other from the Frances Lewis Law Center at Washington and Lee University.

T.L.S.

Notre Dame, Indiana
Lexington, Virginia
January, 1980

Acknowledgments

The earliest version of this book was a manuscript of the same title completed in 1976. I have rewritten all of that manuscript and, in doing so, have used some of the original material in lectures and periodical articles. Much of the substance of those lectures and articles reappears here, although most of what appears here is different than it was in the lectures and articles. I am grateful for kind permissions from the following hosts and copyright holders:

"Christian Theories of Professional Responsibility," 48 Southern California Law Review 721 (1975).

The second annual 'Or 'Emet Lecture at Osgoode Hall Law School, York University, February 1979; later revised and published as "The Practice of Law as Moral Discourse," 55 Notre Dame Lawyer 231 (1979). Reprinted with permission. Copyright The Notre Dame Lawyer, University of Notre Dame.

"Guilty Clients and Lunch with the Tax Collectors," 37 The Jurist 89 (1977).

The inaugural Edward R. Rightor Lecture, Loyola University of the South, March 1979.

Roswell Gallagher Lecture, American Society for Adolescent Medicine, December 1976; later revised and published as "Advocacy as Moral Discourse," 57 North Carolina Law Review 647 (1979).

"The Administration of Justice as a Delusion," 31 Mercer Law Review 459 (1980).

"Moral Moments in Law School," 4 Social Responsibility: Journalism, Law, Medicine 32 (L. Hodges, ed., 1978).

"Law Faculties and the World," at a conference on religion, ethics, and law at Cornell University, April 1979; later revised and published in the Journal of the Legal Profession (1980).

"Hope Meets Power: Thomas More and the King of England," 61 Soundings 456 (1978); reprinted at 54 Notre Dame Lawyer 569 (1979) (with Stanley Hauerwas).

Review of Gordon Zahn's In Solitary Witness, 10 Natural Law Forum 195 (1963). (This journal is now called The American Journal of Jurisprudence.)

"Communities Leave Someone Out," National Catholic Reporter (August 10, 1979). Reprinted by permission of the National Catholic Reporter, P.O. Box 281, Kansas City, Missouri 64141.

Chapter Notes

References are made here only when the text does not lead to the bibliography. I intend that the bibliography be the primary reference, so that documentation in these chapter notes is also meant to lead there rather than to be complete in the notes. Scriptural references are made in the text and quotations are in almost all cases from the New English Bible. The epigraph after the title page is a modest exception; there, for obvious reasons, I translated as "innocent" what the New English Bible translates as "pure." The Greek will support what I did, even if my consequent moral theology will not.

Part One. Clients

Chapter 1. The Ethics of Role

The empirical and theoretical basis for the contrasting views of role presented here are (a) in most of Monroe Freedman's work and in such incidental things as Fortas's little essay on Thurman Arnold—Freedman has been forthright in advancing a public-service rationale for the adversary ethic, although some of his more recent work (e.g., the *Social Responsibility* and *Catholic University* pieces) supports conscientious objection (see Chapter 2)—and, (b) advancing the public-interest role, the Yale note (republished by the American Bar Foundation) and Marks, Leswing, and Fortinsky. Wasserstrom and Redmount ponder both alternatives but endorse neither; part of the explanation for Wasserstrom's position is that he cannot find a moral justification for the professional's preferring his client over other people. This is not an easy question; Hazard (*Ethics*) says it is the fundamental question in legal ethics, and Novak seems to argue that excessive worry about it is a disservice to the public good. My own answer is theological–i.e., I may prefer those whom God sends my way; cf. John 19:27. Stringfellow's essay is a valuable supplement to Wexler.

The law for the disinheritance example is in the wills chapter of my *Planning and Drafting*. The principal theological sources here are Barth (*Word of God* and *Dogmatics in Outline*), Lewis (*World's Last Night* and *Four Loves*), Bonhoeffer and Hauerwas (*Truthfulness*). Cihlar, May, Kaplan, and Beauchamp are also useful; Palmieri and Crock provide examples from the business world for discussion about lawyers (and clients) acting in the public interest. I don't mean here to endorse a "Social Darwinian" view of what justice is (see Chapters 13 and 21) but to suggest that such a view of justice is implicit in the adversary ethic. Several examples are excerpted in the first chapter of Brown and Dauer. The idea of paternalism suggested here is mostly from Eric Berne, whose *Transactional Analysis in Psychotherapy* (1961) is more useful in this regard than *Games*; I attempted to apply Berne's system to the law-office setting, in *Estate Planning Games,* 47 Notre Dame Lawyer 865 (1972), and to a social setting in *The Law and Order Game,* Transactional Analysis Bulletin, April, 1970, p. 41. Tybor's essay on the *Skokie* case is a valuable view of the law-reform situation.

Chapter 2. The Ethics of Isolation

Role ethics, subtopic need, is my attempt to describe paternalism as it operates in law practice; see Chapter 1 notes. Particularly important here are Beauchamp, Dworkin, and Cheatham. Brown and Dauer excerpt readings that pose three further examples–drafting a deceptive lease, advising a client to violate a trivial or unenforced law, and defeating a child-custody order by helping a client to kidnap his own children. In each of these the moral choice is seen, in the authors whom Brown and Dauer quote, as a problem for the lawyer rather than as a matter for moral discourse with the client. The choice for the lawyer comes to be whether to dominate the client or be dominated by him. The results of that choice (either way) are what I call the ethics of role; the reasoning that leads to the choice itself is the ethics of isolation. Cheatham says, "The interested striving of two contending parties is, in the long run, an infinitely better agency for the ascertainment of truth than any species of paternalistic inquiry," but the assumption he makes is that the contenders are *lawyers*; from the client's point of view the choice is between contending paternalisms. My son Joseph Shaffer suggested that the scene between Josiah Bounderby and Stephen Blackpool, in Dickens's *Hard Times,* illustrates this point. Bounderby, the industrial squire, tells Blackpool, the loom weaver, that divorces in England are only for the wealthy, that it is better for society that the poor do not have divorces. Blackpool grumbles that the law is a muddle. "Don't call the institutions of your society a muddle," Bounderby says. "The institutions of your country are not your piece-work, and the only thing you have got to do is mind your piece-work." Trollope's *The Warden,* in the contrasting coercions on Septimus Harding from the archdeacon and the attorney general, is another; see my essay on that novel (*A Lesson*).

Brown and Dauer also reproduce several examples that illustrate the ethics of isolation. At a systematic and theoretical level, the ethics of isolation is illustrated in the recent essays of Harry Jones and Murray Schwartz, is the position Wasserstrom takes, is the view of Hazard's *Ethics,* and is characteristic of most "post-Watergate" moral sensitivity in the profession. The student version of this theory is in Chapter 16. Freedman characterizes the moral concern of this work when he asks whether it is possible for a person to be a lawyer and a good person; I don't object to that question, but I do object to the assumption that the goodness of the client is irrelevant to the answer and I object to the frequent implication that clients are subversive to the lawyer's moral purpose. See also Bliven's review and most of the work of Redmount and of L. Brown. I am helped in thinking about this by a lecture, "Appeals to Conscience," given by James F. Childress, November 29, 1977, at Notre Dame, particularly in his pointing out that the assertion of conscience tends to be thought of as final, definitive, and private. My view is that the conversation that follows from an assertion of conscience is where professional ethics begin; that it is there where one begins to find "the truth about the truth." Barth (*Word of God*) told a group of ministers, in 1922: "It is our acquaintance not with savage and immoral man so much as with moral man that makes us none too proud of his achievements." See Gustafson (*Christian Ethics*), too.

The professional basis for conscientious objection, despite such common promises in oaths as "I will never reject, from any consideration personal to myself, the cause of the defenseless or oppressed" (Indiana Oath for Attorneys), is in the *Code* (E.C. 2-2, 2-16, 2-25 through 2-29, 7-8, and 7-9) and in the *Canadian Code of Professional Conduct* 51-55 (1974). The U.S. *Code* also supports the view that lawyers should, at least in the first instance, work toward discourse rather than withdrawal; E.C. 7-7 through 7-9. The Hazard quotation is from his *Social Responsibility* essay.

The historical perspective is supported, I think, by Miller, Edman (Finney), Timothy Smith, Marty, and Rodes, although I have it mostly from Shriver and Ostrom. See also Heller's biography of Rabbi Wise, and Roof's essay.

Chapter 3. The Ethics of Care

The theology here is mostly from Buber, from Barth's *Romans,* and from Hauerwas's *Character* and his *Truthfulness*; I also used Gustafson

(*Christian Ethics*) and depended on the assertion that the idea of the value of a relationship is both a moral assertion and a political one. In the last connection see Robert Rodes's and my essay in the Feifel book. Hauerwas, in helping me with this chapter, suggested that my position on the hope I have for the client is not consistent with my position (in Chapter 1) that professional service is by definition service to only part of a person. I think, first, that it is possible to sell bolts to a person or fill the gas tank in his automobile and, despite the slightness of my service, to treat him as a child of God. (I once saw a convincing skit done by a cursillo group in which Christian service was illustrated by a gas-station attendant at work in his trade.) A more substantive answer, suggested by L. Brown, might be this: One subject for the moral discourse between a lawyer and his client is why the client came to the lawyer, and whether, now that he is with the lawyer, he should remain. The "jurisdiction" of the law office is defined by what the client seeks there; the moral discourse that follows on his coming to the office can be one in which the lawyer and client decide together which part of the client is served by the lawyer, and that process of deciding jurisdiction is a process that involves the client as a (whole) person.

Dworkin's essay contains quotations from and references to Plato and depends in part on Piaget's *The Moral Judgment of the Child* (1932). The allusion to moral development shows that it is possible for a person to be free substantively but not free procedurally. A child can come "to view in a critical and rational manner his situation." The idea resembles Yoder's description of early Christian slaves and women, who were told to endure their situation and to be free in it; Yoder refers to this status as "revolutionary subordination" (*Politics*).

The contracts dialogue is from L. Brown's unpublished teaching materials; similar material is reproduced in part and discussed in my *Legal Interviewing* (the Carl Tonio case). Brown made the transcript when he was a visiting teacher, for a day, in a first-year contracts class; he used the device to demonstrate that a case can be put with a lawyer-client conversation as well as with an appellate opinion; there are obvious advantages to the law-office alternative. The horsewhip-lawyer case is at Freeman and Weihofen 183-194, which pages include several discussions of the case by experts in counseling, including Redmount.

Interdependence of lawyer and client, as an empirical and psychological reality, is not central to the discussion in this chapter; I mean to focus more on the theological realities involved. However, there is inevitable theology in behavioral discussions claiming to be "scientific"— e.g., Rosenthal, Redmount, Carl Rogers (both titles), Jung (*Analytical Psychology*), and Watson (*Psychiatry for Lawyers*). Interdependence as a *fact* is the central thesis in my *Legal Interviewing*. These titles also discuss—some of them thoroughly—the development of the skills necessary to conduct law-office discourse. These are skills in both the psychological and theological (Chapter 18) senses. The important thing, theoretically, is to see the lawyer-client interaction as more than intellectual. Buber described it as erotic (*Between Man and Man* 29): "We should live not towards another thinker of whom we wish to know nothing beyond his thinking but, even if the other is a thinker, towards his bodily life over and above his thinking—rather, towards his person, to which, to be sure, the activity of thinking also belongs.... The two are loyal to the Eros of dialogue, who love one another, receive the common event from the other's side as well, that is, they receive it from the two sides, and thus for the first time understand in a bodily way what an event is."

Chapter 4. A Theology of the Client

Much of my thinking depends on what one might call theories of humanistic counseling—Simons and Reidy, Wise, Redmount, Jung (particularly *Analytical Psychology*), both Rogers references, the Brown-Shaffer piece, and my work, particularly *Legal Interviewing* and *Death, Property*. Wise and Simons and Reidy provide some theological links, but my most useful theological link here has been the unpublished notes on pastoral counseling of my friend and colleague Morton Kelsey. Other theology comes from Dunne, Burtchaell (*Philemon*), and, of course, Buber. Hazard (*Historical Perspective*) collects and discusses legal and empirical sources on confidentiality and privilege, as does McCormick's *Evidence* (ch. 10, 2nd ed. 1972). Crock and Palmieri are two popular sources on a requirement that lawyers disclose the business misdeeds of their clients; there is, of course, a vaster professional literature on that issue. Lefstein makes the interesting suggestion that lawyers should warn clients that confidentiality is limited by duties to the state. It is important, considering the possibility that a lawyer may be punished because he believes, or professional rules provide, that the confidence he holds as a lawyer is not protected by the privilege provided by the law of evidence. The existing *Code* preserves the distinction between confidence (or, as it says, "secret") and privilege, and the *Canons* preserved it even more clearly. What might have happened was that the eighteenth-century habit of identifying the two was abandoned as American lawyers began to have more to do with their clients than English barristers do, but that the difference has been narrowed in recent decades as our "society of strangers" became one in which lawyers answer moral questions by seeing what the law provides. See Chapter 15, the notes to Chapter 7, and Morton Deutsch's work on conflict resolution.

Chapter 5. The Problem of Revulsion

The most readily available edition of *Orley Farm* is probably the 1950 Knopf edition, which has a foreword by Drinker. *Phineas Redux* is one of the Palliser novels and is available in the new Oxford set (paperback) of that series. I have my Durkheim from Erikson, who seems to rely principally on "The Rules of Sociological Method" (1895); he also discusses and relies on Erving Goffman's *Asylums* (1962) and Gresham Sykes's *Society of Captives* (1958). The annotation is "Rights and duties," etc. This chapter introduces Stanley Hauerwas's special use of the adjective "tragic"; it might be useful to notice (in reference to *Truthfulness*) that he develops the idea of tragedy as a comment on medical ethics, particularly on the delusion that medicine can cure, that it should seek to cure. Hauerwas argues that medicine should seek to care and should be prepared to make moral choices which may result in suffering and death. The morality of being willing to make such choices is what he calls tragic. He defines tragedy as "the triumph of meaning over power." "If we are determined to do good," he says, "we must be prepared to will our own and others' suffering and death." See my review at 23 American Journal of Jurisprudence 245 (1978).

Chapter 6. The Problem of Representing the Guilty

The historical theory here rests on Bloomfield (both pieces), Marty, Timothy Smith, Chroust, and Miller; a contemporary source that suggests the importance of English influences is Story's review of Hoffman's 1817 *Course.* The connection between the political development Bloomfield describes in his piece on Hoffman and the revival is less well established in these sources, although it is implicit in some of them (e.g., in Hoffman's advertent, thorough, careful consideration of the Bible—something Jefferson would not have bothered to do in a law book). Marty's concept of "Righteous Empire" makes the connection in broad thematic strokes; however, finding it expressed in such mundane detail as generalizations about legal ethics is not easy. The Hazard reference is to his *Ethics*; his essay on the evidentiary privilege is also useful on these points, as is Selinger's analysis; see also Wasserstrom, particularly on the ethical problem of preferring one person over another. The situation of the barrister is described a bit in Hazard's essay on privilege and more thoroughly in Mellinkoff; my favorite description of the English legal profession is Sir Robert Megarry's *Lawyer and Litigant in England* (1962). Both Mellinkoff and Patterson quote the Brougham speech, and Mellinkoff discusses it. The Freedman references are to his *Lawyers' Ethics*; his developing theory of conscientious objection is clearer in his later essays, though. On the argument that office lawyers should give moral witness to their clients, see Harry Jones and Schwartz. On the allusion to the rule permitting diminished representation on appeals for indigent criminal defendants, see Anders v. California, 386 U.S. 353 (1963).

Chapter 7. The Problem of Ministry to the Guilty

The argument that social issues, as they are taken up in the practice of law in America, take on an interpersonal focus they do not have in the explication of the British-barrister ideal is illustrated in Chapter 5 of Bloomfield's *American Lawyers in a Changing Society,* particularly in reference to the outpouring, prior to the Civil War, of fiction and popular biography about lawyers. Bloomfield's point is that this literature reflected an effort by lawyers to reconcile the Jeffersonian notion of the lawyer as an aristocrat with a Jacksonian demand for leaders who were also folk heroes—so that the lawyer heroes of nineteenth-century fiction and biography came from humble origins, used common sense, disdained (or did not need) formal learning, and enjoyed success. His analysis makes the incidental point that these lawyers exhibited social compassion, as the revivalists did, interpersonally, rather than in efforts to reform government. The hero of Frederick W. Thomas's novel, *Clinton Bradshaw: The Adventures of a Lawyer* (1835), identified with his clients as a barrister would not have. Thomas not only has Bradshaw volunteer to help the poor, but "he views the problem of the indigent defendant from an individual, rather than an institutional, perspective, and is content to balance Bradshaw's volunteer public interest work against the unscrupulous activities of the pettifogger." In a conversation between the hero of a story for children, *Marco Paul's Adventures in Pursuit of Knowledge* (1843), a young tutor says to the boy Marco, "Why I know that lawyers have not the credit, generally, of preventing many disputes, but I believe they do. Perhaps it is because I am going to be a lawyer myself. But I really believe that lawyers prevent ten disputes, where they occasion one." (Louis Brown would rejoice at that sentiment.) Such confrontations with the community as these lawyer-heroes have is a confrontation with and through clients. There is a resemblance here, although Bloomfield does not discuss it, between lawyer heroes and revival preachers—a resemblance both in origins and aspirations and in theories for social reform. Charles Grandison Finney could have been the hero of one of these stories, either as a lawyer or as a preacher. Bloomfield's Chapter 9 describes the career of John Mercer Langston, founder and first dean of Howard University Law School, one of the country's first black lawyers who had, incidentally, also been the first black graduate student in theology (at Oberlin). He was in many ways a protégé of Finney's; Finney was, as Langston was growing up in

Ohio, the guiding light at Oberlin, and Oberlin was a center for Christian social reform, one of four American colleges which admitted blacks and one of the few which admitted women.

The Gustafson point is from his *Christian Ethics*. My essay on Snow's fiction relates to the points made here. Barth's social theology is described by Will Herberg. Finney's autobiographical and theoretical pieces are cited by Timothy Smith; the Edman biography of Finney is useful, particularly in providing several lengthy excerpts from theoretical pieces and sermons. Finney's and several other relevant sermons are included in the two-volume collection *Great Gospel Sermons*.

Chapter 8. The Problem of Collaboration

See the notes to Chapter 5 for discussion of Hauerwas's concept of tragedy. The Freedman quotations (on Wasserstrom) are in the *Catholic University* essay; Jones and Schwartz lean to Wasserstrom's view. The Lefstein essay on perjured testimony is an interesting suggestion among several contemporary expressions of the idea that lawyers can control the issue of loyalty by warning their clients that lawyer loyalty is a limited commodity. See also Selinger's essay. The use of fidelity, as I use it here, is helped by May's essay but is a more pervasive ethics of character than I think May espouses; my reliance is largely on Hauerwas's *Character*, and on Neuhaus and Gaffney; Jones's arbitration opinion on employee loyalty is an oblique view of what I would argue is the virtue of faithfulness.

Chapter 9. An Example on the Problem of Collaboration

The Hillel and Kant formulations are as translated by Donagan. The Leviticus renderings are from the New English Bible and from Mackie (at 243). Fingarette's idea about the significance, for law, of the Book of Job is the idea I mean to suggest in references to "the God of Job." Relevant support from Hauerwas is in *Character* and in *Truthfulness*. The version of the proposed *Rules* I use here is that published by the American Bar Association in January, 1980. The 1978 proposals of the Criminal Justice Section are not, at this writing, published, but are in the section's files. The 1970 positions of the section are in *Standards Relating to the Defense Function*, published by the ABA in 1970. The Freedman quotations are from his *Adversary Ethics* 35–42; he mentions that Noonan's 1966 piece is in disagreement with him. See Tom Bower's recent report on trials of Nazi war criminals, and a recent case that poses these issues (discussed by Brian), State v. Robinson, 290 North Carolina 56, 224 S.E.2d 174 (1976).

The conclusion I suggest at the end of the chapter is that the crucial issue—which I see exemplified in the moment of testimony—is one that is solved not by rules but by character. This way of looking at the issue is explained precisely and eloquently by Hauerwas (*Character* 195–215). The point is this: I am comfortable with having Atticus Finch negotiate this difficulty, not comfortable in having Mr. Chaffanbrass negotiate it. The difference, seen externally, is a matter of expectations; Mr. Chaffanbrass "cannot be trusted to act faithfully," although he will predictably behave in such a way as to keep himself out of trouble. One way to put this is as Hauerwas does: "The self at once helps determine the kinds of limits and possibilities of a situation it confronts by the very description of the situation it supplies." That is, Atticus will come to see the situation as one of care, Mr. Chaffanbrass will come to see it as a role, and the difference cannot be understood in the principles each of them announces. Another way to put this is to say that I am afraid that Mr. Chaffanbrass will corrupt the counseling relationship—that he will, for example, train his client how to lie effectively. "The problem is not just applying the correct norm to a situation, but rather it is a matter of how the situation is to be seen at all. It is not just a matter of conforming ourselves to what is, but rather it is a matter of conforming what is to our beliefs and desires." Hauerwas and I describe this, in reference to Thomas More (Chapters 18 and 19) as the skill to see the possibilities in the situation—to *imagine* them, if you like—and to see that these involve more than alternative views of fealty to power. "The significance of character for the Christian points to the fact that the Gospel is for the Christian the criterion of the imagination." I am helped here by Reed. The importance of description and imagination is important, too, in the actions of a community; the legal profession, in such enterprises as drafting the new *Rules,* should be imagining new possibilities in definitions of the civil liberties the profession will follow, not waiting to see what the courts do. If the profession cannot or does not do that, the believer then resorts, as he always has to anyway, to more adequate systems of description and imagination. "To have our character determined by Christ," Hauerwas says (*Character* 223), "is to have acquired an orientation that gives us direction in such a way that we are not dependent on the world's set patterns and values. It means that our character receives its form in relating to a community that is not subject to the wider community in which it exists." The relevant community of description and imagination for Christians is the church, but there is a sadness in the necessity to resort to the Christian community for what the profession, even in this "society of strangers," should still be able to provide. A reflection on the task of community, in the perjurious-client problem as the proposed *Rules* and the Criminal Justice Section deal with it, has become less a matter of admonition than of judgment. "The community must indicate the kind of character commensurate with its purposes by providing ethical arguments that create appropriate reasons for the members' actions and practices. Such arguments, however, are not just for observer-determined judgment but to enliven the imagination of the constituents of community for their future orientation.... If the function of ethical discourse and argument is limited to judgment about specific action, it cannot help but pervert rather than enliven men's lives. Ethical argument concerned solely with discrete acts minimizes the moral life as it gives no direction or context of significance for why we should refrain from some things and do others" (*Character* 232). Rodes's *Christian Magistrate* essay is more optimistic on this point than Hauerwas and I are.

Part Two. Advocacy

The historical image here depends on sources not otherwise relevant in this book: J. Thayer, *"Older Modes of Trial,"* in II *Select Essays in Anglo-American History,* 56 Selden Society, *Rolls of the Justices in Eyre for Yorkshire, 1218-1219* (1937); G. Neilson, *Trial by Combat* (1891); Glanville's *De Legibus et Consuetudinibus Regni Angliae*; and J. Beames, *A Translation of Glanville* (1900).

Chapter 10. The Practice of Reconciliation

Theological sources are Barth (*Romans, Humanity of God*), McClendon, and Rodes (*Legal Enterprise*). The "society of strangers" idea is Hauerwas's, depending to some extent on MacIntyre (see *Truthfulness,* particularly in reference to the practice of medicine). Rodes's *Christian Magistrate* piece is more optimistic. My biblical source is Vawter. It may be important, in getting an image of the Old Testament prophets, to notice that they were almost deviant in their ecstatic or charismatic character and at some times even affected distinctive dress. The Hebrew word for prophet ("one made to speak") suggests this quality; the fact of their speaking *for* someone (the Latin root of the word) also gives them detachment and a client; in some cases—e.g., the prophets of Balaam in Numbers 22-24—they were even aliens. Still, it is characteristic of the Old Testament prophet, and notably of Nathan, that he enjoyed an intimate office within the "corridors of power."

The empirical discussions on power on which I depend are Domhoff (all three books), Wexler, and Donnell; see my discussion of Snow's novels (*Snow's Justice*), my review of Donnell's book, at 46 Indiana Law Journal 562 (1971), and Stringfellow. My sources for claims on intraorganizational lawyers and others are from Wall Street Journal discussions, notably Crock, Palmieri, and *The Image Makers*. The history is from the second volume of S. E. Morison's *The Oxford History of the American People* (1965).

Chapter 11. Advocacy of the Person

Cases: Supt. of Belchertown State School v. Joseph Saikewicz, 370 N.E.2d 417 (Mass. 1977); In re Quinlan, 70 N.J. 10, 355 A.2d 647 (1976); Strunk v. Strunk, 445 S.W.2d 145 (Ky. App. 1969) (the kidney case); Stump v. Sparkman, 98 S.Ct. 1099 (1978) (judicial immunity). Jackson v. Indiana, 406 U.S. 715 (1972), and State v. Lang, 325 N.E.2d 305 (Ill. App. 1975), discussed in L. Myers, *The Strange Case of Daniel Lang,* 64 American Bar Association Journal 1198 (1978), both involve understanding of the judicial process by defendants who were mentally impaired. My favorite case of that genre is Thompson v. Louisville, 362 U.S. 199 (1960). I had additional information on *Saikewicz* from stories in The New York Times—July 14, 1976, p. 26, col. 2; Dec. 1, 1977, p. A18, col. 6; and in the McCormick-Hellegers article. For a parallel situation involving a competent client see Harris's essay.

Theology: Hauerwas's several essays on the mentally retarded (in *Truthfulness*); McCullough; Hauerwas, *Reflections on Suffering*; MacIntyre; and Kaplan. The criticism that the Saikewicz decision arrogates power to judges, and takes it away from doctors, seems to me to miss the point that the Massachusetts court made—that patients should not be made to suffer for the dignity of the medical profession. The point is the preservation of moral discourse in these "bioethical" cases; the Massachusetts court did that in *Saikewicz*; the Supreme Court of the United States refused to do it in the 1973 abortion cases. In both it was apparent that the medical profession had not preserved moral discourse. The court in *Saikewicz* took nothing away; it filled a vacuum.

The good-moral-character cases (from immigration law) are discussed in Bradley and in O'Meara. It is incidentally interesting that the *Code* has a good-moral-character requirement for membership in the profession but that the requirement is dropped in the proposed *Rules*.

Chapter 12. Moral Discourse and the Community

This chapter was improved when it was, in an earlier version, edited for the North Carolina Law Review by Billy Leonard, then an editor and law student, now a lawyer in Atlanta. Charles Morgan's career is described by Powledge. The theology in this chapter comes from Yoder, Hauerwas (*Character* and *Truthfulness,* particularly the chapter on Speer), and Churchill. I also found useful Tillich, Kaplan (i.e., on these points), Buber, Wasserstrom, Maritain, Häring, and Lewis (particularly "Christianity and Culture," which is in *Christian Reflections*). The footnote comparison, at the end, on love and justice depends on Haring's essay on justice in *The Catholic Encyclopedia* and on the article on justice in *Encyclopedia Judaica.* Jurisprudential sources here are primarily Rodes and Fuller. One difficulty I have with Fuller's "neo-natural-law" thought is that he seems unable to get beyond procedure; he seems unable to get, theoretically, to the place where Socrates got when he said "we shall unite the officer of judge and advocate in our own persons." But perhaps that difficulty is mainly one of concept; it is interesting to me that the novelist John Jay Osborne, Jr., using Fuller's view of contracts, was able to construct a metaphor for a diverse array of personal and institutional relationships (*The Associates*).

The phenomenon of imputed competence was identified by Rosenthal. It can survive among lawyers only if they retreat into delusion, a symbol for which is Soames Forsyte leading his daughter Fleur into court for the jury trial of her libel case (*The Silver Spoon*). "The great thing is to keep still," Soames says, "and pay no attention to anything. They're all behind you, except the jury—and there's nothing in them really. If you look at them, don't smile." An interesting comparison is the short prescription for lawyer-client relationships promulgated by the National Organization of Women; I quote it in my *Interviewing and Counseling*. Imputed competence works only in a world which is not real, where people are things not to be looked at. Part of the way into that world is what Churchill and I identify as group consensus in the professions; see the notes to Chapter 9 for a theological excursus on how groups can operate to widen imagination rather than to still it—an important point for me to make, because I do not argue—nor does Churchill—that groups implacably corrupt the individual professional. On the contrary, both the individual professional and the broader community (in which the professional group operates) need organized professions that can widen the imagination. Professional groups tend, though, to depend on justification by power, and that dependence leads them into constricted imagination. The individual professional then resorts to some other community, other than the professional group, which can serve the moral purposes the group should be performing. In my opinion, the proposed new *Rules* are a corrupting development in just this sense.

The Barth quote is from *Romans* (395). Colman McCarthy's column on Mother Teresa of Calcutta ("People before Programs") is an interesting supplement to the Buchwald column (which I have from the South Bend Tribune, Sept. 12, 1976, p. 12, col. 5): "The poor, we think, are those for whom we create 'programs,'" McCarthy said. "Agencies and departments do the work. The god is cost-effectiveness.... When she visited the Zacchaeus soup kitchen in Washington a few years ago, Mother Teresa reminded people that programs are for a purpose, but Christian love must be for a person. Then she began ladling the soup into the bowls of the poor.... None of the news accounts about the peace prize going to Mother Teresa mentioned her prayer life. It was as if this woman were merely an exceptionally zealous social worker." He quotes her: "The biggest disease today is not leprosy or tuberculosis, but rather the feeling of being unwanted, uncared for and deserted by everybody."

Chapter 13. The Administration of Justice

My thesis here depends on Robert Rodes's idea of what law is (*Legal Enterprise*) and on Louis M. Brown's and Robert Redmount's ideas of what the practice of law is; my *Planning and Drafting* is a program for teaching one piece of substantive law, and my *Interviewing and Counseling* is a program for teaching legal skill, from these perspectives. I have parts of my theory from the article on justice in *Encyclopedia Judaica,* Reisman, Walter Kaufmann (Buber's editor), Yoder, and Barth. Barth's political theology is in *Community, State,* and *Dogmatics in Outline,* among other places, and is discussed in Herberg's essay and in the Busch biography. The Cary novel is *Not Honour More* (1955). The generalization of legal ethics as involving faithfulness to client, candor to court, and fairness to others is one I fashion from Patterson's typology. My concept of the political theology of the Puritans comes from an eccentric synthesis fashioned from Marty, Miller, T. Smith, and Bloomfield's instructive essay on David Hoffman as one who believed in maintaining the identity of public and private morality. (Hoffman was not consciously Puritan, but there is a good deal of Puritan political theology in his legal and ethical writing.) The idea in this chapter is also developed in a short article which appeared in the Indiana State Bar Association magazine, 22 Res Gestae 394 (1978) and in The Journal of Current Social Issues 51 (Summer 1979). The "rescue doctrine in tort" is the rule that a wrongdoer who puts me in danger is liable for the damages incurred by one who rescues me, or tries. It is sometimes rationalized as a rule that says that the wrongdoer should have foreseen that someone would try to rescue me and is, out of general principles of foreseeability, liable to the rescuer. The better rationale is probably that the rule stands on its own footing. Prosser, *Torts* 258–259, 276–281 (4th ed. 1971) discusses it; its most eloquent explication was by Chief Judge Cardozo in Wagner v. International R. Co., 232 N.Y. 176, 133 N.E. 437 (1921). The referee view of what judges are for is examined empirically in my "Judges, Repulsive Evidence, and the Ability to Respond," 43 Notre Dame Lawyer 503 (1968).

Relating a difference in what "justice" means to the two principal elements in our Western moral thought is not to claim that Greek moral thought was narrow, but it is to claim that the Greek idea of justice is an idea and that the Jewish idea of justice is derivative from something that is not really an *idea* at all. I also mean to identify a radical difference in *why* one should render what is due, a difference that sees universal justice as either an intellectual argument (what I am calling Greek) or as a source of value prior to argument, prior even to value (what I am calling Jewish and could call Mosaic). I think this specification with respect to justice follows from H. Richard Niebuhr's saying (in *Radical Monotheism*) that Greek and Jewish moral thought differed radically (at the roots). To Jews, he said, "All human relations were transformed into covenant relations ... religious observance became fundamentally an affair of promise-keeping, or of keeping faith, in carrying on covenanted practices of worship and sacrifice. Domestic, commercial, and political relations were no less covenantal in character.... Man was understood, in this whole context, as Martin Buber has pointed out, not first of all as rational animal but as promise-making, promise-keeping, promise-breaking being, as man of faith. All life was permeated by the faith in the fundamental covenant between God and man and in every activity some phase of that covenant was re-enacted." He suggests that neglect of the universality of justice was, in Greek thought, a matter of error; but in Jewish thought it was a failure to be faithful; it was a matter, there, not of error, but of sin. I mean to suggest that justice as it was understood in the earliest American democracy, that of the Puritans, was a Jewish notion in this radical sense. Justice, in that view, is not the special province of government.

Chapter 14. On Being Effective

Dan Carter discusses his authorities, many of them original, at pp. 417–421 of his book on the Scottsboro case. I have my ideas about Judge Horton mainly from Carter, and from Patterson and Conrad, but also from the television program (which appeared April 22, 1976) and from a good sermon preached, shortly after the television program, by my friend L. George Reed, a lawyer and minister who was then pastor of the Mountain Plain Baptist Church, Mechums River, Virginia. The theology I advert to is, besides Yoder, from Barth (*Romans, The Great Promise*), Hauerwas, both Niebuhrs, Dillenberger's Luther, Ebeling, and an unpublished outline on the theology of obedience to law in Calvin and Luther, done by a friend and former student, a young minister in the Church of the Brethren, Steven Agee, now in law practice in Roanoke, Virginia. The idea of hope implicit here is developed more conceptually in Chapters 18 to 20, with reference to Thomas More and Franz Jagerstatter, and with help from Hauerwas. My idea that the modern depredations of the American government can only be explained by a political philosophy that says that it is impossible to act without doing wrong is, I'm afraid, personal. It came to me, in the period 1967 to 1970, when I realized that it made very little difference that Senators Robert Kennedy and Mike Mansfield finally joined Senators Morse and McCarthy in saying that the Vietnam War was immoral. The common answer, even then, was, "All war is immoral."

A narrow legal question that arises in consideration of the *Patterson* case is whether Judge Horton could have set the verdict aside, or directed a verdict of acquittal, rather than granting the motion for a new trial. The difference would have been that, after a judgment of acquittal, Patterson could not have again been put to trial. I am assuming that Judge Horton believed he could not have entered a judgment of acquittal; if he could have, even though that action would have been an excessive use of trial-judge power, and if he could have gotten away with it—that is, if Patterson would in fact have gone free—my analysis will have to broaden, as part of the judge's heroic behavior, its emphasis on his belief that the state would not put Patterson to trial a second time. His extra-judicial suggestion to the prosecution, before he ruled on Patterson's motion, suggests to me that Horton did not believe he had the power to enter a judgment of acquittal.

Part Three. Lawyer Culture

The Niebuhr quotations are from *The Responsible Self.* The translation of the Benedictine Rule is from *The Holy Rule of Our Most Holy Father Benedict* (Grail Publications, St. Meinrad, Indiana, 1937). See also "Law Office Organizations," which I wrote with Robert Landies and Richard F. Hennessey, in Law Office Economics and Management, Summer, 1976.

Chapter 15. A Theology of Lawyer Culture

The C. S. Lewis material is from the essay "Christianity and Culture," in *Christian Reflections.* My supplements are from Brown's and my essay on law-office jurisprudence; Shriver and Ostrom; Reinhold Niebuhr's lectures on irony in American history; Bonhoeffer's *Ethics,* especially his theory of penultimate moral action; chapters 8 and 9 of Robert Redmount's and my study of law students; my *Legal Interviewing*; and my essay on having children in James T. Burtchaell's *Marriage among Christians* (1976). Bloomfield's theory about the loss of the republican (Jeffersonian) image in American political and legal thought (developed both in his book and in his essay on Hoffman) is useful, too, in reconciling the fact that lawyer culture has always been, but in the nineteenth century was more prominently than it is now, part of American and English popular culture, with the fact that our popular culture lost its nonsectarian Christian character after the demise of what Reinhold Niebuhr calls innocence and Martin Marty calls the

Righteous Empire. This is in part the theory of Perry Miller on the secularization of American law; compare Rodes's essay on the nonsectarian consensus.

Chapter 16. Moral Moments in Law School

This chapter derives from Redmount's and my book, although I would not want to blame my coauthor for my theology or for my ethical theory. See William Bennett's solid little essay on "teaching values." The Bowen biographies are discussed in my review at 73 Yale Law Journal 537 (1963).

Chapter 17. Law Faculties and the World

I use Daniel-Rops to supplement Acts on biographical facts about Paul. Paul's last few years, and his death, are not reported in the New Testament; the Roman Catholic tradition is that he left Rome after the period described in Acts but later returned there and was a victim of Nero's persecution of Christians; he probably was beheaded near Rome in A.D. 67. My theology here refers to Barth (*Romans*), Churchill, Yoder, and May, as well as to studies of law teachers referred to and discussed in Redmount's and my book.

Part Four. Institutions

Chapter 18. Thomas More's Skill

Hauerwas and I concluded, after some investigation, that Bolt's More is an accurate picture of the historical More. Colleagues more steeped in English history, particularly Marvin O'Connell, of the Notre Dame history department, and Rodes disagree in some respects, but not in matters essential to our thesis in this chapter and Chapter 19. Biographical references on More include Chambers, Reynolds, Roper, and Harpsfield's *The Life and Death of Sir Thomas More* (1550–1553). Theological, philosophical, and jurisprudential sources here are Rodes, Lynch, Barth (*Evangelical Theology* and the Gollwitzer selections from *Church Dogmatics*), and John Dewey's *Logical Method and Law*, 10 Cornell Law Quarterly 17 (1924). We are talking about law as an activity; too often considerations of the relation between law, religion, and morality concentrate on law only as a system of rules. As a result, claims of moral or religious support for law have little to do with law as it is practiced by citizens (including lawyers). The soil in which law grows includes the client and the client's character meeting the lawyer and the lawyer's character. See the Brown-Shaffer essay; my *Legal*

Interviewing; and Redmount's essay on psychological jurisprudence.

The anecdote from Bruges was given to us by our colleague Edward F. Barrett and is mentioned by Blackstone (vol. 3, p. 148, 1916 ed.). Our use of skill here is both in the obvious (lawyer's) sense and also as a meaning for what is otherwise called virtue. Hope is a skill, in both senses, and in both senses is a skill one learns from a master. Hope is part of an initiation into a way of life (see Hauerwas's *Truthfulness*). From a Christian perspective, the traditional theological virtues—faith, hope, and love—are understood as reminders of the narrative of the master, Jesus, a narrative that schools the self to serve God rightly. Such virtues become distorted if they are treated as independent norms of behavior. In using skill in the sense of craftsmanship, we are aware of the issue of lawyers serving this way in a corrupt system. Our view of More's "exit" from the Tudor system, discussed here and in Chapter 19, might suggest that we do not think that this skill can be exercised in a corrupt system. While some legal systems are doubtless so corrupt that it is impossible to practice law in them, we argue that the use of lawyer skill is possible if the regime is one in which people have both a means to control and limit power and a means to resolve interpersonal conflicts short of violence. More's exit (see Chapter 19) was a political act, we think: He did not exit from the practice of law.

The view of law implicit here and in Chapter 19 is largely that of Rodes (*Legal Enterprise*), who says, "The very coherence of the community in which laws operate seems to depend on some common experience or common consciousness of history." This would say that the existence of means to control and to resolve conflicts depends to some extent on a common interpretation of history. See also his *Christian Magistrate* essay. From this perspective, the recent attempt, by both natural-law and positivistic theorists, to secure the "autonomy" of the law from the vicissitudes of history can be interpreted as an attempt to save the morality of the law from a community that no longer shares a common interpretation of its history. We sometimes admire the attempt, but it seems to us to be destined to fail and, worse, it seems to prevent lawyers from facing the moral challenge of practicing law in a pluralistic society.

Chapter 19. Thomas More's Hope

Many of the notes to Chapter 18 bear on this chapter. The epigraph is from Murdoch's novel *The Red and the Green* 113 (1965). The theology is in Hauerwas (*Truthfulness, Character,* and *Virtue*), Barth (*Romans*), Yoder, and Hannah Arendt's *On Violence* (1969). The points about compromise to attain or retain power are illustrated in literature, perhaps better than in theoretical essays—e.g., Snow's *Corridors of Power*

(1964) and LeCarré's *Tinker, Tailor, Soldier, Spy* (1974). See also Chapters 13 and 16. There is an issue with respect to More here that would notice that he appears not to have sought reform in Tudor government through the exercise of his office as the highest judge in England and as "the conscience of the King." His political career seems to have been unremarkable. (See Reynolds and Chambers.) The curious fact about this is that while he pursued a more or less ordinary political career, he was a member of the European humanist intelligentsia and assayed political reform in his *Utopia*. Scarisbrick finds some evidence, even, that More was a compromiser. (See the discussion of shadows in the life of a lawyer-hero, with respect to Judge Horton, in Chapter 14). We argue that More was a reformer at least in that he was honest, publicly and privately, and that this honesty was both unusual and promising. Compare, for example, the life and career of Francis Bacon in Bowen, *Francis Bacon: The Temper of a Man* (1963). My review of the Bowen book discusses this comparison, 73 Yale Law Journal 537 (1963).

Chapter 20. Franz Jagerstatter's Hope

Zahn collected and included in his biography all of Jagerstatter's essays; they are nine, all written in Saint Radegund, apparently in 1942. The theology here (aside from Zahn's adequate description of just-war theory) is in Barth, particularly Herberg's and Busch's rendering of Barth's political theology; in Hauerwas (*Truthfulness,* especially in Hauerwas's and Burrell's essay on Speer, which is where the epigraph comes from); in McClendon; and in Calvin, who on this point is quoted and discussed by Herberg. The More quotation is from Rogers's collection of letters; the Sartre quotations are from *Existentialism* and Barrett's *Irrational Man,* the James quotation from *A Pluralistic Universe* (1932). The unattributed quotation on propaganda is from a Nazi propaganda officer who is a character in C. P. Snow's *The Light and the Dark* (1947). The allusion to Gethsemane is to C. S. Lewis's essay "Christianity and Culture" (see notes to Chapter 15). The discussion on the leadership of churches is supported to some extent by Clasen's history of Anabaptism.

Chapter 21. Tragic Communities

Most of the Barth quotations are from *Romans*; the political theology is in *The Word of God,* in *Community, State, and Church,* and in reports of and quotations from letters, lectures, and articles in the Busch biography. Herberg's introductory essay in the 1968 Peter Smith edition of *Community, State, and Church* is helpful. The syndrome of the two kingdoms appears in Barth's thought in a number of places; I was reading

Evangelical Theology when I wrote this chapter. Stanley Hauerwas is the source of the idea that tragedy is the triumph of meaning over power—he first derived it in discussions of medical ethics, but I take responsibility for adapting it to a theory about communities. I have had help in the adaptation, of course, from mainline sociological deviance theory, such as that of Durkheim and Kai Erikson; see the notes to Chapter 5. Reilly's essay on homosexuals illustrates what I mean by tragedy. The Billy Sunday sermons are in *Great Gospel Sermons*.

Bibliography

I. Abrahams, Hebrew Ethical Wills (1954 ed.)

American Bar Association, Code of Professional Responsibility (1979 printing).

———, Formal and Informal Opinions (looseleaf; formal opinions 1969 to date; informal opinions 1973 to date).

———, Informal Ethics Opinions (2 vol. 1974).

———, Opinions of the Committee on Professional Ethics (1967; this includes the Canons of Legal Ethics, with annotations on amendments to the Canons, and, apparently, all formal and informal opinions to 1967).

American Bar Foundation, "The New Public Interest Lawyers" (1970); this is a reprint of a student note of the same title from 79 Yale Law Journal 1069 (1970).

American Law Reports, "Attorney's Failure to Promptly Report Receipt of Money or Property Belonging to Client as Ground for Disciplinary Action," 91 A.L.R.3d 975 (1979).

———, "Attorneys at Law: Fee Collection Practices as Ground for Disciplinary Action," 91 A.L.R. 3d 583 (1979).

———, "Compliance with Federal Constitutional Requirement that Guilty Pleas Be Made Voluntarily and with Understanding, in Federal Cases Involving Allegedly Incompetent State Convicts," 38 A.L.R.Fed. 238 (1978).

———, "Modern Status of Admissability, in Statutory Rape Prosecution, of Complainant's Prior Sexual Acts or General Reputation for Unchastity," 90 A.L.R.3d 1300 (1979).

———, "Propriety and Prejudicial Effect of Impeaching Witness by Reference to Religious Belief or Lack of It," 76 A.L.R.3d 539 (1977).

———, "Rights and Duties of Attorney in a Criminal Prosecution, where Client Informs Him of Intention to Present Perjured Testimony," 64 A.L.R.3d 385 (1975).

———, "Who May Dispute Presumption of Legitimacy of Child Conceived or Born during Wedlock" 90 A.L.R.3d 2032 (1979).

J. Apfel, "Ethical Wills: A Forgotten Tradition Worthy of Recall," Pennsylvania Bar Association Quarterly, January 1978, p. 171.

T. Aquinas, Summa Theologica (Benziger Bros. 1947).

W. Armstrong, "A Century of Legal Ethics," 64 American Bar Association Journal 1063 (1978).

M. Aultman, "The Lawyers' Time Bomb: Will It Explode or Fizzle?" The National Law Journal, Dec. 18, 1978, p. 19.

J. Ayer, "Do Lawyers Do More Harm than Good?" 65 American Bar Association Journal 1053 (1979).

D. Baly, Geographical Companion to the Bible (1963).

W. Barrett, Irrational Man (1958).

B. Barry, "And Who Is My Neighbor?" 88 Yale Law Journal 629 (1979) (a review of Fried's Right and Wrong).

K. Barth, Anselm: Fides Quaerens Intellectum (Knox ed. 1960).

——, Church Dogmatics: A Selection (Gollwitzer ed., Bromiley tr., 1960).

——, Community, State, and Church (Smith ed. 1968) (includes Herberg's essay on Barth's political theology).

——, Dogmatics in Outline (Thomson tr. 1959).

——, The Epistle to the Romans (6th ed. Hoskyns tr. 1968).

——, Evangelical Theology: An Introduction (Foley tr. 1965).

——, The Faith of the Church (Vahanian tr. 1958).

——, The Humanity of God (Wieser, Thomas, and Wieser tr. 1960).

——, The Word of God and the Word of Man (Horton tr. 1978).

K. Barth and E. Thurneysen, Revolutionary Theology in the Making (Smart tr. 1964).

J. Barzun, "The Professions under Siege," Harpers, Oct. 1978, p. 61.

T. Beauchamp, "Paternalism and Bio-Behavior Control," in T. Beauchamp and L. Walters, Contemporary Issues in Bioethics: Its Nature and Significance (1977).

S. Benn, "Justice," 4 Encyclopedia of Philosophy 298 (1967).

W. Bennett, "When Values Are Substituted for Truth," Wall Street Journal, July 25, 1978, p. 20, col. 4.

E. Berne, Games People Play (1967).

N. Bliven, review of Janowitz's The Last Half Century: Societal Change and Politics in America, The New Yorker, June 18, 1979, p. 106.

M. Bloomfield, American Lawyers in a Changing Society, 1776–1876 (1976).

——, "David Hoffman and the Shaping of a Republican Legal Culture," 38 Maryland Law Review 673 (1979).

R. Blum, "A Perspective on the Bar," 53 California State Bar Journal 98 (1978).

R. Bolt, A Man for All Seasons (1962).

D. Bonhoeffer, Creation and Fall and Temptation (Fletcher and Downham tr. 1976).
——, Ethics (N. H. Smith trans. 1955).
C. Bosk, Forgive and Remember (1979).
T. Bower, "They Were Just Following Orders," Washington Post, Oct. 21, 1979, p. C-3, col. 4.
L. Bradley, "Naturalization–Good Moral Character as a Prerequisite," 34 Notre Dame Lawyer 375 (1959).
W. Brazil, "The Attorney as Victim: Toward More Candor about the Psychological Price Tag of Litigation Practice," 3 Journal of the Legal Profession 107 (1978).
D. Brian, "Professional Responsibility–North Carolina's View of the Lawyer and the Perjurious Witness," 55 North Carolina Law Review 321 (1977).
H. Brown and L. Brown, "Disqualification of the Testifying Advocate–A Firm Rule?" 57 North Carolina Law Review 597 (1979).
——, "What Counsels the Counselor? The Code of Professional Responsibility's Ethical Considerations–A Preventive Law Analysis," 10 Valparaiso University Law Review 453 (1976).
L. Brown, "The Case of the Re-Lived Facts," 48 California Law Review 448 (1960).
——, Cases and Materials on Professional Responsibility: Law Practice from Start to Finish (mimeo 1975).
——, The Client in a Contracts Class (unpublished 1971).
——, "Ethical Aspects of Preventive Law," Harvard Law School Record, Dec. 20, 1949.
——, "The Law Office–A Preventive Law Laboratory," 104 University of Pennsylvania Law Review 940 (1956).
——, "The Legal Autopsy," 39 Journal of the American Judicature Society 47 (1955).
——, "The Practice of Preventive Law," 35 Journal of the American Judicature Society 45 (1951).
——, Preventive Law (1950).
——, "Teaching the Low Visibility Decision Processes of the Lawyer," 25 Journal of Legal Education 386 (1973).
L. Brown and E. Dauer, Planning by Lawyers: Materials on a Non-Adversarial Legal Process (1978).
L. Brown and T. Shaffer, "Toward a Jurisprudence for the Law Office," 17 American Journal of Jurisprudence 125 (1972).
M. Buber, Between Man and Man (Smith tr. 1947).
——, I and Thou (Kaufmann tr. 1972).
——, The Knowledge of Man (Friedman and Smith tr. 1965).
J. Burtchaell, Philemon's Problem (1973).

E. Busch, Karl Barth: His Life from Letters and Autobiographical Texts (Bowden tr. 1976).

L. Buzzard, Law and Theology: An Annotated Bibliography (1979).

E. Cahn, "Justice," 8 International Encyclopedia of the Social Sciences 341 (1968).

D. Callahan, "When Friendship Calls, Should Truth Answer?" Chronicle of Higher Education, Aug. 7, 1978, p. 32.

J. Carlin, Lawyers' Ethics: A Survey of the New York Bar (1966).

——, Lawyers on Their Own: A Study of Individual Practitioners in Chicago (1962).

W. Carlton, In Our Professional Opinion: The Primacy of Clinical Judgment over Moral Choice (1978).

D. Carter, Scottsboro: A Tragedy of the American South (1969).

H. Carter, The Methodist Heritage (1950).

R. Chambers, Thomas More (1973).

E. Cheatham, The Lawyer When Needed (1963).

J. Childress, Civil Disobedience and Trust (Poynter Center 1975).

A. Chroust, The Rise of the Legal Profession in America (2 vol. 1965).

L. Churchill, "The Professionalization of Ethics: Some Implications for Accountability in Medicine," 40 Soundings 40 (1977).

F. Cihlar, "Client Self-Determination: Intervention or Interference," 14 St. Louis University Law Journal 604 (1970).

C. Clasen, Anabaptism: A Social History, 1525–1618 (1972).

W. Clebsch, American Religious Thought: A History (1973).

V. Countryman, T. Finman, and T. Schneyer, The Lawyer in Modern Society (2nd ed. 1976).

S. Crock, "S.E.C. to Consider Rule Requiring Lawyers to Disclose Fraud by Corporate Clients," Wall Street Journal, Aug. 3, 1978, p. 3, col. 2.

Daniel-Rops, Saint Paul (Martin tr. 1953).

A. de Toqueville, Democracy in America (Random House ed. 1945).

M. Deutsch, "Conflicts: Productive and Destructive," 25 Journal of Social Issues 7 (1969).

J. Dillenberger (ed.), Martin Luther (Anchor ed. 1961).

J. Dolan, Catholic Revivalism (1978).

G. Domhoff, The Bohemian Grove and Other Retreats (1974).

——, The Higher Circles (1971).

——, Who Rules America? (1967).

A. Donagan, The Theory of Morality (1977).

J. Donnell, The Corporate Counsel (1970).

H. Drinker, "The Lawyers of Anthony Trollope," in Two Addresses Delivered to Members of the Grolier Club (1950).

——, Legal Ethics (1953).

J. Dunne, A Search for God in Time and Memory (1969).

G. Dworkin, "Autonomy and Behavior Control," Hastings Center Report, Feb. 1976, p. 23.
F. Eaton, Shearman and Sterling, 1873–1973 (1973).
G. Ebeling, Luther: An Introduction to His Thought (1977).
V. Edman, Finney Lives On (1951).
K. Erikson, Wayward Puritans (1966).
Ethics and Advocacy (American Trial Lawyers Foundation 1978).
H. Fingarette, "The Meaning of Law in the Book of Job," 29 Hastings Law Journal 1581 (1978).
——, Self Deception (1969).
A. Fortas, "Thurman Arnold and the Theatre of the Law," 79 Yale Law Journal 988 (1970).
J. Frank, "The Legal Ethics of Louis D. Brandeis," 17 Stanford Law Review 683 (1965).
W. Frankena, Ethics (2nd ed. 1973).
M. Freedman, "Are There Public Interest Limits on Lawyers' Advocacy?" II Social Responsibility: Journalism, Law, Medicine 30 (1976).
——, Lawyers' Ethics in an Adversary System (1975).
——, "Personal Responsibility in a Professional System," 27 Catholic University Law Review 191 (1978).
H. Freeman and H. Weihoffen, Clinical Law Training (1972).
S. Freud, The Psychopathology of Everyday Life (Brill tr. 1951).
C. Fried, Right and Wrong (1977).
F. Friedman, "Introductory Essay," in M. Buber, The Knowledge of Man (1965).
L. Fuller, The Law in Quest of Itself (1940).
——, The Morality of Law (1964).
E. Gaffney, "The Gospel in the Law: The Jurisprudence of Pastor Neuhaus," 14 Valparaiso University Law Review (1979).
M. Galson (ed.), Professional Responsibility of the Lawyer: The Murky Divide between Right and Wrong (1977).
W. Garrett, "Politicized Clergy: A Sociological Interpretation of the 'New Breed,'" 12 Journal for the Scientific Study of Religion 383 (1973).
E. Gaustad, Dissent in American Religion (1973).
——, The Great Awakening in New England (1965).
Great Gospel Sermons (2 vol. 1949).
S. Greenleaf, The Testimony of the Evangelists (1965).
J. Guillet, Themes of the Bible (LaMothe tr. 1960).
J. Gustafson, Christian Ethics and the Community (1971).
——, "Introduction," in H. R. Niebuhr, The Responsible Self (1963).
——, "Mongolism, Parental Desires, and the Right to Life," 16 Perspectives in Biology and Medicine 529 (1973).

———, Protestant and Roman Catholic Ethics: Prospects for Rapprochement (1978).
W. Hamilton, Anglo-American Law on the Frontier: Thomas Rodney and His Territorial Cases (1953).
B. Haring, The Law of Christ (3 vol. 1963).
———, "Justice," 3 New Catholic Encyclopedia 68 (1967).
R. Harris, "Annals of Law: A Scrap of Black Cloth," The New Yorker, June 17, 1974, p. 37.
S. Hauerwas, Character and the Christian Life: A Study in Theological Ethics (1975; paperback ed. 1979).
———, "Ethics and Ascetical Theology," 61 Anglican Theological Review 87.
———, "Jesus: The Story of the Kingdom," 26 Theology Today 303 (1978).
———, "Reflections on Suffering, Death, and Medicine" (unpublished).
———, "A Tale of Two Stories: On Being a Christian and a Texan" (unpublished).
———, Truthfulness and Tragedy (1977).
———, Vision and Virtue: Essays in Christian Ethical Reflection (1974).
R. Haughton, "Sin, Like Redemption, Springs from Body," National Catholic Reporter, June 15, 1979, p. 11.
G. Hazard, "Conscience and Circumstance in Legal Ethics," I Social Responsibility: Journalism, Law, Medicine 36 (1975).
———, Ethics in the Practice of Law (1978).
———, "An Historical Perspective on the Attorney-Client Privilege," 66 California Law Review 1061 (1978).
J. Heller, Isaac M. Wise: His Life, Work, and Thought (1965).
W. Herberg, "The Social Philosophy of Karl Barth," in K. Barth, Community, State, and Church (1968).
D. Hoffman, biographical sources: 7 The National Cyclopaedia of American Biography 129 (1897); 9 Dictionary of American Biography 111 (1932); Who Was Who in America, Historical Volume 324 (rev. ed. 1967).
———, An Address to Students of Law in the United States (1824).
———, A Course of Legal Study (1st ed. 1817) (2nd ed. 2 vol. 1836).
———, Chronicles Selected from the Originals of Cartaphilus, The Wandering Jew (3 vol. 1853).
———, Introductory Lectures and a Syllabus of a Course of Lectures Delivered in the University of Maryland (1837).
———, Legal Outlines (1836).
———, Miscellaneous Thoughts on Men, Manners, and Things, by Anthony Grumbler, of Grumbleton Hall, Esquire (1841).
———, Viator, or A Peep into My Note Book (1841).
M. Horwitz, The Transformation of American Law (1977).

M. Howe, review of R. Swaine, The Cravath Firm and Its Predecessors, 1819–1947, 60 Harvard Law Review 838 (1947).
S. Huber, "Competition at the Bar and the Proposed Code of Professional Standards," 57 North Carolina Law Review 559 (1979).
R. Hunt, "Problems and Processes in the Legal Interview," 50 Illinois Bar Journal 726 (1962).
J. Hurst, Law and Social Process in United States History (1960).
———, The Growth of American Law: The Law Makers (1950).
The Image Makers, Wall Street Journal, Aug. 1, 1978, p. 1, col. 1.
E. Jones (labor arbitrator), Los Angeles Herald-Examiner, 49 Labor Arbitration Reports 453 (1967).
H. Jones, "Lawyers and Justice: The Uneasy Ethics of Partisanship," 23 Villanova Law Review 957 (1978).
A. Jonsen, Responsibility in Modern Religious Ethics (1968).
C. Jung, Analytical Psychology (1968).
———, Memories, Dreams, Reflections (Winston tr. 1963).
———, "The Psychology of the Transference," in The Practice of Psychotherapy, 16 Collected Works (Bollingen, 2nd ed. 1966).
"Justice," 10 Encyclopedia Judaica 476 (1971).
B. Kaplan, "Martin Buber and the Drama of Otherness: The Dynamics of Love, Art, and Faith," 27 Judaism 196 (1978).
S. Kaplan, "Legal Ethics Forum: The Case of the Unwanted Will," 65 American Bar Association Journal 484 (1979).
A. Kaufmann, Problems in Professional Responsibility (1976).
W. Kaufmann, introduction to M. Buber, I and Thou (1972).
M. Kelsey, Pastoral Care in the Ministry (unpublished).
A. Kinsey, Sexual Behavior in the Human Male (1948).
E. Kraeling, Rand-McNally Bible Atlas (1966).
I. Kristol, "Business Ethics and Economic Man," The Wall Street Journal, Mar. 20, 1979.
H. Kung, On Being a Christian (Quinn tr. 1975).
R. Lawry, "Confidences and the Government Lawyer," 57 North Carolina Law Review 625 (1979).
B. Leete, A. Francia, and R. Strawser, "A Look at Lawyers' Need Satisfaction," 57 American Bar Association Journal 1193 (1971).
N. Lefstein, "The Criminal Defendant Who Proposes Perjury: Rethinking the Lawyer's Dilemma," 6 Hofstra Law Review 665 (1978).
S. Levinson, "The Specious Morality of the Law," Harper's, May, 1977.
A. Lewis, Gideon's Trumpet (1964).
C. Lewis, Christian Reflections (1967).
———, The Four Loves (1960).
———, God in the Dock (1970).
———, letters, in S. Vanuken, A Severe Mercy (Bantam ed. 1979).
———, Letters to Malcomb, Chiefly on Prayer (1964).

———, Mere Christianity (1958).
———, Surprised by Joy (1958).
———, The World's Last Night (1960).
H. Lewis, "The Baltimore Police Case of 1860," 26 Maryland Law Review 215 (1966).
K. Llewellyn, The Bramble Bush: On Our Law and Its Study (1951).
T. Lynch, Images of Hope (1965).
A. MacIntyre, "Patients as Agents," in S. Spicker and H. Engelhardt, Philosophical Medical Ethics: Its Nature and Significance 197 (1977).
J. Mackie, Ethics: Inventing Right and Wrong (1977).
J. Maritain, Man and the State (1951).
K. Marks, K. Leswing, and B. Fortinsky, The Lawyer, The Public, and Professional Responsibility (1972).
B. Martin, If God Does Not Die (Farley tr. 1966).
J. Martin, "Miss Manners" (four reasons for family loyalty), The South Bend Tribune, July 1, 1979, p. 10S, col. 1.
M. Marty, Righteous Empire: The Protestant Experience in America (1970).
W. May, Notes on the Ethics of Doctors and Lawyers (Poynter Center 1977).
M. Mayer, The Lawyers (1967).
L. Mazor, "Power and Responsibility in the Attorney-Client Relation," 20 Stanford Law Review 1120 (1968).
C. McCarthy, "People before Programs," Washington Post, Oct. 28, 1979, p. H.-6, col. 3.
J. McClendon, Biography as Theology (1974).
R. McCormick and A. Hellegers, "Specter of Joseph Saikewicz: Mental Incompetence and the Law," 138 America 257 (1978).
L. McCullough, "Pain, Suffering, and Euthanasia" (unpublished).
R. McNemar, The Kentucky Revival, or A Short History of the Late Extraordinary Outpouring of the Spirit of God in the Western States of America (1808).
D. Mellinkoff, The Conscience of a Lawyer (1973).
R. Merhighe, "Delivery of Legal Services," 2 Social Responsibility: Journalism, Law, Medicine 40 (1976).
P. Miller, The Life of the Mind in America (1965).
E. Mould, Essentials of Bible History (1966).
L. Myers, "The Strange Case of Donald Lang," 64 American Bar Association Journal 1198 (1978).
"The New Public Interest Lawyers," 79 Yale Law Review 1069 (1970).
R. Neely, "Your Moral Obligation to Make Money," Juris Doctor, Feb.-Mar., 1979, p. 46.
W. Neil, Harper's Bible Commentary (1963).

R. Neuhaus, "Law and the Rightness of Things," 14 Valparaiso University Law Review 1 (1979).
H. R. Niebuhr, The Responsible Self (1963).
——, Radical Monotheism and Western Culture (1960).
R. Niebuhr, The Irony of American History (1962).
——, An Interpretation of Christian Ethics (1935).
——, Moral Man and Immoral Society (1932).
J. Noonan, "The Purposes of Advocacy and the Limits of Confidentiality," 64 Michigan Law Review 1485 (1966).
W. Notestein, The English People on the Eve of Colonization, 1603–1630 (1954).
H. Nouwen, Creative Ministry (1973).
M. Novak, In Praise of Cynicism (or) When the Saints Go Marching Out (Poynter Center 1975).
J. O'Meara, "Natural Law and Everyday Law," 5 Natural Law Forum 83 (1960).
V. Palmieri, "Officers of the Board," Wall Street Journal, Aug. 14, 1978, p. 12, col. 3.
S. Passamaneck and L. Brown, "The Rabbis–Preventive Law Lawyers," 8 Israel Law Review 538 (1973).
H. Patterson and E. Conrad, Scottsboro Boy (1950).
L. Patterson, "A Preliminary Rationalization of the Law of Legal Ethics," 57 North Carolina Law Review 520 (1979).
G. Petter, review of Clebsch's American Religious Thought: A History and of Gaustad's Dissent in American Religion, Cross Currents, Winter, 1975, p. 493.
Plato, The Republic (Jowett tr. 1937).
F. Posner, "Charity: In the Talmud and Rabbinic Literature," 5 Encyclopedia Judaica col. 343 (1971).
F. Powledge, "Something for a Lawyer to Do," The New Yorker, Oct. 25, 1969, p. 63.
"Privileged System of British Law Is in the Public Dock," The New York Times, Mar. 18, 1979, p. 38, col. 1.
W. Probert and L. Brown, "Theories and Practices in the Legal Profession," 19 University of Florida Law Review 447 (1966).
R. Redmount, "Attorney Personalities and Some Psychological Aspects of Legal Consultation," 109 University of Pennsylvania Law Review 972 (1961).
——, "Humanistic Law through Legal Counseling," 2 Connecticut Law Review 98 (1969).
——, "Perception and Strategy in Divorce Counseling," 34 Connecticut Bar Journal 249 (1960).
——, "Psychological Views in Jurisprudential Theories," 107 University of Pennsylvania Law Review 472 (1959).

R. Redmount and T. Shaffer, Cases in Legal Interviewing and Counseling (1980).
L. Reed, "God's Good Servants: Opinions and Beliefs about the Call to the Christian Life and the Role of the Christian Attorney" (unpublished).
R. Reilly, "Homosexuality and Nature's Laws," Wall Street Journal, Jan. 22, 1979.
E. Reynolds, St. Thomas More (1958).
D. Riesman, "Some Observations on Law and Psychology," 19 University of Chicago Law Review 30 (1951).
P. Roberts, "A Theology for Christian Critics," 45 Journal of the American Association for Religion 275 (1977).
R. Rodes, "The Last Days of Erastianism—Forms in the American Church-State Nexus," 42 Harvard Theological Review 301 (1969).
——, The Legal Enterprise (1976).
——, "The Passing of Non-Sectarianism—Some Reflections on the School Prayer Case," 38 Notre Dame Lawyer 115 (1963).
——, "Pluralistic Christendom and the Christian Civil Magistrate," 8 Capital University Law Review 413 (1979).
C. Rogers, Client-Centered Therapy (1951).
——, On Becoming a Person (1961).
E. Rogers (ed.), St. Thomas More: Selected Letters (1961).
W. Roof, "Traditional Religion in Contemporary Society: A Theory of Local-Cosmopolitan Plausibility," 41 American Sociological Review 195 (1976).
W. Roper, The Life of Sir Thomas More, Knighte (1556).
C. Rosenberg, "The Lawyer as Hired Gun," Los Angeles Lawyer, July–Aug. 1979, p. 11.
D. Rosenthal, Lawyer and Client: Who's in Charge? (1974).
J. Sartre, Existentialism (Frechtman tr. 1947).
R. Schnackenberg, The Moral Teaching of the New Testament (1965).
M. Schwartz, "The Professionalism and Accountability of Lawyers," 66 California Law Review 669 (1978).
C. Selinger, "Criminal Lawyers' Truth: A Dialogue on Putting the Prosecution to Its Proof on Behalf of Admittedly Guilty Clients," 3 Journal of the Legal Profession 57 (1978).
W. Seymour, "The First Century of the American Bar Association," 64 American Bar Association Journal 1041 (1978).
T. Shaffer, Death, Property, and Lawyers (1970).
——, Legal Interviewing and Counseling (1976).
——, The Planning and Drafting of Wills and Trusts (2nd ed. 1979).
——, "Snow's Justice," 4 California Western Law Review 76 (1968).
T. Shaffer and R. Redmount, Lawyers, Law Students, and People (1977).

T. Shaffer and R. Rodes, "Law for Those Who Are to Die," in H. Feifel (ed.), New Meanings of Death (1977).

G. Sharswood, "An Essay on Professional Ethics," 32 Reports of the American Bar Association (1907).

D. Shriver and K. Ostrom, Is There Hope for the City? (1977).

W. Simon, "The Ideology of Advocacy: Procedural Justice and Professional Ethics," 1978 Wisconsin Law Review 29.

J. Simons and J. Reidy, The Human Art of Counseling (1972).

E. Smigel, The Wall Street Lawyer (1964).

J. Smith, review of Horwitz's The Transformation of American Law, 1977 Wisconsin Law Review 1253.

T. Smith, Revivalism and Social Reform in Mid-Nineteenth Century America (1958).

A. Solzhenitsyn, "A World Split Apart," National Review, July 7, 1978, p. 836.

M. Steinberg, Basic Judaism (1947).

J. Story, review of Hoffman's Course of Legal Study, The North American Review, p. 76 (1817).

W. Stringfellow, "Christianity, Poverty, and the Practice of Law," 8 Capital University Law Review 451 (1979).

J. Sutton, "How Vulnerable Is the Code of Professional Responsibility?" 57 North Carolina Law Review 497 (1979).

R. Swaine, The Cravath Firm and Its Predecessors, 1819–1947 (3 vol. 1946).

H. Thielicke, Christ and the Meaning of Life (Doberstein tr. 1962).

P. Tillich, Systematic Theology (1963).

J. Tybor, "A Matter of Conscience—and the First Amendment," South Bend Tribune, Apr. 29, 1979, p. 17 col. 1 (Associated Press).

J. Updike, review of Busch's biography of Barth and of the Paucks' biography of Tillich, The New Yorker, Mar. 12, 1979, p. 135.

S. Vanuken, A Severe Mercy (Bantam ed. 1979); with several letters of C. S. Lewis.

B. Vawter, "Introduction to Prophetic Literature," in R. Brown, J. Fitzmyer, and R. Murphy (eds.), The Jerome Biblical Commentary (1968).

A. Watson, Psychiatry for Lawyers (2nd ed. 1978).

——, "Some Psychological Aspects of Teaching Professional Responsibility," 16 Journal of Legal Education 1 (1963).

——, "The Quest for Professional Competence: Psychological Aspects of Legal Education," 37 University of Cincinnati Law Review 93 (1968).

S. Wexler, "Practicing Law for Poor People," 79 Yale Law Journal 1049 (1970).

E. Wiesel, Four Hasidic Masters and Their Struggle against Melancholy (1978).
J. Wilson, review of Strick's Injustice for All, Fortune, July 31, 1978, p. 131.
C. Wise, Pastoral Counseling: Its Theory and Practice (1951).
J. Yoder, Liberating Must Come First: Exodus Precedes Sinai (mimeo, Associated Mennonite Biblical Seminaries, Elkhart, Ind., 1972).
——, The Politics of Jesus (1972).
G. Zahn, In Solitary Witness: The Life and Death of Franz Jagerstatter (1964).

Index of Names

This index covers the text and chapter notes. It does not cover the acknowledgments or the bibliography. References to the chapter notes are to authors and do not include the names of books or periodicals.

Abraham, 9, 102
Act of Supremacy, 193–94, 200
Acts of the Apostles, 52, 177–83, 222
Affair, The (Snow), 73, 74, 119
Agee, Steven, 227, 244
Alabama, 133, 144–52
Alabama National Guard, 147
A Man for All Seasons (Bolt), 175, 189–206
American Bar Association (ABA), 5, 7, 16, 37, 38, 42, 44, 63, 67, 68, 90, 95, 99, 100
American Law Reports, 54–55, 69, 71, 72
Anabaptists, 9, 248
Anders v. *California,* 237
Anschluss (Austria, 1938), 207–16
Anti-Mormon, 219
Antioch, 36, 43
Apostles' Creed, The, 137
Aquinas, Thomas, 22, 25, 35, 52, 54, 116, 190, 192
Arendt, Hannah, 247
Aristotle, 90, 96, 116, 157, 172
Arnold, Thurman, 7, 231
Athens, 36
Athens, Ala., 145

Auchincloss, Louis, 18, 74
Augsburg Synod of 1935, 221

Bacon, Francis, 176, 248
Bailey, F. Lee, 76
Balaam, prophets of (Old Testament), 240
Baptist Church (Baptists), 17, 170, 187, 217–26
Barrett, Edward F., 247
Barrett, William, 248
Barth, Karl, 9, 19, 21, 25–31, 35, 53, 76, 111, 116, 128, 144, 150, 152, 181, 192, 198, 202, 209, 221, 224, 225, 232, 233, 238, 240, 242, 243, 244, 246, 247, 248
Bathsheba (Old Testament), 112, 113
Bauer, Joseph, 227
Beames, J., 240
Beauchamp, T., 232
Belchertown State School, 121, 125, 128
Benedict, Saint, 154, 245
Benét, Stephen Vincent, 195
Bennett, William, 246
Berne, Eric, 14, 232
Bersin, Richard, 227

Birmingham, Ala., 187–88
Blackpool, Stephen, 232
Blackstone, Sir William, 58, 59, 247
Blane, James, 227
Bliven, Naomi, 233
Bloomfield, Maxwell, 74, 236, 237, 243, 245
Bolt, Robert, 104, 175, 189–206, 246, 247, 248
Bonhoeffer, Deitrich, 27, 104, 232, 245
Booker, Frank E., 227
Boston Bar Association, 166
Bounderby, Joseph, 232
Bowen, Catharine Drinker, 176, 246, 248
Bower, Tom, 238
Bracton, Henry de, 108, 205
Bradley, L., 241
Bradshaw, Clinton, 237
Bramble Bush, The (Llewellyn), 165
Brandeis, Louis D., 7
Brougham, Lord (Henry Peter), 59, 68, 71, 72, 236
Brown, Louis M., 232–35, 237, 243, 245, 246
Bruges, University of, 106, 247
Bryan, William Jennings, 117
Buber, Martin, 22, 28–32, 35, 55, 94, 104, 233, 235, 241, 243, 244
Buchwald, Art, 129, 130, 242
Burger, Warren E., 76
Burrell, David, 175, 207, 248
Burtchaell, James T., 37, 104, 235, 245
Busch, E., 243, 248

Caesarea, 178
Calvary, 52, 53, 54, 55, 78, 216
Calvin, John, 213, 244, 248
Calvinism, 60, 89
Calvinists, 209

Campeggio, Cardinal (Lorenzo), 196
Camus, Albert, 192
Canons of Legal Ethics (American Bar Association), 37, 59, 63, 67, 68
Cardozo, Benjamin N., 243
Carter, Dan, 146, 147, 148, 244
Carter, Jimmy (former president of U.S.), 218
Cary, Joyce, 140, 167, 243
Chaffanbrass (Trollope's *Orley Farm*), 48, 49, 53, 54, 57, 62, 66, 72, 77, 88, 239
Chambers, R., 246, 248
Chapin, Samuel, 59
Charles (king of England), 194
Chavez, Cesar, 203
Cheatham, E., 232
Childress, James, 227, 233
Christian Anti-Communist Crusade, 4, 5, 8, 13, 15, 17
Christian Law-Student Fellowship (University of Virginia), 227
Chroust, Anton-Hermann, 236
Churchill, Larry, 130–32, 227, 241, 242, 246
Cihlar, Frank, 232
Civil War (U.S.), 77
Clasen, C., 248
Cochran, Robert, 227
Code of Professional Responsibility (American Bar Association), 5, 7, 11, 16–18, 37, 38, 42, 56, 86–88, 95, 98, 100, 102, 111, 132–33, 170, 180, 192
Coke, Sir Edward, 176
Communism, 136, 149
Conrad, E., 244
Conscience of the Rich, The (Snow), 73
Constantine, Emperor, 219
Constitution of the United States, 54, 56, 88, 98, 99, 101, 102
Corinth, 36, 37, 43, 180

Index of Names 265

Cornelius, 52
Cox, Archibald, 157
Cozzens, James Gould, 74
Criminal Justice Section (American Bar Association), 100-103
Crock, S., 232, 235, 240
Cromwell, Thomas, 175, 191-92, 197, 198, 200, 201, 203

Daily Worker, 148
Daniel-Rops, 246
Dartmouth College, 164
Darwin, Charles, 8, 232
Dauer, Edward, 232, 233
David (Old Testament), 112, 113, 115
Decatur, Ala., 144-52
Declaration of Independence, 58
de Toqueville, Alexis, 8
Deutsch, Morton, 235
Dewey, John, 175, 246
Dickens, Charles, 232
Dillenberger, J., 244
Dismas, 78, 79
Dockwrath (Trollope's *Orley Farm*), 45, 46, 81
Domhoff, William, 240
Donagan, Alan, 89, 238
Donne, John, 19
Donnell, John, 240
Dresden, 9, 144
Dreyfus Case, 74
Drinker, Henry, 66, 72, 236
Duke's Children, The (Trollope), 22
Dunne, John, 235
Durkheim, Emile, 50, 57, 236, 249
Dutile, Fernand N., 227
Dworkin, Gerald, 25, 26, 28-30, 232, 234

Ebeling, G., 244
Edman, V., 233, 238

Eichmann, Adolf, 78, 99, 207
El Greco, 198
Eliot, Lewis, 73, 119
Elizabeth (New Testament), 152
Ephesus, 36, 180, 198
Episcopal Church, 216
Erasmus (Desiderius), 196
Erickson, Kai, 50, 55-57, 117, 236, 249

Faulkner, William, 73, 74, 76, 167
Feifel, Herman, 234
Finch, Atticus (Lee's *To Kill a Mockingbird*), 74, 164, 239
Fingarette, Herbert, 238
Finn, Phineas (Trollope's *Phineas Redux*), 49, 73, 77
Finney, Charles Grandison, 75, 237, 238
Fleisser, Bishop, 211, 215
Fletcher, Joseph, 172
Forsyte, Fleur, 242
Forsyte, Soames, 73, 242
Fortas, Abe, 7, 10
Fortinsky, B., 231
Frances Lewis Law Center (Washington and Lee University), 228
Frank, John P., 7
Frankfurter, Felix, 17
Freedman, Monroe, 68, 69, 71, 72, 74, 78, 85, 86, 90, 93, 94, 98, 103, 231, 233, 236, 238
Freeman, Harrop, 234
Frick Museum, 198
Frost, Robert, 166
Fuller, Lon, 242
Furnival, Thomas (Trollope's *Orley Farm*), 45-49, 51, 52, 54, 57, 62, 66, 72, 81, 82
Fussa, Anthony, 227

Gaffney, Edward, 227, 238

Galatia, 180
Gandhi, Mohandas, 113–15, 131, 133
Garrison, William Lloyd, 75, 114
German army, 207–16
Gethsemane, 159, 211, 248
Gideon, Clarence Earl, 10
Glanville, 240
Glenn, John, 227
Glenn, Peter, 227
Goessler (Madame) (Trollope's *Phineas Redux*), 77
Goffman, Erving, 236
Golden Rule, The, 89, 93–96, 100–103
Gordon, Croxton, 227
Graham, Billy, 221
Graham, Felix, 48, 49, 51, 53, 54, 57, 61, 66, 67, 72
Grolier Club, 66
Groot, Roger, 227
Gustafson, James, 73, 233, 238

Hand, Leonard, 125
Harding, Septimus (Trollope's *The Warden*), 22, 233
Hargis, Reverend Billy, 15
Haring, Bernard, 133, 241
Harpsfield, 246
Harris, Richard, 241
Hauerwas, Stanley, 56, 84, 123, 138, 150, 155, 174, 175, 189–207, 223, 227, 232–34, 236, 238–41, 244, 246, 247, 249
Hauptmann, Bruno, 78
Hazard, Geoffrey, 16, 20, 37–39, 58, 231, 233, 236
Hebrew Christians, 181
Heidegger, Martin, 165
Hellegers, A., 241
Heller, J., 233
Hennessey, Richard, 245

Henry (king of England), 190, 194, 210, 213
Herbert, Will, 238, 243, 248
Hillel, Rabbi, 93, 96, 238
Hiroshima, 9, 144
Hitler, Adolf, 148, 175, 207–16, 225
Hodges, Louis, 227
Hoffman, David, 6, 7, 39, 59–63, 66–68, 72–75, 99, 102, 236, 243, 245
Holbein, Hans, 198
Holmes, Oliver Wendell, Jr., 137, 138, 156, 166, 172
Holocaust, the, 9, 136
Holy Ghost, the, 161, 192
Horsewhip Lawyer, the, 22–24, 27
Horton, James Edwin, 97, 104, 144–52, 174, 209, 212, 213, 225, 244, 245, 248
Howard University, 237
Hutchinson, Ann, 50, 52, 57, 117

Indiana, 125
Indiana State Prison, 41
Inherit the Wind (Lawrence and Lee), 117
Injustice for All (Strick), 139
Inns of Court, the, 197
International Labor Defense, 148
Intruder in the Dust (Faulkner), 73
Isaac (Old Testament), 9, 102
Israel, 75, 113, 177–83, 217
Israelites, the, 77

Jackson, Andrew, 58, 237
Jackson v. Indiana, 241
Jacob (Old Testament), 9, 102
Jaggerstatter, Franz, 57, 97, 104, 187, 207–16, 225, 244, 248
James, Saint (New Testament), 1, 178
James, William, 214, 248
Jaworski, Leon, 157

Index of Names

Jefferson, Thomas, 59, 74, 236, 237, 245
Jehovah's Witnesses, 209
Jenner, Albert, 157
Jerome, Saint (Eusebius Hieronymus), 198
Jerusalem, 159, 174, 178
Jesus, 9, 27, 28, 36, 37, 43, 50, 52, 53, 56, 57, 75–79, 88, 93, 96, 117, 130, 137, 143, 158, 160, 174, 175, 179, 190, 192, 198, 199, 203, 208, 212, 214, 217–20, 239, 247
Jimson, Gulley (Cary's *The Horse's Mouth*), 167
Joan of Arc, 213
Job (Old Testament), 102, 103, 238
John (king of England), 107
John, Saint (New Testament), 130
Johnson, Samuel, 163
Joint Conference on Professional Responsibility (1956), 86
Jones, Edgar, 238
Jones, Harry W., 86, 180, 233, 237, 238
Judah, 113
Jung, C. J., 234

Kant, Immanuel, 25, 93, 96, 97, 102, 172, 238
Kaplan, B., 232, 241
Kaufmann, Walter, 28, 138, 243
Kelsey, Morton, 235
Kennedy, Robert F., 245
Kentucky, 125
King, Martin Luther, Jr., 113, 114, 115, 131, 133, 203
Kingsfield, Professor (*The Paper Chase*), 4, 166
Kirgis, Frederick L., Jr., 227
Klinefelter, Donald, 227
Kluger, Richard, 176
Knights of Columbus, the, 219
Korean War, 155

Kuntsler, William, 127
Landies, Robert, 245
Lang, Daniel, 241
Langston, John Mercer, 237
LaRue, Lewis, 227
Last Chronicle of Barset, The (Trollope), 81
Latter, Capt. James (Cary's *Not Honor More*), 140
Law Day, 136, 159, 162
LeCarré, John, 248
Lee, Harper, 74, 76
Lefstein, N., 235, 238
Lemons, Donald, 227
Leonard, Billy, 241
Leswing, K., 231
Lewis, Anthony, 10
Lewis, C. S., 157–64, 211, 232, 241, 245, 248
Lilly Endowment, the, 228
Lincoln, Abraham, 74, 195
Linz, Austria, 207
Llewellyn, Karl, 165, 166
Luther, Martin, 150, 200, 244
Lynch, T., 246

Machiavelli, Niccolò, 196
MacIntyre, Alistair, 240, 241
Mackie, J., 238
Mafia, the, 57, 75, 76, 78
Mansfield, Mike, 245
Maritain, Jacques, 241
Marks, K., 231
Marshall, Thurgood, 164, 197
Martin, Raymond, 227
Marty, Martin, 59, 60, 140, 233, 236, 243, 245
Mary (Virgin), 152
Maryland, University of, 60, 62
Mason, Lady Mary (Trollope's *Orley Farm*), 45–53, 56–58, 61, 66, 72–73, 76–78, 81–85, 90, 91, 93

Mason, Lucius (Trollope's *Orley Farm*), 45, 49, 52, 81, 82, 84
Mason, Sir Joseph (Trollope's *Orley Farm*), 45
Massachusetts Bay Colony, 50, 55, 117
Matthew, Saint (New Testament), 52, 223
May, William, 77, 78, 232, 238, 246
McCarthy, Colman, 242
McCarthy, Eugene, 245
McClendon, James, 240, 248
McCormick, Charles, 235
McCormick, R., 241
McCullough, L., 241
McThenia, Andrew W., 227
Megarry, Sir Robert, 236
Mellinkoff, David, 236
Mennonite Church (Mennonites), 216
Methodist Church (Methodists), 59, 216
Miller, Perry, 59, 62, 77, 233, 236, 243, 246
More, Alice, 202
More, Margaret (Mrs. William Roper), 193–94, 202, 205
More, Sir Thomas, 57, 97, 104, 175, 187, 189–206, 209, 210, 212, 213, 225, 239, 244, 246, 247, 248
Morgan, Charles, 131, 187–88, 241
Morgan County, Ala., 144–52
Morison, Samuel E., 240
Morse, Wayne, 245
Moses, 27, 77, 130, 179, 217, 222, 244
Moses v. *Macferlan*, 155
Murdoch, Iris, 199, 247
Myers, L., 241

NAACP, 148
Nathan (Old Testament), 112, 113, 114, 115, 116, 120, 131, 240
Nazis, 187, 207–16
Neil, William, 36
Neilson, G., 240
Neuhaus, Richard, 139, 238
New English Bible, the, 231, 238
New Jersey, 123
Newman, John Henry, 157
New Testament, the, 50, 177, 192, 220, 223
New York (state), 148
Niebuhr, J. Richard, 144, 153, 172, 244, 245
Niebuhr, Reinhold, 17, 71, 75, 76, 144, 146, 149, 151, 162, 244, 245
1984 (Orwell), 151
Nixon, Richard M., 156
Noonan, John T., 238
Norfolk, Duke of, 191–92
Notre Dame, University of, 155, 228, 233, 246
Nouwen, Henri, 160
Novak, Michael, 231

Oath of Supremacy, the, 104
Oberlin College, 237–38
O'Brien, John A., 220
O'Connell, Marvin, 246
Old Bailey, the, 48
Old Testament, the, 114, 115, 117, 150, 177, 179
O'Meara, Joseph, 172, 241
O'Neill, Nena and George, 84
Open Marriage (O'Neill), 84
Orley Farm (Trollope), 45, 52, 73, 81, 90
Orme, Edith (Trollope's *Orley Farm*), 49, 51, 52, 77, 82–85, 90, 91, 93
Orme, Sir Peregrine (Trollope's *Orley Farm*), 49, 51, 82, 83
Orwell, George, 151
Osborne, John Jay, Jr., 242
Ostrom, Karl, 18, 233, 245

Index of Names 269

Owen, David, 227

Palliser, Plantagenet, 22, 236
Palmiere, V., 232, 235, 240
Paper Chase, The, 166
Passant, George, 73
Patterson, Haywood, 144–52, 244, 245
Patterson, Raymond, 236, 243
Paul, Saint, 2, 8, 28, 29, 32, 36, 40, 43, 52, 77, 113, 131, 137, 139, 177–83, 192, 198, 202, 220, 246
Pennsylvania, University of, 63
Peter, Saint, 52, 222, 223
Pharisees, 49, 75, 114, 177, 220, 221, 226
Phariseeism, 220–21
Philippi, 180
Phineas Redux (Trollope), 49, 73, 81
Piaget, Jean, 234
Piggun, Elias, 108
Plains, Ga., 218
Plato, 234
Powledge, F., 187–88, 241
Presbyterian Church (Presbyterians), 59, 216
Prosser, William, 172, 243
Protestantism, 220
Public Broadcasting System, 137
Puritans, 9, 51, 138, 139, 243, 244

Quakers, 50, 51, 55, 57, 216
Queen Caroline's Case, 59
Quinlan Case, 123, 241

Rabbi and the Horsewhip Lawyer, the, 22, 23, 24, 27
Rawls, Frank, 227
Rebecca (Rebekah) (Old Testament), 45
Redmount, Robert S., 165, 166, 231, 233, 234, 235, 243, 245, 246, 247
Reed, George, 227, 239, 244

Reformation, the, 220, 221
Reidy, Jeanne, 235
Reilly, R., 249
Reisman, David, 173, 243
Revelation (New Testament), 143–52
Reynolds, E., 246, 248
Rhinelander, Phillip, 90–91
Rhodesia, 114
Richardson, E., 157
Righteous Empire (Marty), 59, 140, 144
Rodes, Robert E., Jr., 10, 114, 227, 233, 234, 240, 242, 243, 246, 247, 248
Rogers, Carl, 234, 235
Rogers, E., 248
Rolls of the Justices in Eyre, 107
Roman army, 139, 178, 219, 222
Roman Catholic Church (Catholics), 207–16, 246
Roman Christians, 177–83, 192, 202, 213
Roper, William, 193–94, 197, 198, 200, 203, 246
Rosenthal, Douglas, 129, 234, 242
Rules of Professional Conduct (American Bar Association), 42, 44, 68, 97, 98, 100, 103

Saikewicz, Joseph, 121–25, 127, 131, 132, 241
Saint Radegund, Austria, 207–16
Samaritans, 55, 78
Sanhedrin, the, 139
Sartre, Jean-Paul, 212, 248
Saul (king) (Old Testament), 112
Saul of Tarsus (Saint Paul), 177–83
Schnackenberg, R., 175
Schwartz, Murray, 71, 86, 233, 237, 238
Scott, Sir Walter, 107
Scottsboro Cases, 144–52

Securities and Exchange Commission (SEC), 118, 119
Seliger, C., 236, 238
Selma, Ala., 115, 133
Sermon on the Mount (New Testament), 66, 160
Shaffer, Francis D., 155
Shaffer, Joseph P., 228, 232
Shaffer, Nancy J., 223, 228
Shaffer, Thomas L., 234, 235, 236, 238, 240, 242, 243, 245, 246, 248
Shaffer, Thomas M., 155
Shahinian, Dean, 227
Sharswood, George, 7, 59, 60, 62, 63, 64, 65, 66, 67, 68, 72, 73, 74, 102
Shriver, Donald, 18, 233, 245
Simons, Joseph, 235
Simple Justice (Kluger), 176
Sirica, John, 157
Skokie Case, 232
Sleep of Reason, The (Snow), 73
Smith, Timothy, 62, 75, 77, 233, 236, 238, 243
Snow, C. P., 22, 73, 74, 118, 119, 238, 240, 247, 248
Snow, Daniel, 227
Socrates, 30, 117, 203, 242
Solomon (Old Testament), 113
Solzhenitsyn, Alexandr, 178
Speer, Albert, 175, 241, 248
Standiford, Debi, 227
State v. *Lang* (Illinois), 241
State v. *Robinson* (North Carolina), 238
Statute of Distributions (England), 19
Statute of Frauds, 135
Statute of Limitations, 66
Stephen, Saint (New Testament), 178
Stevens, Gavin, 73, 164, 167
Stone, Jabez, 78

Story, Joseph, 236
Strangers and Brothers (Snow), 73
Strick, Ann, 139
Stringfellow, William, 231, 240
Strunk v. *Strunk,* 241
Stump v. *Sparkman,* 241
Sunday, Billy, 218-19, 221, 222, 249
Supreme Court of Alabama, 145
Supreme Court of the United States,, 96, 99, 101, 124, 125, 145
Supreme Judicial Court of Massachusetts, 122-25
Superintendent of Belchertown v. *Saikewicz,* 121-27
Sykes, Gresham, 236
Szasz, Thomas, 128

Teresa, Mother, 242
Thayer, J., 240
The Masters (Snow), 118, 119
Third Reich, the, 99, 207-16
Thomas, Frederick W., 237
Thompson v. *Louisville,* 241
Thoreau, Henry David, 210
Tigar, Michael, 127
Tillich, Paul, 30, 132, 144, 241
To Kill a Mockingbird (Lee), 74
Tonio, Carl, 234
Trollope, Anthony, 22, 45-49, 53, 57, 60, 66, 72, 73, 77, 81, 82, 88, 233, 236
Trollope, Frances, 60
Truthfulness and Tragedy (Hauerwas), 223
Tudor monarchs, 187, 248
Tybor, J., 232

Uniform Commercial Code, 165, 179
Uniform Probate Code, 179
Urbana, Ill., 220
Uriah the Hittite (Old Testament), 112

Index of Names 271

Vawter, B., 115, 240
Victorian England, 50, 51
Vietnam War, 113, 114
Vietnam, 9, 144, 210, 215, 216, 245
Virginia, University of, 167, 227

Wagner v. *International R. Co.,* 243
Walworth, Clarence, 60
Warden, The (Trollope), 22, 81
Wasserstrom, Richard, 85, 86, 90, 175, 228, 231, 233, 236, 238, 241
Watergate, 9, 156, 157, 233
Watson, Andrew S., 176, 234
Webster, Daniel, 164, 195
Weihofen, Henry, 234
Wesolowski, Nancy, 228
Wexler, Steven, 5, 7, 8, 18, 128, 129, 160, 231, 240
Whiting, Steven, 227
Williams, Margaret, 228
Wilson, James, 78
Wilson, James Q., 139
Wise, C., 235
Wise, Isaac, 233
Wolsey, Thomas, 190-92, 196, 197, 203
Wootton, James, 227

Yoder, John Howard, 9, 52, 143, 150-52, 234, 241, 243, 244, 246, 247

Zacchaeus Soup Kitchen (Washington, D.C.), 242
Zahn, Gordon, 210, 211, 214-16, 248
Zealots, 78, 198
Zechariah (New Testament), 152